Enlightened Absence

D0937850

Enlightened Absence

Neoclassical Configurations
of the Feminine

RUTH SALVAGGIO

University of Illinois Press
Urbana & Chicago

89992

© 1988 by the Board of Trustees of the University of Illinois

Manufactured in the United States of America
C 5 4 3 2 1

This book is printed on acid-free paper.

Library of Congress Cataloging-in-Publication Data

Salvaggio, Ruth.
  Enlightened absence : neoclassical configurations of the feminine /
Ruth Salvaggio.
    p. cm.
  Bibliography: p.
  Includes index.
  ISBN 0-252-01541-X (alk. paper)
  1. English literature—18th century—History and criticism.
2. Women in literature. 3. Sex role in literature. 4. Classicism—
Great Britain. 5. Enlightenment. 6. Feminism and literature—
Great Britain—History—18th century. 7. Feminist criticism.
I. Title.
PR449.W65S25   1988   88-4726
820'.9'352042—dc 19   CIP

FONTBONNE LIBRARY

PR
449
.W65
S25

For Alison, Joan, Marleen, Minrose, and Terry

$19.95

1-1990

07992

Contents

Preface

I OFFER in this book a feminist critique of the English Enlightenment, or, to put the matter in a larger context, a critique of classical systems epitomized in Enlightenment science and literature. In arguing that this age was infected with a profound sexual bias, I am not simply suggesting that women were not allowed a voice in the construction of its systems—a fact that would now be generally acknowledged—but that the exclusion and displacement of what the age regarded as feminine was *necessary* in order for these systems to exist and thrive.

I use the terms *classical* and *enlightened* to describe systems of thought built on notions of order and hierarchy. These systems have, to some degree or other, influenced the development of Western thinking from ancient times well into our own—but they enjoyed their most precise expression during the seventeenth and eighteenth centuries.[1] It was during this time in England that Isaac Newton explained the workings of the physical universe, and Jonathan Swift and Alexander Pope dominated the literary world. These men—reflecting the spirit of their own age, but also reflecting classical modes of thought that have long permeated the very construction of Western ideas—were involved in a great consolidation of systems. In terms of English history, this particular consolidation had been in progress at least since England's rise to world power during the Renaissance. In terms of its larger Western heritage, the effort was modeled on the glory of classical times, which these men fancied themselves mimicking in their "Augustan" literature and neoclassical values. But in both its immediate historical and more extensive cultural contexts, the consolidation necessitated the firm cohesion of certain ideas and phenomena, and the inevitable exclusion of "others"—specifically, an assortment of "other" material that did not fit the classical paradigm. Enlightenment men were continually purging their systems of this material. They were also continually representing it in terms of something feminine.

My purpose is to explore the nature and effects of their sexually exclusive representational schemes. I argue that Enlightenment discourse in particular, and classical systems of thought that it reflects, participate in woman's suppression by configuring that which violates cohesive, systematic structure as feminine. In concerning myself primarily with forms of representation, I do not directly address here the predicament of actual females who were, for various reasons, prevented from playing a part in the age's scientific revolution or from assuming positions in its major literary circles—women such as Margaret Newcastle, Mary Astell, or Lady Mary Wortley Montagu. Instead, and as a complement to recent feminist studies that are uncovering the ignored women of our past, I treat "woman" and all her feminine associations in terms of a figure, a figure that is repeated, varied, and continually reshaped into "configurations" of those phenomena that never found a place in England's classical age, but that nonetheless strongly influenced its development through their very displacement. Some of these configurations were enforced by women's historical connections with witchcraft and hysteria. Others were enforced through systems of representation in which phenomena that proved difficult to control—madness, fluidity, color, shade, and darkness—took on a feminine demeanor.

Yet while my primary concern is with representations of woman, implicit in my argument is the belief that configuration and reality are always infused in each other—making it impossible to talk about the plight of women without also understanding the ways in which they and their gender have been represented, and just as impossible to talk about schemes of representation without constantly keeping in mind the effects of these configurations in the real world. The suppression of what I call the feminine—ideas and associations that took on the attributes of the female gender—is inevitably and intricately connected to the suppression of women. One could hardly exist without the other, and classical discourse could not exist without both of them.

My subject, then, is discourse in the fullest sense of the term, but specifically the discourse that we have come to recognize as the "major" literary and scientific works of this age—Swift's and Pope's satires, Newton's treatises—as well as the poetry of a woman writer, Anne Finch, who has recently enjoyed some recognition in literary studies. I seek, through readings of their texts, the configurations of that which was rendered absent within the systematic language of these men, and which infused the poetry of a woman whose writing resists placement in classical systems. It was, after all, in the search for classical order and for the light of Enlightenment that Newton, Swift, and Pope played out their part in a history dominated by men, and that Finch inevitably found no place in that history. Yet rigid as England's classical age was in the construction of its systems, it could not entirely ignore the feminine material that functioned as its "other." The notable men of the Enlightenment acknowledged this otherness again and again, often in disparaging ways, at times with a kind of vengeance. I read their texts for the otherness that they suppressed and yet, in so suppressing, continually acknowledged—for the woman who was absent, yet whose absence fueled their discourse. In exposing the feminine configurations of this otherness, I try to recover the feminine energies that the Enlightenment placed in pejorative contexts. I try "to go back," as Luce Irigaray writes, "through the masculine imaginary, to interpret the way it has reduced [women] to silence," and "from that starting-point and at the same time, to (re)discover a possible space for the feminine imaginary."[2]

This task involves a reclaiming of woman's image, an attempt to expose feminine representations as the construction of a dominant sex that figures its desires and fears through metaphors of the other sex. From Medea and Medusa to Pope's Belinda, Swift's Celia, and Newton's Lady, the classical mind has been plagued by the woman through whom it figures its most precious fear—the fear that something, perhaps something desirable, will destroy its neatly ordered systems. So woman has haunted classicism, and classicism has kept her suppressed. We underestimate the oppressive power of classical systems if we believe that we can rid them of their ghosts, and change these feminine figures into proper ladies. It is not the Enlightened mind that rescues woman from her historical obscurity, but rather the suppression of woman and all her feminine associations that allows Enlightenment to thrive. I therefore do not want to restore woman to some rightful place in the classical order of things. I want instead to question the value of a classical vision that constructs itself at the expense of the feminine, and to suggest that we open ourselves and our discourse to processes that our culture has long suppressed—processes that seep through and exceed its systematic structures.

Irigaray, speaking about the power of discourse to suppress that which does not fit into its discursive system, says that we must question "*the conditions under which systematicity itself is possible.*"[3] As I have pondered the conditions necessary for Enlightenment discourse to flourish, I have found that its classical systematicity is possible only when the feminine remains absent. We need to contemplate the disturbing implications of this absence if we are ever to come to terms not only with the condition of "women," but with "woman"—that is, her configuration of the feminine—as the very condition of her own suppression. The exclusion of woman from Enlightenment systems, seen from this perspective, is not ultimately a matter of any feminine configuration or metaphor, but of the predicament of actual women who lived and who continue to live in a culture built on classical systems of representation. The political dimension of my argument must be clear: there can be no place for women in any culture whose discourse has already rendered displaced phenomena as feminine. Underlying my argument about "configurations of the feminine" is the belief that we seriously need to question *both* the intellectual and political ramifications of the ways in which ideas are gendered, and the effects of a gendered discourse on the lives of people. This means that we need to question the connections between language and power, between classical discourse and the effects of its inherent exclusionary tactics.

In trying to recover what the English Enlightenment excluded and rendered absent, I do not want to provide a fuller picture of our classical past. Instead, I want to offer a means of breaking with that past and with modes of thinking that construct barriers to intellectual revision and political action.

Acknowledgments

IT SEEMS appropriate that this book began, long ago, as a study of literary time and space. Though my concerns have moved in a very different direction, I find myself most grateful to those who allowed me the time to transform my thoughts, and who encouraged me to explore the fascinating spaces I came to regard as feminine.

For fellowship and research support, I thank the American Society for Eighteenth-Century Studies, the Folger Institute, the National Endowment for the Humanities, and the William Andrews Clark Memorial Library. I also want to thank the English Department at the University of Oregon for inviting me to teach eighteenth-century courses there for a year, and my own department at Virginia Polytechnic Institute for reduced teaching loads and for increasingly stimulating teaching opportunities. At both institutions, I've had the privilege of engaging with students whose enthusiasm proved to be a continual source of energy.

I'm grateful to Professors Julia Epstein and Ellen Pollak for the attention they devoted to my manuscript, and especially for their numerous suggestions which helped me bring together the theoretical and historical contexts of my argument. Professor Ellie Ragland-Sullivan's support and direction were crucial in helping me transform a manuscript into a book. I owe special thanks to Ann Lowry Weir, senior editor at the University of Illinois Press, for her remarkable efficiency and her assistance in ushering the book through to publication, and to Elizabeth Rubenstein for combining her editorial expertise with a genuine interest in my subject.

The configurations that I explore in this study have grown out of a dialog with special friends who also happen to be the very best of colleagues. Alison Sulloway helped me attempt to shape my initial perceptions into the kind of refined intellectual argument that characteristically informs her books, and that continues to serve as a model for my thinking and writing. With Joan Randall, I managed to find my way through some particularly abstract areas of critical theory, but only because she was there to remind me of their cultural and political significance. Louis Gwin has been a good and supportive friend, in more ways than I could begin to name here. Of the wealth of experiences and ideas I've shared with Marleen Barr, I'm most grateful for learning with her the value of collegial support. Our

Acknowledgments

involvement in practical feminist matters gave meaning and urgency to the theoretical issues I explore in this study. Terry Brown provided me with a special kind of space for my writing—one in which, under the best of conditions, I could finally complete the manuscript. That only seems appropriate, since her ideas and suggestions were a shaping influence from the very beginning. Finally, I cannot imagine having written this book without Minrose Gwin. She read so many versions of the manuscript that at times I could not differentiate our ideas—though I know that whatever is valuable in this study owes its articulation to her generous engagement with my work, and to the creative processes she incites in herself and in others.

I

Woman Displaced

. . . I can see a strange, provoking, formless sort of figure, that seems to skulk about behind that silly and conspicuous front design. . . .

It is always the same shape, only very numerous.

And it is like a woman stooping down and creeping behind that pattern.

CHARLOTTE PERKINS GILMAN

1

Histories, Theories, Configurations

Representation of the world, like the world itself, is the work of men; they describe it from their own point of view, which they confuse with absolute truth.

SIMONE DE BEAUVOIR

. . . a woman cannot "be"; it is something which does not even belong in the order of *being*. . . . something that cannot be represented, something that is not said, something above and beyond nomenclatures and ideologies.

JULIA KRISTEVA

. . . there is no possible place for the "feminine," except the traditional place of the repressed, the censured.

LUCE IRIGARAY

Night to his day—that has forever been the fantasy. Black to his white. Shut out of his system's space, she is the repressed that ensures the system's functioning.
    . . . somehow "outside." But she cannot appropriate this "outside" (it is rare that she even wants it); it is his outside: outside on the condition that it not be entirely outside, the unfamiliar stranger that would escape him. . . . Within his economy, she is the strangeness he likes to appropriate.

HÉLÈNE CIXOUS

THE ONE HISTORY AND THE OTHER

THE HISTORY of science and literature in the English Enlightenment, like most historical accounts, concentrates almost entirely on the activities and achievements of men. Not only has the "rise of modern science" centered on the story of Isaac Newton and several other notable men of the Royal Society, but our sense of "neoclassical" literary history primarily derives from the story of recognized male writers—some of whom gathered to-gether in their own literary clubs, all of whom are now safely canonized by the literary establishment. It is not that women did not play a part in the science and literature of this period—for we know that they were in-volved in both endeavors, and that the eighteenth century in particular marks the emergence of a number of recognized women writers.[1] It is simply that women have not been given any prominent place in the history of this age. They do not "figure" directly in that history.

Women's absence, considered from this perspective, might be viewed as a sort of historical oversight, an omission in the official historical record. Or from another perspective, one which I will be assuming throughout this book, we might see women "figuring" quite prominently in Enlight-enment discourse. It is certainly true that if we follow what Dominick LaCapra calls a "documentary model" of history, one that involves the accumulation of data and facts,[2] we are not likely to find the details that have been recorded about women assuming any prominent position in the history of this age. Yet if we take into account the language—metaphors, tropes, figures of speech—that is inherently a part of the historian's equip-ment, we might find ourselves gaining access to a subject that was osten-sibly omitted from the historical record, but that emerges in the very lan-guage used to construct and describe Enlightenment discourse.

Consider, for instance, the questions that several prominent historians and theorists are posing about what Paul Ricoeur calls "The Reality of the Historical Past," and particularly the effects of metaphoric and figurative language used to reconstruct that past. Hayden White describes a "tropics of discourse" in which tropes deviate "from literal, conventional, or 'proper' language use" and in the process "generate figures of speech or thought by their variation from what is 'normally' expected."[3] These trop-ical concerns, leading us away from what we might expect to encounter, remind us, as Ricoeur says, that history is involved not so much in docu-mentation as "representation," a "referential mode" that is "inseparable from the work of configuration itself: for it is only by means of the un-ending rectification of our configurations that we form an idea of the in-exhaustible resources of the past."[4] Poet Cynthia Ozick, writing not simply about the effects of metaphor, but its "necessity," claims that met-aphor—by facilitating "the leap into the Other"—allows us to root his-tory in figures of speech.[5] The medium of language, we might say, tells more about and beyond the subject than the teller ever intended to relate. It deviates from the normal, exceeds documentation, leaps into the realm of the "other." Could it be that implied messages about women have long been part of this language of excess? If men, who seem always to be directly talking about themselves and their achievements, have also indirectly been talking about woman—figuring her into their discourse in ways that we are only now beginning to recognize, it may be no accident that the recent interest in the role language plays in shaping historical discourse is paralleling the feminist project of recovering women's roles in history.

My own sense of Enlightenment history is not only that women have been excluded from its notable "documents," but that the very idea of woman became a metaphor and figure of the essence of exclusion—of not being, of absence. She was figured as, and assumed the configuration of, whatever was perceived as "other" to the major documents of Enlightenment thought. When Newton and Jonathan Swift wrote about systematic universes and islands, dispersive and fluid phenomena assumed a feminine configuration. When Newton and Alexander Pope wrote about light, darkness, shade, and color assumed a feminine configuration. Women may have been excluded from discourse, but discourse is filled with references to woman. So it is that while a documentary history may have excluded women, theories of language are now facilitating her emergence.

Yet she is proving difficult to locate in historical categories and discursive systems. Carroll Smith-Rosenberg, for instance, argues that "women's history challenges traditional history" by forcing us "to reconsider our understanding of the most fundamental ordering of social relations, institutions and power arrangements within the society we study."[6] Instead of assuming some fixed place within these systems, woman seems to occupy a place at the intersection of history and theory—the place where theory exposes history to the omissions inherent in its ordering. It is at this intersection, I believe, that woman emerges in the form of configurations of all that has been suppressed in systematic discourse. What are the implications of her emergence? How will she affect our understanding of a discourse that has long kept her suppressed?

We might begin to ponder these questions by considering the ways in which some recent literary critics have explored the question of "woman" and her representation in eighteenth-century literature. Take the critical engagement with Swift's poetry, for example, a poetry notable for its disparaging and often gross portrayals of women. As late as 1978, when these poems were attracting a good deal of attention, there seemed to be little in the poetry that was generating what one commentator called "fuel for feminist fires."[7] Around that same time, however, one particular feminist critic was supplying this fuel. Susan Gubar argued that Swift's poetry about women not only reflected his own personal misogyny, but was symptomatic of the tendency among Augustan writers to portray women as "monstrous."[8] It is easy to understand today how such depictions of women take their place in a more general tradition of antifeminist writing during this age, an argument later advanced and elaborated by Felicity Nussbaum.[9] But what I find more interesting, now that the question of woman and her representation has finally ignited as a critical issue, is the possible relationship between the view of woman as "monstrous" and our perception of Enlightenment discourse as ordered, balanced, and controlled. In other words, if women were portrayed as monsters, if the very notion of monstrosity was associated with woman, might we not also say that the concept of monstrosity assumed a gender and became a feminine configuration of that which functioned as "other" to contained and controlled Enlightenment systems?

I would suggest that such feminine configurations emerge not only in the discourse of a man who was all too explicit in his disparaging portrayals of women, but in the discourse of other writers who might seem more sympathetic in their descriptions. Samuel Richardson, for instance, appears to be especially sympathetic to the plight of his heroines. Yet Terry Eagleton argues that Richardson's "'exaltation' of women" in his novels actually served the bourgeois goal of maintaining women's passive submission—in both marriage and the nuclear family.[10] And Terry Castle, arguing that Richardson's Clarissa becomes a text or "cypher" for everyone's exegesis, describes her "oppression" in terms of "the tyranny of a sexual ideology that inscribes the female body itself. . . ."[11] Ellen Pollak, bringing this kind of argument to bear on the works of Pope and Swift, argues in a similar fashion that a "myth of passive womanhood" defined the "sexual ideology" of the age—a myth that had its basis in the history of real women's lives and that shaped literary portrayals of woman as "lack," as "an extension of male desire."[12] It is just as true, I would add to all of these observations, that the very notion of "lack" took on the attributes of the feminine gender, and can be seen as a feminine configuration of that which functioned as "other" to everything assuming an active and organizing function in Enlightenment systems. The men of the Enlightenment, in other words, not only saw themselves giving shape to a well-structured system of the world, but regarded everything lacking in that world in terms of a submissive wife or passive creature who might function as the object of their desire.

It is in this double sense, the sense of woman as both "other" and desirable, that we can begin to understand the implications of her suppression in discourse. For it was the very suppression of woman—and the ways in which she assumed such configurations as excess and absence—that kept the system alive and thriving. She excited the desire for refining its structure and bringing it to its goal of perfection—a desire to appropriate those "other" forces and make them conform to universal laws and principles. To understand the logic of this economy, we need to imagine a narrative of our past different from the one that history has recorded, bringing theories of discourse to bear on that recorded history. And so I turn to Hélène Cixous who explains how woman has functioned within this sexual economy throughout the history of discourse and the discourse of history. Woman, she says, is the thing outside the system from the very start, the "other" and different thing that makes the very definition of systems possible—that makes it possible to say what *is* in the system by knowing what is *not* to be allowed in its parameters. It is because woman exists outside, Cixous explains, that she can function as the object of desire. In this way, the one who controls the system from within can reach out to her, attempt to capture, conquer, and thus consolidate his empire. This "desire for appropriation" functions according to a certain logic: desire comes from "a mixture of difference and *inequality*." If both the one and the other are equal, there is no movement of one toward the other. But there is more. There is what Cixous calls a "little surreptitious slippage"—not simply inequality, but the "*sexual* difference" that combines with an inequality of force. There is the one sex—the stronger, desiring the other sex—the weaker. That is what "triggers desire, as a desire—for appropriation."[13]

In writing at the intersection of history and theory, I find myself attempting to write part of a "history of the other"—a narrative account of the phenomena that were suppressed by Enlightenment men, variously rendered by them as feminine, and that served as the object of their desire. Catherine Clément, seeking the history of women through woman's historical connections with the sorceress and hysteric, says that "every culture has an imaginary zone for what it excludes, and it is that zone we must try to remember *today*." She has a new history in mind, one that "will necessarily be from other points of view . . . taken from what is lost within us. . . ."[14] "There is phallocentrism," Cixous writes, as she too speaks about the exclusivity of history. "History has never produced or recorded anything else. . . . And it is time to change. To invent the other history" (p. 83).

It is within this other history that I want to locate my own study. And yet such a place is difficult to locate at all. We will have to read through what has been recorded with an eye for what has been left out—phenomena not simply omitted in scientific discourse or in literary texts, but purposefully excluded so that they could function as objects of appropriation. This effort involves me in a seemingly paradoxical predicament. I will obviously be working within the domain of a documentary history, and yet at the same time, I will be writing about something outside its parameters—a situation not foreign to that of contemporary theorists who question the narrative construction of any systematic discourse. I am particularly thinking of Michel Foucault, especially his rejection of the traditional expression of history in favor of "archaeology." Tracing the "epistemological mutation of history" through its various methods of questioning "the *document*," Foucault argues that developments in other fields—linguistics, psychoanalysis, literary analysis—are making the very project of history problematic. "It is as if it was particularly difficult, in the history in which men retrace their own ideas and their own knowledge, to formulate a general theory of discontinuity. . . ." Accustomed to seeking the connections among events that forge totalities and unities, it is as if historians—in their very nature—"felt a particular repugnance to conceiving of difference, to describing separations and dispersions, to dissociating the reassuring form of the identical." Could it be that the historian does not know how to deal with woman, the configuration of that dispersion? Foucault adds: "As if we were afraid to conceive of the *Other* in the time of our own thought." [15]

Can we conceive of woman's history as "other"? Alice Jardine suggests as much when she calls attention to the ways in which a "new conception of history" among postmodern writers is pronouncing the end of "Man and History." [16] For Foucault, she explains, what will come after the demise of this history is unclear and apocalyptic. For J.J. Goux, however, who is more explicit about this issue, the end of such a history will signal "'the crossing-over into the place of the Other'" and "'the coming into symbolic existence of *woman* as such—that is, *beyond* the phallic symbolism which represented her.'" [17] The connections linking such notions of the end of "Man's" history with the "other" history of woman described by Clément and Cixous must be obvious. Woman-as-other is not only emerging at the intersection of history and theory, but she is providing the matrix at which a new and different history can emerge—a history that aims not at a totalizing mastery of the past, but is itself involved in the experience of otherness, the expression of difference and discontinuity.

But is it also possible to approach scientific discourse in this way? Can we open scientific systems to an engagement with their own otherness? Since I will be tracing feminine configurations in science as well as literature, I want to consider conceptual models that might provide us with a means for understanding the dynamics of what is inside and outside scientific systems of discourse—what we might regard as the "one" and the "other" science. In particular, I want to look at two different models used by historians of science, taking these models not as definitive or accepted explanations of the way in which scientific thought proceeds, but as notable examples of different accounts of that process. The first is Thomas Kuhn's famous notion of the "paradigm" that he used to identify the assumptions shared by a scientific community, and that has since been used to identify assumptions shared within other intellectual communities and even between communities.[18] Whatever its specific reference, the very notion of paradigm brings with it the idea of spatial enclosure. With respect to science, for instance, a paradigm constitutes a kind of common ground, an intellectual space, providing scientists with the boundaries for their theories and experiments. What is inside the paradigm, Kuhn tells us, will contribute to the production of "normal science," and what is outside will remain largely unaccepted until something forces a "crisis" and ultimately a "revolution" in science, marking the rejection of an older paradigm and the inauguration of a new one. The process of revolution in this way itself becomes a "structure" encompassing paradigm shifts.

As we try to conceptualize this process, we are forced to think in terms of the very spatial model that both the "paradigm" and the "structure" supply. Both enclose a space in which science functions, one that will ensure the development of new spaces. Revolutions, far from breaking out of this accepted scientific space, actually enforce and account for its very structure. The implications of Kuhn's theories, we might say, are therefore themselves both "revolutionary" and "normal." While, in one sense, he has offered a description of scientific change notably different from that conventionally given by historians of science who trace science's linear development, in another sense his conceptual model only confirms the spatial structure of the history of science as we know it—that is, as it extends from Copernican to Newtonian and on through Einsteinian revolutions. We end up with a different understanding of how science progresses, but we also end up with the same science and the same historical space it occupies.

Yet if there is a space outside science, perhaps resembling the domain that constitutes history's "other," then how might we envision it? Let me try to explain my own sense of this space by turning to the work of Michel Serres, French historian of science who has written extensively on the connections among science and other intellectual pursuits. Like Kuhn, Serres relies on metaphoric constructs to explain the space of science and also to account for the space in which the connections between science and other discourses are forged. Yet Serres seems to pay more attention to a different space as well, to that outside the domain in which scientific and other intellectual pursuits are undertaken. Envisioning himself on an excursion, he views his search for "passages" between and among different discourses

in terms of sea travel. "I am looking for the passage among these compli-
cated cuttings. I believe, I see that the state of things consists of islands
sown in archipelagoes on the noisy, poorly-understood disorder of the
sea. . . ." As an historian, Serres seeks these connections: "Passages exist, I
know, I have drawn some of them in certain works using certain opera-
tors. . . ." And yet, in a way that violates the principles of orderly, historical
method, he refuses to bring these "passages" into the formal domain of a
general theory, a "structure" that might account for their connections:
"But I cannot generalize, obstructions are manifest and counter-examples
abound."[19]

The conceptual model that Serres uses to explain his perspectives—if
we can call it a model—would be that of an uncharted world in which he
seeks passages, but a world that will ultimately remain uncharted, unstruc-
tured. He is interested in the "islands," to be sure, the places safely enclosed in space, whose parameters recall the safely enclosed space of the
paradigm—the space inside. But Serres appears even more drawn to the
disorder of the sea, the phenomena outside that, strangely enough, facilitate his excursion. He views the "Classical Age," the age of Descartes and
seventeenth-century science, as one in which the notion of structure and
its varied political and social orders dominate the quest for knowledge, a
quest which itself is an attempt to dominate the natural world and attain
the power of mastery (pp. 15–28). This age, he says, boasts of structure
and closure. Yet as such, it differs from what Serres calls "the living organism." To describe this organism and its difference from theoretical systems, he again relies on the metaphor of water, which also helps him
conceptualize his own historical excursions. "The living system is ho-
meorrhetic," he says, because instead of seeking stasis, it is engaged in
continual movement. It flows perpetually. It "combines sea and islands"
(pp. 74–75).

In this fluid movement, both island and sea, both inside and outside,
are forces to be reckoned with. But one can never precisely demarcate the
parameters of the island, or define the material inside the paradigm that
has always constituted the stuff of which history is made, because it is
perpetually changed by the sea—by what is unknown, by the displaced
phenomena of classical systems. "The 'rational,'" Serres explains, "is a tiny
island of reality, a rare summit, exceptional, as miraculous as the complex
system that produces it, by a slow conquest of the surf's randomness along
the coast. All knowledge is bordered by that about which we have no
information" (p. 83). For Kuhn, as for traditional historians of science as
well, scientific knowledge is bordered by the very parameters of the paradigm and structure. But for Serres, knowledge is an island bordered by

the disordered sea that effects its very design through "randomness," and about which we can have no information. What drives an historian like Kuhn, we might say, is the desire to account for paradigms by seeing them within a larger structure that explains scientific progress. What drives Serres, however, is a desire to travel the random motions of the sea. Serres is interested in the islands—the stuff of history. But he is intellectually engulfed by the disordered space outside—the space that captures his imagination and fuels his excursions.

It is within this space beyond the borders of knowledge that we can begin to envision the location of the other history. "Space" seems a particularly appropriate term, since the recent feminist critique of systems long dominated by men—historical, literary, and scientific—is often described as an effort to seek out new spaces. Luce Irigaray, for instance, claims that she is attempting "to (re)discover a possible space for the feminine imaginary," and Alice Jardine explains "the crisis in the discursive itineraries of Western philosophy and the human sciences" as "a problematization of the boundaries and spaces necessary to their existence. . . ." What this crisis involves, Jardine goes on to say, is "a disruption of the male and female connotations upon which the latter depend."[20] As these connotations are disrupted, so are the spaces neatly enclosed within boundaries. And yet, as we will see, other spaces emerge.

The Enlightenment mind, I will argue, figured this "other" space as a fluid realm outside the pristine islands and systems of men. It was the very fluid quality of this space that marked it as distinctly feminine, problematizing both Enlightenment boundaries and our own discursive attempts to describe their systems. Displaced and seeping throughout these systems, woman inevitably became a sign and symptom of everything that would not conform to systematic structures. For the Enlightenment, these systematic structures defined the spirit of the age—and woman, inevitably, defined its absence.

FEMININE CONFIGURATIONS: MADWOMAN, HYSTERIC, WITCH

When Foucault studied the period that he labeled *"l'âge classique,"* he did not explore the phenomena we traditionally associate with Enlightenment or classicism. Instead, he was drawn to the age's preoccupation with and confinement of "madness."[21] Foucault tells us that this "Age of Reason" was distinctive for initiating the massive institutionalization of the insane, and in so doing, for coming to isolate and define the nature of madness and its social accommodation. He explains this historical event in terms of the age's response to its otherness, for madness was understood as a kind of "unreason," especially that associated with persons who were considered shameful and beastial—those who, in other words, scandalized and threatened the orderly world of rational men. If the "madman" presents us with the most conspicuous portrayal of "unreason," I would suggest that "woman" presents us with the least conspicuous. To a large extent, I believe, the story of "madness and civilization" can also be written in terms of "woman and civilization," since woman, like the madman, represented the very phenomenon that became the object of the age's repression and fascination.

We might consider, for instance, Foucault's description of insanity, specifically his notion that there was "something which refers elsewhere, and to *other things*" in the classical conception of madness (p. 58). Was woman part of this "elsewhere," and were her feminine associations among the "other things" to which madness referred? Foucault dates the official beginnings of this massive confinement as 1656, the year that marks the establishment of the Hôpital General in Paris, as well as the larger movement across Europe to solidify the social order by confining those who did not serve that order. The numerous establishments founded in the late seventeenth and throughout the eighteenth centuries were not medical institutions, but "establishments of religion and public order, of assistance and punishment, of governmental charity and welfare measures," especially aimed to house "a population without resources, without social moorings, a class rejected or rendered mobile by new economic developments" (pp. 43, 48). Considering the economic predicament of this social element, it should come as no surprise that women—especially pregnant women and those with young children—constituted a large number of the confined. One establishment, Foucault records, "housed 1,460 women and small children," another "lodged 530 pregnant women, nursing women, and very young children," and at another, "there were 98 boys, 897 girls between seven and seventeen, and 95 women" (p. 49). As these places of confinement were spreading across Europe, the age was also coming to define its notion of "madness"—the nature and manifestations of otherness that society would isolate and exclude. What I want to consider is not simply the fact that these women were among those who populated the establishments, but the ways in which their gender became associated with the very definition of madness.

Is it merely coincidence, I wonder, that in Foucault's description of insanity, he most frequently cites women as examples of the insane—"madwomen" who were found with their feet, hands, and faces bitten by rats; "madwomen" whose ankles were chained to the wall; "madwomen" seized with fits and "chained like dogs" (pp. 71–74). There were, of course, many different groups of people confined during these years, each reflecting a peculiar kind of otherness that reasonable men considered manifestations of "unreason"—beggars, vagabonds, and criminals had all assumed a place in the confinement of the mad.[22] I do not want to suggest that woman's outcast position in the social and economic order should in any way eclipse the predicament of different "other" social elements suppressed by this reasonable age. I will be arguing, however, that the classical notion of madness was strongly linked to a sexual ideology in which women were represented as both lack and excess—lacking in their economic predicament as well as in their intellect and reason, yet at the same time excessive in their emotional intensity and reproductive capacity. In these ways, the female gender became emblematic of an "unreason" that influenced the very definition of madness and in turn shaped madness into a feminine configuration of otherness. That configuration, as Foucault's descriptions of "madwomen" suggest, still haunts the mind, shaping woman into an example of that which her gender has come to represent.

Catherine Clément would seem to be commenting on exactly these kinds of associations when she writes: "Societies do not succeed in offering everyone the same way of fitting into the symbolic order; those who are, if one may say so, between symbolic systems, in the interstices, offside, are the ones who are afflicted with a dangerous symbolic mobility. Dangerous for them, because those are the people afflicted with what we call madness, anomaly, perversion. . . . And more than any others, women bizarrely embody this group of anomalies showing the cracks in an overall system."[23] Woman's embodiment of "madness, anomoly, perversion" would help explain her specific associations in Enlightenment representational schemes with notions of excess—as the monstrous female, and with passivity—as the submissive creature confined in both social institutions and in the institution of marriage. It also helps account for the emphasis that feminists critics have been placing on two divergent positions that woman occupies in the cultural imagination. Sandra Gilbert and Susan Gubar describe these poses as the "angel in the house" and the "madwoman in the attic"; Nina Auerbach finds them in depictions of woman as "corpse" and "demon." For an Enlightenment articulation of such perceptions, consider Nicolas Malebranche's statement: "'L'imagination est la folle du logis'—imagination is the madwoman of the house. . . . "[24] Whatever the particular configuration, the general sense is that women not only inhabit places outside the "normal" social order, but that woman herself takes on the representation of otherness. She becomes an embodiment of the other world.

The idea that women "embody" otherness is especially suggestive, since woman's physical body was intimately connected with one of the most famous diseases of the age—hysteria. The classical notion of hysteria, we should keep in mind, differed from that which we now commonly associate with the mental phenomenon described by Freud, principally because in the eighteenth century hysteria was still strongly connected to the body. "The space in which [hysteria] assumed its dimensions," Foucault explains, was "that of the body" (p. 143). Yet it was specifically the body of woman that figured this space. Because hysteria constituted one of the major manifestations of insanity during this age, and because of its close associations with woman's body, hysteria became a disease that both forged the connections between woman and madness, and helped to shape madness into a feminine configuration of otherness. Although the old myths that hysteria was caused by the displacement and movement of the womb were largely rejected, physicians nonetheless believed that the uterus and the womb effected hysteria through a diffusion of humors and nerves. Perhaps the most distinctive manifestation of this diffusion—one that, as I will show later, was especially important in shaping Enlightenment configurations of the feminine—concerned fluid instability. Foucault explains that the womb, in generating this instability, effected a disease "dispersed throughout the entire body," through the irregular flow of menstrual blood, and through a general mobility of bodily fluids in the stomach and intestines, blood and vital humors, even the brain (pp. 143–45). What distinguished "female hysteria" from the "male variety," or hypochondria, was the very infirm and less resistant quality of the female body—a body that was more accommodating to these fluid motions. "The entire female body," Foucault says, "is riddled by obscure but strangely direct paths of sympathy; it is always in an immediate complicity with itself . . . it encloses a perpetual possibility of hysteria" (pp. 149, 153–54). Might we not also say, then, that the entire female body also encloses a perpetual possibility of madness and unreason? And if this is the case, then would not madness generate the possibility of becoming like a woman and assuming the fluid disorder of her body?

If woman came to "embody" the disease of madness, we need to take account of the cultural effects of both her real and figurative associations with the very concept of disease itself. Foucault, who relates the history of insanity within the larger history of disease, suggests that societies define and isolate various incarnations of disease so that they can renew their "rites of purification and exclusion" (p. 3). Thus in his scheme of things, madness replaced leprosy—the disease that had necessitated confinement in earlier centuries—in the social effort to exclude the diseased and purify

the healthy. Yet his comments on the otherness of the lepers, those diseased predecessors of the mad, recalls for me the perpetual otherness of
woman. "What doubtless remained longer than leprosy, and would persist
when the lazar houses had been empty for years, were the values and images attached to the figure of the leper as well as the meaning of his exclusion, the social importance of that insistent and fearful figure which was
not driven off without first being inscribed within a sacred circle" (p. 6).
I want to suggest that we might well read "woman" for "leper," and understand woman as that "insistent and fearful figure" who has always represented what did not fit in men's systems. The associations linking woman
and disease, after all, have a long background in woman's reproductive
history. Consider Carroll Smith-Rosenberg's observation that nineteenth-
century male physicians "had followed the eighteenth century's latitudi-
narian attitudes toward sex in general and female sexuality in particular"
in diagnosing several aspects of women's reproductive capacity as "path-
ological." [25] Mary Ann Doane draws on these same historical connections:
"Disease and the woman have something in common—they are both socially devalued or undesirable, marginalized elements which constantly
threaten to infiltrate and contaminate that which is more central, health or
masculinity. There is even a sense in which the female body could be said
to harbor disease within physical configurations that are enigmatic to the
male." [26]

The disease to which Doane refers, of course, is hysteria—a "physical
configuration" that became "enigmatic" to the Enlightenment mind,
which regarded itself as healthy. In exploring the enigma of this disease,
Foucault associates it with guilt—a guilt then regarded as "'the torment
of all effeminate souls whom inaction has plunged into dangerous sen-
suality'" (p. 157). To understand the bearing of this association on
woman and her history, let me return to Clément who, writing more than
a decade after Foucault's study of madness was published, appropriately
entitles her history of woman "The Guilty One."

Like Foucault, Clément also explores the social dimensions and conceptions of disease. But she specifically focuses on the connections linking the
contagion of disease and the agency of sorceress and witch—both predecessors to the hysteric, both "embodying" the history of woman. Drawing
on the ideas of Jules Michelet, Clément describes how the great epidemics
of the middle ages—especially the diseases of the skin such as leprosy and
syphilis—were "signs of repressed desire boiling up." [27] But it is the sorceress and witch, Clément explains, who spread the contagion, particularly
through their circulation of bodily waste and odors. Among the waste
products Clément identifies are "menstrual blood, excrement, a lock of

hair," products that will assume an important place, as we will see, in classical configurations of the feminine. Because this waste derives from woman's body, because it is "bound by bodily geography to orifices; voice, spit, tears, shit, a cry, anything secreted and emitted" (p. 35), the spreading of this waste, or the failure to contain it within the body, is associated with the very idea of the uncontained, hysterical woman. So it is, Clément explains, that the hysteric inherits the role of the witch. For her transgression and violation of boundaries, woman becomes the "The Guilty One," the very embodiment of the disease and contagion she fosters.[28] To the classical mind, hysteria became a disease that not only infected woman's body, but that threatened the social order as well—generating the dangerous movement of fluids that might exceed the bounds of contained systems. This would explain not only why hysterical women were among those confined during the age, but also why the very notion of bodily and social disorder became inscribed in representations of woman. The attempt to control a contagion that might result from the spreading of woman's bodily fluids thus finds its literary expression in Swift's horrified response to the fluid and excremental properties of women's bodies, just as Pope's fascination with a young woman who lost a lock of her hair—and also lost control of her emotions—finds its realistic complement in the actual plight of the hysterical woman.

If we can regard hysteria as a feminine configuration of madness, then woman's body becomes an object not only to be confined in the real world, but an object representative of a diseased and contagious otherness that the age felt compelled to contain. In this sense, we might think of feminine configurations of disease as constituting a kind of "dis-ease," an unsettling of material—bodily and social—that reasonable men tried to keep in place. It was, I would suggest, the very possibility that an ordered world could easily become an hysterical one—the possibility that something lurked within society that could at any moment destroy the symmetry of its system—that made it so necessary for the age to isolate and confine this disruptive feminine phenomenon. The hysterical woman became a kind of "other" man—a "mad" man inside the normal man—who threatened the very order of his being, and who became the diseased part that he would have to differentiate from himself and isolate. Later, I will explore the theoretical implications of such notions in larger, mythic accounts of woman's nature—particularly the story of Genesis and its account of woman as created from material excessive to man's body. Having her very origin in Adam's rib, man's excess, Eve comes to embody excess and transgression. Is it any wonder that she and her effects need to be contained, or that the age most distinctive for its schemes of confinement would figure madness and disease through the body of woman?

These feminine configurations also infiltrated the imagination and language of science, a topic that has lately received much attention from those involved in the feminist critique of scientific methods and pursuits. Like those historians who have been exploring the effects of language in historical discourse, several feminist critics have called attention to the metaphors and figures in scientific discourse that have had the effect of excluding woman and all her feminine associations. In tracing this exclusion, they are especially concerned with the development of experimental modes of scientific investigation that derive their epistemology from the philosophy of Francis Bacon and the founding of the Royal Society. The "rise of modern science" that we associate with these men was consumed with the penetration and domination of Nature—a realm long associated with the generative forces of woman. Describing the scientist's need "'to follow and as it were hound nature in her wanderings,'" Bacon speaks in revealing terms to the "man" of the new science, instructing him not "'to make scruple of entering and penetrating into these holes and corners, when the inquisition of truth is his whole object. . . .'"[29] Viewed from this perspective, the scientific enterprise is seen not only regarding itself as masculine, but fearing any association with the feminine. Evelyn Fox Keller cites several explicit claims by founders of the new science that betray these specific anxieties, among them Henry Oldenburg's announcement that the Royal Society would "'raise a Masculine Philosophy . . . whereby the Mind of Man may be ennobled with the knowledge of Solid Truths,'" and Joseph Glanvill's warning that "'The *Woman* in us, still prosecutes a deceit, like that begun in the *Garden*; and our *Understandings* are wedded to an *Eve*, as fatal as the *Mother* of our *miseries*.'"[30]

It seems inevitable, then, that this peculiar scientific anxiety about woman was connected to seventeenth-century debates about witches—women representative of yet another feminine configuration outside the domain of science. Noting the practical disappearance of witchcraft after the mid–1660s, Brian Easlea argues that the new science had achieved victory over the supernatural and "occult" forces that were associated with woman. In its victory, modern science joined forces with the Christian attack against "Satan and his (in)human, mostly female allies."[31] During the famous seventeenth-century debates about witchcraft, as Keller explains, a new "mechanical science" that "sought to divorce matter from spirit" distinguished itself from and replaced a "hermetic tradition" in which "material nature was suffused with spirit" (p. 44). Alchemy, firmly rooted in that hermetic tradition, allowed that natural magic could serve as a method for studying nature. Since spirit and matter were merged, witchcraft might be accepted as a form of natural magic and therefore as a means of understanding the natural world. The new mechanical science, however, in separating spirit and matter, conveniently disassociated itself both from the demonology of witchcraft and the magical lures of alchemy. Not only had witchcraft, as Keller puts it, "attested to the gravity of the dangers represented by women—dangers against which reason and the new science promised protection," but in so doing it "reinforced the arguments for banishing Woman, sexuality, and the correlative 'unsober' inquiry of the alchemists from science" (p. 60). Science, we might say, became the grand witch hunter.

The very conceptualization of science as a hunter seems particularly relevant, since in configuring woman as other, science sought both to exclude and appropriate her. Just as the disease of hysteria allowed the age a means for defining the domain of reason, so the witch and sorceress made it possible for science to establish its intellectual domain. It was the exclusion and desired appropriation of the madwoman, in other words, that facilitated the system of the reasonable man. She was not simply excluded from science because a group of seventeenth-century men happened not to allow her admission to their circle. She was excluded *because she is the very other thing that man desired to appropriate,* to conquer, and, as Cixous puts it, "to give him the pleasure of enjoying . . . the return to himself which he, grown greater—reassured in his own eyes, is making."[32]

In calling attention to this feminine world that scientists omitted, the feminist critiques of science explain how this omission is related to various historical and cultural factors. Keller, for instance, observes how science has developed within a "network of gender associations" that connected masculinity with objectivity, reason, and power (p. 12). And Sandra Harding writes: "Yet there is another world hidden from the consciousness of science—the world of emotions, feelings, political values; of the individual and collective unconscious; of social and historical particularity explored by novels, drama, poetry, music, and art—within which we all live most of our waking and dreaming hours under constant threat of its increasing infusion by scientific rationality."[33] What we should add to these insights is an awareness that science could not have had it any "other" way. It was necessary to exclude women because woman was already figured as the very material of exclusion. In its desire to define itself and appropriate the other thing that was not itself, science played out its masculine role in the sexual economy of classicism.

THEORIES OF THE FEMININE

An other history, composed of varied configurations that all seem to bear the shape of woman—should we envision the story of woman as entirely outside of, completely other than, man's history? This possibility has recently informed much writing that goes under the name of "feminist theory," whose authors explicitly identify woman with those cultural elements that have been omitted from and displaced throughout man's account of his world. If we can think of intellectual history as composed of narratives about the past, what Jean-François Lyotard calls "grand narratives" through which knowledge is organized and passed on,[34] then the women who are now theorizing the feminine could be regarded as writing those narratives that never found a place among the "grand narratives." This feminist theory—commonly associated with the "French Feminisms" of Hélène Cixous, Luce Irigaray, and Julia Kristeva, and more recently associated as well with a variety of women writers from several academic disciplines and from both continental and Anglo-American contexts of feminist thought,[35] finds the story of woman intricately linked to individuals, ideas, and values that have been excluded from the systems that dominate Western culture. Informed by the discourses of psychoanalysis and poststructural philosophy, feminist theory not only tells the story of the other elements outside the domain of "grand narratives," but breaks in every way from the orderly modes of discourse typically used to construct narrative, historical, and theoretical writing. In this sense, it has become an "other" theory altogether—and is, not surprisingly, both influencing and becoming a subject of much contemporary intellectual revisionism, or what some might more appropriately regard as a revolution in theoretical discourse.

For the purposes of my own search for Enlightened Absence, I want only to sketch the outlines of this other narrative whose specific unfolding in England's classical age impresses me as a crucial episode in the articulation and suppression of the feminine. This sketch will take us from the story of Genesis—which typically figures in accounting for the predicament of woman as outside man's systems, to contemporary poststructural philosophy—which is locating the very deconstruction of metaphysical systems in the phenomenon of woman.

"No other civilization," Julia Kristeva writes of Judeo-Christian culture, "seems to have made the principle of sexual difference so crystal clear."[36] In the separation of man and woman in Eden, man assumes the position of God and father—the role of lawmaker, and woman plays out her role in the subservient positions of mother, wife, daughter. Through the adoption of these identities, sexual division becomes cultural construction. It is only to be expected, since without something outside the system, and different from its law, how else could the system define itself? "The economy of this mechanism," Kristeva explains, "requires that women be excluded from the single true and legislating principle, from The Word . . . excluded from knowledge and from power" (p. 21). The economy of man's world, we might say, does not simply delegate woman to a position outside. It requires her exclusion. Where men's ideas are, she is not; where men's history is, she is not; where men's world is, she is not. As Claudine Hermann puts it, woman's space is *"empty,"* constituting "a sort of *no man's land.*" [37]

Kristeva's notion of Eve not simply as the woman who violated God's law, but as the very embodiment of violation that man has figured as woman, relies on the story of Genesis—a "grand narrative"—to find terms with which we can begin to tell an other story. Speaking in these terms, Kristeva is engaging a kind of theoretical discourse that Alice Jardine calls "postmodern," a discourse through which theorists not only write about elements that have been omitted, but that are explicitly connected to the idea of woman. Jardine describes this notion of woman as a "configuration," a means of delineating and giving shape to the thing that resists being placed. In particular, she finds this configuration of woman permeating the discourse of postmodern thought in its "search for that which has been 'left out,' de-emphasized, hidden, or denied articulation within Western systems of knowledge." [38] The tendency to regard things "left out" in terms of "woman" becomes all the more intriguing not only because it parallels the cultural event of the contemporary women's movement, but also because, as Jardine explains, it "problematizes" the very concept of woman. "Woman" now assumes at least two meanings: that of *"woman as sexual identity,"* and woman as concept—or, as Jardine puts it, *"woman as process."* On the one hand, we have a classification of humans defined as "women." On the other, we have an assortment of concepts figured as "woman," specifically as the woman who signifies "those *processes* that disrupt symbolic structures in the West." [39]

This notion of "woman as process" helps us conceptualize feminine displacement in terms of a space that annihilates its own space. Just as Serres was able to conceptualize unknown forces by describing them in terms of the disordered sea, so we may be better able to regard woman's displacement not so much as a fixed *place,* but as a fluid *process* that effects the very construction of solid systems. To regard woman as process also makes it easier to understand why she appears threatening to the established world of stasis and order. In her very nature—her identity as other and her process of behaving otherwise—she violates the code of man and God. Eve again comes to mind, along with all the figurations of evil entering the world through woman. She is the prototype of the woman who threatens a systematic world not because she has somehow decided to violate the code of order, but because her separation, her otherness, makes her the very material of that violation. And yet it is precisely because of her threatening nature that she becomes an object of desire. Kristeva explains: "The myth of the relationship between Eve and the serpent is the best summary of this exclusion: the serpent stands for the inverse of God, since he invites Eve to transgress God's prohibition. But it is also this very desire to transgress which Adam represses, which he dares not act out, which is his shame: the sexual symbolism helps us understand that the serpent is that which, in God or Adam, remains outside or beyond the sublimated content of the Word. Eve has no relationship except with that—precisely because she is its opposite, the 'other race.'" [40] Writing about this "other race" is much like writing about an "other history"—the story of the woman displaced by a culture that must at once exclude her so that it can define itself, and yet reach out to appropriate her so that it can reinforce its own sense of self. Playing her role in these dynamics, woman remains perpetually outside this world, hovering on its margins.

But this world—what is it? In one sense we might think of it as "the world of man," because the memorable men of history—philosophers, historians, scientists—are largely responsible for its construction. And in this sense we might well describe such a world as *patriarchy,* a term that resounds throughout much feminist scholarship, since it describes a social order constructed by men who, like their father God, preserve its symmetry and order through law and the passing on of that law from father to son. Such descriptions typically emphasize that this world—of men, of patriarchs—is a cultural construct, one that has, for various historical reasons, excluded women, but one that can nonetheless be reconstructed, modified, reformed. The system, in other words, is to be preserved in the process of its reformation. What is "wrong" with the system is that it has failed to account for the role of women. Therefore, once it begins to take account of her accomplishments, it can somehow be fixed.

Envisioning the problem is this way focuses more attention on woman's place outside the systems of men rather than on her complicitous displacement as other in the very construction of systems—that is, the fact that she *must* be outside the system in order for it to exist and thrive. These two perspectives about woman's position, while they are not diametrically opposed, obviously generate very different accounts of what woman's role *should* be once she is recognized as having been excluded from men's systems. From one perspective, woman should be allowed to enter the patriarchal world and in the process change its construction. From another perspective, however, even if woman were allowed entrance into the world of man, there would still have to be something outside, something else functioning as other—excluded, repressed, desired, dominated—in order for the system to prosper. The question of "woman," then, may be more than the question of whether "women" will enter and potentially transform patriarchy. For if all the women of the world were suddenly inside, there would remain the thing "like a woman" outside. The issue here is one of domination and oppression, appropriation and repression—of the insidious connections between those in power and their subordinates who make the acquisition of power possible.

This world, then—what is it? When Luce Irigaray says that "women diffuse themselves according to modalities scarcely compatible with the framework of the ruling symbolics," she uses a term that echoes throughout much recent poststructural writing: *symbolics*—the world that is represented through language, or as Irigaray puts it, "the structuration of language that shores up its representations."[41] Regarded from this perspective, symbolic systems and representational schemes order the world, providing it with its symmetrical framework. Whatever does not enhance this symmetry is therefore excluded, placed outside. As such, the symbolic consolidates a patriarchal world that in turn becomes the material of the symbolic order. No wonder Irigaray says that we must question *"the conditions under which systematicity itself is possible."*[42]

Western culture has, of course, a "grand narrative" to account for the structure of this symbolic order, both for what it includes and excludes. A father God is created, "in the beginning was the Word," Father and God and Word. The universe is then created, and it will function according to the law of Father and God, who places a man in this perfectly symmetrical, ordered world. But the law is violated, through the agency of a woman, herself created from the substance of man. She is different from man. It is this woman, this thing different from man, his other side, that violates the law of a God and Father who is, from the beginning, himself the Word. Different from man, woman is also different from God and Father and Word. She is not of the world of language, of the structured representation of the world. She is, and she must be, outside the symbolic order.

This world, then—let us call it the symbolic order of things—is the world that men order through symbols, through structured representations. It is the world of the word, of language, of the use of language to achieve the structuration that is its substance. The psychoanalyst Jacques

Lacan, who is largely responsible for rewriting Freudian theory in terms of language theory, explains the sexual dimensions of the structuration of language by describing "man" not only as the agent who supplies order and structure through language, but who actually becomes the material of that order. He suggests that "in man and through man *it* speaks [*ça parle,*] that his nature is woven by effects in which is to be found the structure of language, of which he becomes the material. . . ."[43] To begin to understand this "structure of language," this construction of the symbolic order, we have to go back, Irigaray says, to philosophy—"to try to find out what accounts for the power of its systematicity, the force of its cohesion, the resourcefulness of its strategies, the general applicability of its law and its value. That is, its *position of mastery*. . . . " (p. 74).

Philosophy—the vehicle for man's pursuit of knowledge and truth. If history, in recording man's story, places woman outside its narrative, then where is woman in philosophy? I pose this question because while history has isolated the age I want to study, philosophy fathers the two discourses I will be exploring—that of a modern science and a classical literature. And if history, at least in the hands of some contemporary historians, is beginning to look back at just those things that were "left out" of its story, then philosophy—in its questioning of its own construction, in its deconstruction—has also taken notice of its omissions. Its pursuit of truth has become strangely linked to its pursuit of something that never figured in the kind of knowledge perceived as leading to truth. We might think of this other concern of philosophy as an other discourse altogether.

The contemporary philosopher perhaps most recognized for his critique of Western metaphysics is Jacques Derrida, a man whose questions about "the conditions under which systematicity itself is possible" have much in common with the feminist critique of the symbolic order. Rejecting the total space of philosophical discourse for the spaces and spacings within discourse that make it ceaselessly generative and impossible to fix, Derrida's writing—like Foucault's history—becomes part of an other world, one that exceeds the boundaries of systematic and structured discourse. It takes account of the displaced element, that elusive interval of deferral, and it does so while assuming its own role in the dispersive process of writing—since that condition is "always already" the condition of discourse.[44]

To what extent, and in what ways, is this dispersion in and of philosophical discourse connected to woman? Gayatri Spivak addresses this issue quite explicitly. Like many of the commentators on Derrida, she believes that what some find particularly troubling about Derridean deconstruction is the sense of "uncertainty" and "indeterminacy" it fosters. Things are not stable in Derrida's writing; his writing itself is a disturbingly mobile process. Yet she distinguishes herself from "most male commentators on Derrida" by suggesting that "the naming of woman . . . has slowly moved into the scene of Derrida's own writing," and that "it is possible to say that 'woman' on the scene of Derrida's writing . . . occupies the place of a general critique of the history of Western thought." [45] This idea not only complements those of other female commentators on Derrida, but also informs several of the recent overviews of "feminist" writing that make much of the connections between "deconstruction" and "feminism." Toril Moi, in surveying the major strands of Anglo-American and French feminism, finds a combination of Derridean and Kristevan theory to be especially promising for feminist writing. [46] Gayle Greene and Coppelia Kahn, introducing their collection of essays on feminist literary criticism, claim that such criticism "may be allied with deconstruction" and that "a deconstructive feminist criticism is potentially revolutionary." [47] Elizabeth Meese finds the "de-centering" implicit in deconstruction vital to feminist criticism if it is to do anything more than preserve "a hierarchal structure of domination." [48] And Alice Jardine considers Derrida—along with Lacan and Deleuze—as providing a "theoretical heritage" for the women theorists in France. [49]

This connection between deconstruction and woman, between Derrida and a group of "feminist" writers, has everything to do with what I have described as the other interest of philosophy—the other discourse. In his essay *Spurs,* Derrida associates woman with what he calls the "untruth of truth"—she lures the philosopher toward truth, but because she "will not be pinned down," she "unseats the philosopher-knight" who seeks meaning and closure. [50] Woman, to use Spivak's terms, becomes "the place" of deconstruction because she herself has no place, is dis-placed, different from, distanced from the truth that systematic philosophy seeks. Because she is outside of man's world, because she has figured as the object of his desire, and—this is most important—because she is associated with all that cannot be "pinned down" by him, woman becomes other to his discourse. She becomes the gaps and holes within philosophical discourse that make it impossible for philosophers to achieve the metaphysical cohesion they seek.

As the other material that is both excluded from and desired by the man, woman makes it possible for philosophy to define its very metaphysical system. Derrida puts it this way: "A woman seduces from a distance. In fact, distance is the very element of her power. Yet one must beware to keep one's own distance from her beguiling song of enchantment. A distance from distance must be maintained. Not only for protection (the most obvious advantage) against the spell of her fascination, but also as a way of succumbing to it, that distance (which is lacking) *is necessary*" (p. 49). Both to ensure his protection from her "untruth," and at the same time to ensure the continuation of his desire, it "is necessary" for woman to be outside of philosophy. Like science, philosophy simply could not have things any other way, or else it would have touched the domain of this other—the forbidden object. The tree of knowledge beckons, but man does not touch it. The thing in him that reaches for the fruit is woman.

The important question here is how woman might escape the role assigned to her in this representational scheme, how she might escape her role as a temptress and seductress in the discursive process. Is the Derridean notion of woman's displacement only another version of the classical configuration and appropriation of woman?[51] My own feeling is that while this particular postmodern identification of woman may only serve to enforce woman's imprisonment in discursive categories, it also holds forth the possibility of liberating her from those categories—by allowing us to reconceptualize woman's displacement not as the object of man's desire, but as the subject of her own actions. Several feminist theorists, for instance, have been able to critique philosophical systems by reading woman as a subject who upsets metaphysical systems, and who promises a radical change in the very way we conceptualize knowledge itself.

And so it is that the women of contemporary theory have transformed postmodern woman from a desired object into a speaking subject. Explaining her perspective in writing *About Chinese Women*, Kristeva says: "Women. We have the luck to be able to take advantage of a biological peculiarity to give a name to that which . . . remains on this side of the threshold of repression."[52] Introducing a collection of her essays, she strikes the same note: "It was perhaps also necessary to be a *woman* to attempt to take up that exorbitant wager of carrying the rational project to the outer borders of the signifying venture of men."[53] There is something about being outside, or at least about being associated with the outsider, that imbues with human urgency the project of seeking what is displaced, distanced, other.

In Luce Irigaray's writing, the distinction between woman-as-object and woman-as-subject has become a crucial one. She believes that we need to listen for the voice of this woman in a symbolic system that has kept her long suppressed. "And yet that woman-thing speaks. . . . It speaks 'fluid,'" Irigaray says. "*Yet one must know how to listen otherwise than in good form(s) to hear what it says*. That it is continuous, compressible, dilatable, viscous, conductable, diffusable, . . . " (p. 111). Irigaray shares with

Cixous this concern with woman's fluid effects. Distinguishing herself from Derrida, Cixous says that "he must jump from concept to concept, or from rock to rock, whereas I allow myself to say, since I do not have any obligation toward philosophy, I really do prefer swimming. I prefer being in the water and openly in the water. . . ."[54] Elsewhere, Cixous describes woman: "Unleashed and raging, she belongs to the race of waves. She arises, she approaches, she lifts up, she reaches, covers over, washes a shore, flows embracing the cliff's least undulation, already she is another. . . ."[55]

While associations linking woman and water have long been part of the mythic and literary imagination, recent "theories of the feminine" are not only calling attention to these associations, but to the *effects* of feminine fluidity—particularly the danger it poses to systems that are enclosed within what Irigaray calls "solid walls of principle. . . ." (p. 106). If we are to seek out this fluid other who—instead of excluding and desiring the one outside—herself continually merges with and becomes "another," who is "viscous, conductable, diffusable," we are going to have to question, at every point, both systematic and solid pursuits. Perhaps they will take us to the fluid realm outside the world of man and his fixed symbolic order, and into the "space" that Hermann aptly calls "womans' space"—*"no man's land."*

Fluidity, we might say, has come to be associated with the threat of woman as other—the danger of a potentially uncontrolled dispersion that cannot be fixed in place, that seeps through the "cracks in the overall system." For a powerful example of this feminine danger, we might consider Klaus Theweleit's fascinating explorations of woman's image as a fluid threat to fascist systems, her embodiment of a "male fantasy" that has long depicted woman in terms of water and floods.[56] We might also return, in a curious way, to Foucault's history of madness. When introducing his study, Foucault tells the story of something new that appeared in the "imaginary landscape of the Renaissance"—the "Ship of Fools," boats on which the insane were placed to keep them in a *"liminal* position," a prison that wandered from country to country, a prison that was the *"threshold"* itself." This was the "other world" of the madman before the "Age of Reason" confined him, a world that, Foucault says, is inevitably associated with water since "water and madness have long been linked in the dreams of European man."[57]

Or might we say that the connection is between water and woman? It is *her* marginal position—as the object throughout history of men's confinement and fascination—that I sense in Foucault's description of the wandering and watery world of the mad, and in Serres's account of the waters of the unknown. There is the "immense literature that stretches from Ophelia to the Lorelei," Foucault remarks, adding to those conspicuous feminine portrayals of madness the analyses "which interpret madness as the manifestation in man of an obscure and aquatic element, a dark disorder, a moving chaos, the seed and death of all things, which opposes the mind's luminous and adult stability" (p. 13). Among the very first acts of the Father God was the transformation of fluid chaos into firm land, and, of course, the creation of light. Not long after that, man was created, and then woman from the substance of man—from within him. It was woman who wandered off, who would not stay in place, who transgressed the Father's law, who brought darkness and death into the world. It was woman who became the transgressive element *of* man, the madness in him, that he would henceforth associate with her and banish from his enlightened and ordered world. "He has his truth," Foucault writes of the madman, "and his homeland only in that fruitless expanse between two countries that cannot belong to him" (p. 11). And so does woman, in her fluid realm, have her own "truth" outside the solid claims of philosophy and science. It is a mad and mobile truth. And it is a space about which we have no information.

And so our search for woman outside not only leads us to the fluid realm surrounding man's islands, but asks that we reconsider the parameters constructed to preserve the domain inside—especially those constructed by the grand system makers of science. "It is already getting around," Luce Irigaray writes, "that women diffuse themselves according to modalities scarcely compatible with the framework of the ruling symbolics." Entertaining the possibility that their "transgression and confusion of boundaries" are implicated in the omissions of science, she claims: "So we shall have to turn back to 'science' in order to ask it some questions. Ask, for example, about its *historical lag in elaborating a 'theory' of fluids,* and about the ensuing aporia even in mathematical formulation." Could it be, she goes on, that science has found it necessary "to minimize certain of these features of nature . . . so as to keep it/them from jamming the works of the theoretical machine" (pp. 106–7). She has caught the reason for the lag, for the omission. If science lets the woman enter its symbolic order, if it lets the woman assume a place, then her processes, he fears, may jam its system. Displaced, she can be sought, and appropriated to a safe degree—just enough to give the illusion that science has achieved the dominion that its system continually asks that it achieve.

Science's lag in developing a theory of fluids—like history's resistance to accounting for the forces of dispersion, like philosophy's necessary exclusion of woman's "untruth"—they are all signs of the ways in which civilization makes "the principle of sexual difference so crystal clear." For the difference between presence and absence, between that which is included and that which is excluded, has all along been represented in terms of the difference between man and woman. The science and literature of Enlightenment England was a model of men's ability to construct universal principles. But we need to understand that these universal principles were also highly exclusive ones, and that they were sexually determined. Newton said as much in his *Principia*, if we can listen to him otherwise than in good form, if we can be sensitive to the fluid world he never managed to accommodate, if we begin to inquire into the conditions that make his systematicity possible.

II

Systematic and Fluid Universes

2

Newton's
Exclusive Principles

Given the success of modern science, defined in opposition to everything female, fears of both Nature and Woman could subside. With the one reduced to its mechanical substrate, and the other to her asexual virtue, the essence of *Mater* could be both tamed and conquered; male potency was confirmed.

EVELYN FOX KELLER

Then everything becomes possible: optics and dioptics, the world and its system, medicine and everything that follows from it. In the game of truth, error has been checkmated; in the game of domination, all is reduced to slavery, including the body.

MICHEL SERRES

This Being governs all things, not as the soul of the world, but as Lord over all . . . and Deity is the dominion of God not over his own body, as those imagine who fancy God to be the soul of the world, but over servants.

ISAAC NEWTON

THE LADY

THE STORY of how Isaac Newton came to write the *Principia* centers, we are told, on two characters—Newton himself and Edmund Halley. According to the story, Halley, one of the secretaries of the Royal Society, visited Newton in 1684, when Newton was Lucasian Professor of Mathematics at Cambridge and a fellow of Trinity College. Halley asked Newton a question about planetary motion, and Newton's reply so excited Halley that the two men continued to correspond on the matter. After this correspondence, Newton agreed to make his ideas public, and with the encouragement and support of Halley, he completed and published the *Principia*.

Other characters emerge in this story—Hooke, Wren, Huygens,

Leibniz—all of whom had been studying the laws of motion and whose findings therefore impinged on the "discoveries" of Newton. The names of such men appear again and again when historians of science tell the story of the *Principia*. There was another character as well. She figures in the story in far less notable ways, and yet in some sense, it was her presence that shaped the development of this narrative.

Among the correspondence between Halley and Newton concerning the publication of the *Principia*, there is a letter in which Halley refers to the part of the manuscript to be entitled "The System of the World," a final section in which Newton would explain his mathematical principles in philosophical terms and thus make them available to "those that will call themselves philosophers without Mathematicks. . . ."[1] Newton, however, wrote to Halley that he had decided to "suppress" this part of the *Principia*, complaining that his involvement with philosophy was troublesome and that he would therefore keep his distance from this subject. Referring to "The System of the World" as the third book of the *Principia*, Newton explained: "The third I now designe to suppress. Philosophy is such an impertinently litigious Lady that a man had as good be engaged in Law suits as have to do with . . . her. I found it so formerly & now I no sooner come near her again but she gives me warning."[2]

Halley was understandably upset. In persuading Newton to retain this third book, he wrote back to him about the value of both the book and the Lady: "I am heartily sorry, that in this matter wherein all mankind ought to acknowledge their obligations to you, you should meet with any thing that should give you disquiet, or that any disgust should make you think of desisting in your pretensions to a Lady, whose favours you have so much reason to boast of. Tis not shee but your Rivalls enviing your happiness that endeavor to disturb your quiet enjoyment. . . ."[3] The argument worked, and Newton agreed to include the book. And yet throughout his life, Newton would continue to be haunted by this Lady.

Perhaps we should say that the real story of the *Principia* involves only the real men who figured in it and the theories with which they were concerned. The *Principia*, after all, is the grand product of the seventeenth-century scientific revolution. It not only uncovered the mathematical principles accounting for the motion of bodies, but applied those principles to laws governing the motion of planetary bodies—producing a perfect mathematical explanation for what Newton called "The System of the World." Several men had theorized about such principles, but only Newton derived the exact mathematical calculation. The story of his formulations of those principles, and of how such principles fulfilled the expectations not only of the Enlightenment scientific community but of an age bent on creating systems that encapsulated an orderly, designed universe, has been told again and again by historians of science and culture. It seems only natural that they should be interested in writing about such systems and about the men who created them, that they should be concerned with the sources of certain theories, the development of ideas, the exchange among members of a scientific community that produced the very "rise" of modern science. They would hardly be interested in some reference to a "Lady," a mere metaphor that Newton used to figure his attraction toward and yet distance from the troubling realm of philosophy. A literary critic might find the metaphor curious, but should a scientist?

Even supposing that this metaphor has some significance, we might nonetheless wonder why Newton, a man who rarely indulged in ornate or metaphoric language,[4] and who spent most of his life alone contemplating the dynamics of the universe, would express himself in such terms. Why, in order to explain the mathematical principles governing the laws of universal motion, and specifically to explain his anxieties about applying them to "The System of the World," did he describe himself as having to wrestle with a woman? I will be suggesting not only that Newton's metaphoric figuring of his undertaking was no accident, but that it was necessary. It would have been impossible for Newton to account for the dynamics of the universe without engaging in a kind of sexual dynamics. The science of his age simply could not have had it otherwise. Sexual difference had already become the unacknowledged basis of scientific investigation.

To understand how these sexual dynamics play their part in the production of systems and theories, we might listen to the commentary of another man who tried to put his world together, but who, as he himself admitted, failed in his attempt. I am thinking of Henry Adams and his famous *Education*, published at the beginning of the twentieth century, in which he attempted to come to grips with a world profoundly altered by science and technology. He described himself as having "greatly preferred his eighteenth-century education when God was a father and nature a mother, and all was for the best in a scientific universe."[5] In his own time, Adams felt, matters were far from being "best." The problem was that the ordered universe had lost its "unity" and given way to "multiplicity." And what made matters more frightening was that scientific concepts of "force"—instead of accounting for principles of cohesion—were unable to deal with the new chaotic powers that had somehow been unleashed in the world.

This sense of chaos, for Adams, was intimately associated with feminine powers beyond the control of men. Adams respected, but also feared, the "Virgin" and her symbolic reproductive capacity. In her fecundity, she represented the source of life and energy; but in her potential for generation, she represented a source of chaos that threatened to exceed the systematic designs of the universe, and that ultimately made it impossible for Adams to chart the history and meaning of his education. Implicit throughout the *Education* is the suspicion that woman—the source of life but also the potential source of chaos—has made science impossible, and has, in a sense, rendered it impotent. She seems always to interrupt and exceed its systematic pursuits. Adams desired a world of order, a world he identified with "his eighteenth-century education when God was a father and nature a mother," the fixed universe of Newtonian science. But instead, he found himself transformed into "a conscious ball of vibrating motions, traversed in every direction by infinite lines of rotation or vibration, rolling at the feet of the Virgin at Chartres . . . a centre of supersensual chaos."[6] Yet there was also something about this image of himself as rendered helpless before the Virgin that fascinated Adams. If he desired an orderly, systematic world, he also desired to know the phenomenon that made such a world impossible. The very story of his life became the search for an elusive and threatening feminine force.

This vision of woman as disrupting the scientific attempt to explain an ordered universe might well be described as a phobia that plagued the men involved in the "rise of modern science," and that accounted for their marked tendency to describe the object of their scientific scrutiny in feminine terms. The world itself—the natural, physical universe—was figured as a woman. The *system* of the world—its unity and structure—was that to be inscribed by the scientist, by man. To delineate this system, to account for *The Mathematical Principles of Natural Philosophy*, it would be necessary to constrain the feminine material of nature and inscribe this material in terms of law and system. For Newton, this enterprise necessitated a confrontation with the Lady. For the seventeenth-century scientific community, such a confrontation was implicit in the very aims and methods of the scientist, and became explicit in the language Newton used to speak of these goals.

The natural world, notably unlike the world of Newton's *Natural Philosophy*, had long been associated with women and feminine powers, something that must have been deeply embedded in the unconscious of the seventeenth-century scientific community since they acknowledged the association again and again in their language. For almost two centuries, however, the connection between this feminine natural world and the distinctly male-dominated world of the new science has gone virtually unrecognized. While the "History of Science" assumed the task of recording developments in scientific knowledge, and more recently—in the work of such men as Thomas Kuhn and Paul Feyerabend—of probing into science's epistemological bases,[7] it was not until the "feminist" interest in science that anyone bothered to inquire into its sexual construction. Only then did things begin to change. Carolyn Merchant, sensing links between the feminist and ecology movements in our own time, argued that the manipulation and control of nature that brought us to our present ecological crisis had its origins in the seventeenth-century scientific revolution and its desire for dominion over the natural world.[8] And not surprisingly, she found the evidence for this sexual appropriation of nature in a whole network of cultural assumptions that continually surfaced in the language of the scientist.

Ever since Merchant called attention to Bacon's sexual imagery "in delineating his new scientific objectives and methods"—images that portray nature as having to be "'bound into service' and made a 'slave,' put 'in constraint' and 'molded' by the mechanical arts"[9]—much has been made of the implications of such language in the shaping of the entire scientific enterprise. Evelyn Fox Keller argues that "we cannot properly understand the development of modern science without attending to the role played by metaphors of gender in the formation of the particular set of values, aims, and goals embodied in the scientific enterprise."[10] And Sandra Harding claims that scientists share unacknowledged assumptions about their undertaking, assumptions revealed in their "gender symbolization," among them that "the best scientific activity and philosophical thinking about science are to be modeled on men's most misogynous relationships to women—rape, torture, choosing 'mistresses,' thinking of mature women as good for nothing but mothering."[11] Lest we consider this metaphoric tendency peculiar only to the men of seventeenth-century science, Harding cites this statement of Richard Feynman, a contemporary physicist, from his Nobel lecture: "'. . . the idea seemed so obvious to me and so elegant that I fell deeply in love with it. And, like falling in love with a woman, it is only possible if you do not know much about her. . . .'"[12]

The implications of such figurations—whether we find them in Bacon "constraining" the feminine, natural world, Newton complaining about the Lady of philosophy, or Feynman falling in love with a distant, womanly theory—would all seem to lead in similar directions. Woman is figured as the object of scientific scrutiny. To achieve scientific knowledge, to prove the theory, the scientist must discover and conquer the woman. Or, using terms that are admittedly charged with sexual implications, we might say that the scientist, if he is to be successful, must "come" "to know" woman. In this way, his desire for knowledge becomes inextricably tied up with his desire for power. As Merchant explains, it was by "penetrating" the mysteries of nature that man could recover the dominion that he lost, through the agency of a woman, in Eden. "Scientific method, combined with mechanical technology, would create a 'new organon,' a new system of investigation, that unified knowledge with material power." [13] The feminine world of nature was to become the object of scientific inquiry and domination. Michel Serres, without addressing any of the gender implications of such scientific quests, nonetheless reaches a similar conclusion about the desire for domination that characterized "classical" science. "These epistemologies are not innocent: at the critical tribunal they are calling for executions. They are policies promulgated by military strategies. To know is to kill, to rely on death, as in the case of the master and the slave." [14] Or, we might say, to know is to gain power, as in the case of the controlling man and the rebellious woman.

Henry Adams, writing at the beginning of the twentieth century, was no longer convinced of science's ability to control these feminine forces—an ability that he specifically associated with the eighteenth century and its neat placement of "father" and "mother" in a "scientific universe" where "all was for the best." Isaac Newton, writing near the beginning of the eighteenth century, seemed determined that these very feminine forces be controlled. The historical connections between these two men are forged through their common fears—the fear that something feminine threatened to disturb a patriarchal system. But while Adams exposed his fear, Newton suppressed his—and it was this suppression that shaped a scientific universe that, two centuries later, Adams would question. For Newton, any disorderly or unprincipled phenomena would have no place in scientific epistemology. Yet in remaining outside a system constructed by men, these disorderly phenomena would take on—as Adams's testimony two centuries later demonstrates—the attributes of a woman. They would be like Newton's Lady.

THE DANGEROUS HYPOTHESIS

I have suggested that this Lady, the metaphor Newton used to figure his anxieties about phenomena that resist systematic closure, would always come back to haunt him. In the *Principia*, she takes the form of hypotheses.

Newton's *Principia* is composed of three books. The first two concern laws of motion, and the third—which at one point he threatened to "suppress"—concerned the application of these mathematical principles to planetary bodies. "In the preceding books I have laid down the principles of philosophy; principles not philosophical but mathematical," Newton writes at the beginning of Book Three. "It remains," he continues, "that, from the same principles, I now demonstrate the frame of the System of the World."[15]

It was the universal application of Newton's mathematical principles, as Halley well knew, that would make the *Principia* a monumental treatise. Yet Newton, associating this particular book with "philosophical inquiries" that plagued him,[16] as the Lady of philosophy had often done when he approached her, seemed willing to drop the book altogether. Why Newton ever suggested suppressing this book involves another character in the story of the *Principia*, Robert Hooke. When Halley presented Newton's treatise to the Royal Society, Hooke accused Newton of plagiarism, insisting that he himself had already deduced as much about the laws of gravity. Halley, offering a compromise and attempting to save the third book, wrote to Newton: "Mr Hooke has some pretensions upon the invention of the rule of the decrease of Gravity, being reciprocally as the squares of the distance from the Center. He sais you had the notion from him, though he owns the Demonstration of the Curves generated thereby to be wholly your own; how much of this is so, you know best, as likewise what you have to do in this matter, only Mr Hook seems to expect you should make some mention of him, in the preface, which, it is possible, you may see reason to praefix."[17]

Newton was clearly angered by Hooke's accusations. It was then that the talk about the Lady began. Finally, through the diplomacy of Halley, Newton's anger was appeased, and he wrote back to Halley that he would "compose" the dispute by acknowledging the insights of Hooke and others not in the Preface, but in the Scholium to the fourth Proposition.[18] The acknowledgment, meager as it was, took care of the problem. And yet at the same time, the dispute itself signaled a more general problem—the question of why Newton would so willingly take the opportunity to suppress what was obviously the most daring and monumental part of the *Principia*. While it is true that Newton had not been the first to conceive of the laws governing universal gravitation, he had nonetheless accomplished something that his fellow scientists could not manage—he had actually figured out the mathematical demonstration and successfully applied it to the workings of the planetary system. And yet when it came time to make his work public, to establish the connection between mathematical principle and philosophical statement, he pulled back—as if such "philosophical inquiries" should have no place in experimental science. Were Hooke's accusations the reason for this retreat? Or is it possible that "philosophical inquiry" truly did disturb Newton, as it threatened—in the guise of a Lady—to disturb the neat and purely mathematical system of his *Principia?*

We can, of course, never know what Newton's motivations actually were; further, if his motivations were at least in part unconscious, even Newton's own statements would not help clarify the situation. To say definitively that he intended to suppress the "philosophical inqueries" of the third book strictly because of the argument with Hooke would dismiss the lurking possibility that Newton did not want to publish ideas that would be anything less than mathematically precise. Frank Manuel has suggested that "two midwives were necessary" to assist in the birth of the *Principia*. One was Halley, with his "encouragement and reassuring affection." The other was Hooke, whose "provocation" and "desire to trounce him, to crush him once and for all," finally "stung Newton into action." [19] Might we, then, think of Halley as the agent who would bring forth Newton as the man of science, the man who would give the age what it so desperately wanted—a perfect system of the world? And if this is possible to imagine, might we then think of Hooke's provocations as bringing forth the woman who seemed always to be hovering around Newton— the Lady who would trouble him and threaten to disturb his neat systems?

In one sense, it might seem futile to engage in such speculations, since the problems surrounding Hooke's argument with Newton were, through Halley's intercession, fairly quickly resolved, and since Newton did ultimately publish his famous third book of the *Principia*. In another sense, however, such speculations linger only to resurface when we see this troublesome Lady return to haunt Newton. The "philosophical inqueries" that formed the substance of Book Three left some important matters unsettled, and on being provoked again, Newton had to confront the Lady once more. This time, the dispute grew much larger in its dimensions, and involved yet other figures. It was also implicated in Newton's adding to the second edition of the *Principia* what is now perhaps the most memorable part of the treatise—the General Scholium.

This story involves yet another notable figure in the history of science, Gottfried Wilhelm von Leibniz who, like Hooke, also staked a claim to theories that Newton set forth in his *Principia*. Some two years after the first edition of the *Principia* appeared, Leibniz published material concerning the laws of motion. One of his essays specifically addressed "the causes of the motions of the heavenly bodies," an essay in which he reached conclusions about certain laws of motion that were remarkably similar to Newton's. Leibniz claimed that he had come to these conclusions twelve years earlier, when he communicated some of them to the Royal Academy of Sciences—but did not publish them until after "Newton's work stimulated me to allow these notes, for what they are worth, to appear, so that sparks of truth should be struck out by the clash and sifting of arguments, and that we should have the penetration of a very talented man to assist us."[20] For Newton, however, the "sparks" were of a different nature, and no doubt reminded him of those that surrounded his dispute with Hooke. As Bernard Cohen explains, Newton was never convinced that Leibniz had been "wholly honest" about his deductions, and on several occasions Newton made it quite clear that Leibniz was guilty of "stealing unjustly" from him, or at the very least of "annoyingly repeating" what he had already said.[21]

I do not want to go into detail about what have become the famous quarrels between Newton and Leibniz,[22] but the substance of this disagreement, I think, can tell us much about what Newton was willing to include among his *Mathematical Principles of Natural Philosophy,* and more important, what he was determined to exclude. The disagreement between the two men, which surely had its origins in their similar interests and competitive spirit, surfaced again shortly before the publication of the second edition of the *Principia,* and this time it involved more than bickering about who discovered what first. This time it concerned arguments about the nature of gravity, involving no less than a controversy about the two traditions that fueled the scientific spirit of the age—the mechanical and the hermetic. Roger Cotes, who orchestrated the publication of the second edition of the *Principia,* brought to Newton's attention a letter that Leibniz had written to Hartsoeker and that had appeared in a London weekly. Leibniz here accused Newton of failing to offer a mechanical explanation of gravity. In deserting "Mechanical causes," Leibniz claimed, Newton built his theories on "Miracles" and "Occult qualitys"—a charge that would upset any scientist who aligned himself, publicly at least, with a systematic empirical philosophy.[23] Cotes, coming to Newton's defense, responded to such complaints in his Preface to the second edition. There are those who "mutter something about occult qualities," Cotes writes. "They continually are cavilling with us, that gravity is an occult property, and occult causes are to be quite banished from philosophy. But to this the answer is easy: that those are indeed occult causes whose existence is occult, and imagined but not proved; but not those whose real existence is clearly demonstrated by observations. Therefore gravity can by no means be called an occult cause of the celestial motions, because it is plain from the phenomena that such a power does really exist."[24]

The answer seems not to have been so "easy" for Newton, who wrote and kept revising several drafts of the General Scholium in which he wrestled with this issue. The result was his famous "*hypotheses non fingo*"—his claim not only that he would not frame hypotheses, but that they did not belong in experimental science.

> Hitherto we have explained the phenomena of the heavens and of our sea by the power of gravity, but have not yet assigned the cause of this power. This is certain, that it must proceed from a cause that penetrates to the very centres of the sun and planets. . . . But hitherto I have not been able to discover the cause of those properties of gravity from phenomena, and I frame no hypotheses; for whatever is not deduced from the phenomena is to be called an hypothesis; and hypotheses, whether metaphysical or physical, whether of occult qualities or mechanical, have no place in experimental philosophy. (pp. 546–47)

What is particularly interesting about this statement, as Cohen points out, is that in looking through Newton's several drafts of the General Scholium, we can see Newton "increasing the number of types of hypothesis he will shun from the original pair (mechanical, and of occult qualities), first to three (by adding those that are metaphysical), and then to four (including physical ones too)."[25] Clearly Newton wanted nothing to do with *any* kind of hypothesis, with any form of speculation that could not be explained in terms of the mathematical principles that kept his *Principia* perfectly inscribed.

Newton obviously had reasons for not wanting to engage in hypotheses and speculations, reasons that derived from his own training at Cambridge and from the commonly accepted assumptions of his scientific community—what Kuhn might call the "paradigm" that Newton at once helped to establish and within which he himself worked.[26] Yet I find myself seeking other reasons for his adopting such an exclusive position, and for deliberately excluding from his mathematical propositions the kind of philosophical speculation that he had earlier associated with the Lady. To engage in "philosophical inquiry" that could not be deduced from observation would entail stepping outside the domain of science, perhaps even into the realm of the occult and miraculous. And that very step beyond boundaries would mean entering a world over which science could not, at least yet, claim dominion. If knowledge was a form of power for the scientist as he sought to "know" the phenomena of the world, then this realm outside his dominion was that of the unknown.

It was also the realm that was both fascinating and disturbing to Newton, at once constituting the source of his curiosity and the parameters of his science. Manuel suggests that a "chief source of Newton's desire to know" was his "fear of the unknown," which accounted for, among other pursuits, his desire to seek the origins of ancient kingdoms through chronology, and to seek certainty through mathematical calculation.[27] Is it possible that this "other" world was for Newton somehow feminine? Did the Lady—the philosophical inquiry that he was once willing to suppress, and later insistent on keeping outside the parameters of the *Principia*—have any bearing on the nature of his scientific enterprise?

Figured as the phenomena not to be included in a purely mechanical science, bordering—as Leibniz would have it—on the very occult world that was so opposed to the methods and goals of experimental science, Newton's Lady seems to hover everywhere around his scientific enterprise without ever assuming a place in it. As such, she not only becomes that which is excluded (the unknown), but that which must be displaced so that it can function as an object of desire and appropriation (the thing to be known, to be conquered by science). She is necessary, as is the hypothesis, because she makes science possible. Yet she is dangerous, as is the hypothesis, because once she enters the scientific system, she distorts its mathematical certainty and symmetry. Like the woman perpetually displaced throughout the systems of Western discourse, Newton's Lady lures him to the realm where he can achieve his greatest conquests, where he can enjoy the pleasure of confirming his knowledge. Yet if she were to enter his systems, he would no longer be able to engage in a purely systematic science. The Lady, for Newton, had to be absent.

Newton, I think, understood the appeal of this Lady all too well. He also recognized that she was dangerous. It is intriguing to consider Frank Manuel's ideas about Newton's relationship with his mother in terms of what I find to be his curious relationship with this Lady. Manuel believes that Newton's mother was "the central figure in his life," and that her absence during Newton's childhood years explains his lifelong desire to return to her—a desire that became "one of the most powerful psychic drives in his nature and manifested itself in a variety of scientific forms."[28] If we were to follow this line of speculation, and if we were to consider Newton's desire for a return to his mother as a similar manifestation of his anxieties about the Lady, it might be possible to begin to understand the longing for certainty that motivated Newton's intense scientific spirit as a desire to reach out for something feminine, so that he could appropriate this other thing for his fixed and systematic theories.

That Newton himself was far from being a purely mechanical philosopher is now commonly acknowledged. His fascination with chemical mixtures or with the figurative language of biblical prophecy shows us a man who was drawn not only to precise mathematical studies, but to phenomena and ideas profoundly mysterious. Perhaps, as his biographer Richard Westfall suggests, the *Principia* had given shape to Newton's earlier and more private indulgences in alchemy and theology, and had "redirected Newton's intellectual life . . . into an unexpected and concrete realm of thought where the rigor of mathematical precision could help . . . reshape natural philosophy." In this way, Westfall continues, the *Principia* transformed Newton's life "as much as it had transformed the course of Western science."[29] Clearly what we know as science, as a precise and methodical discourse, is Newton's legacy. But it was only part of Newton's own imagination, and only part of the scientific imagination of his age. As Margaret Jacob explains, the scientific Enlightenment was actually composed of two elements: the Newtonians who believed that a systematic universe was regulated by a providential creator, and a diverse group of radical thinkers who subscribed to a more "pantheistic" notion of the universe—"a metaphysic that conflated spirit and matter and tended to proclaim nature, and not God, as the sole object of worship and study."[30] In addition to these radical thinkers who, despite their differences with the Newtonians, nonetheless maintained strong connections with the mechanical philosophers, we also need to take account of those who more clearly aligned themselves with the hermetic tradition and all its associations with witchcraft and magic. While these individuals were largely purged from the entire scientific endeavor, their cultural influence, as Brian Easlea explains, played an important role in the shaping of science.[31] We need to remember that there were such "other" forces informing Enlightenment science if we are to discover an "other" side of Newton himself—a possible feminine quality that he suppressed, yet one that drove him on.

THE OTHER NEWTON

The Newtonian imagination—what Frank Manuel described as "a compelling drive to find order and design in what appeared to be chaos, to distill from a vast inchoate mass of materials a few basic principles that would embrace the whole and define the relationships of its component parts"[32]—defined, to a large extent, the cultural imagination of the English Enlightenment. And it was Isaac Newton and his *Principia* that captured the cultural imagination, that "transformed," as Westfall explained, "the course of Western science." To begin to understand the "other" side of that imagination, I want to reverse the terms we use to speak of it. Instead of acknowledging the fact that Newton captured the cultural imagination, I want to consider the possibility that the cultural imagination—an imagination consumed with the idea of system—captured Isaac Newton.

Bent on securing control over an unwieldy natural world, the new science would find everything it needed in Newton's mathematical principles. And the prominent position given to Newton in the history of science only shows how he and his theories have come to stamp the science of that age. Manuel says as much when he suggests that Newton's "closed scientific system . . . affected the evolution of Western science by excluding alternatives—the looser models of a Hooke or a Leibniz,"[33] or, we might add, the chemical world of Boyle, even Newton's own fluid domain of optics. It was the Newton of the *Principia* who became the great scientist of the age. And it was the closed system of the *Principia* that came to define the world of science.

Yet if the age created this Newton, it did so by ignoring another side of him. Newton's interests far exceeded the world of mathematical philosophy, and though it is the author of the *Principia* who continues to dominate our modern sense of the man, the "other" Isaac Newton has begun to attract the attention of recent historians—the Newton who wrote a chronology of the world, who studied and commented on Biblical manuscripts, who kept his Arian beliefs and his alchemical interests secret throughout his life, who was fascinated with the "spirit" of aether, the processes of fermentation, and the reflections of color. Westfall, who is all too sensitive to the shaping influence of the *Principia* on both Newton and Western science, nonetheless finds himself unable to "avoid the question: Have we perhaps mistaken the thrust of Newton's career? To us, the *Principia* inevitably appears as a climax. In Newton's perspective, it may have seemed more like an interruption of his primary labour."[34]

Let us entertain the question to see how this "perhaps mistaken" notion about Newton might radically alter our assumptions about the history of modern science. If, as historians tell us, the Newtonian revolution is responsible for ushering in the systematic world of classical physics—providing a "brilliant synthesis of Galilean terrestrial mechanics and Copernican-Keplerian astronomy"—[35] it is Newton, in whose name the revolution is inscribed, who should be rightly credited with the inauguration of this new worldview. The world became Newtonian as he stamped it with his mathematical principles. Yet if we consider Newton himself as a scientist whose interests far exceeded those of mathematical principles, then the world that bears the stamp of his name would become a very different place. The Newtonian world would no longer exclusively be the domain of the *Principia* and related systems of fixed social and religious order, but would be more complex and multifaceted, less precisely defined, less rigid and systematic. The borders of its paradigm would be less distinct, more susceptible to what Serres envisioned as the random encroachment of the waters that surround it. We might consider the age to be "amphibious"—as Hugh Kearney describes Newton himself caught between the demands of a science seeking an ordered, mechanical universe and the lures of magic and alchemy.[36] Brian Easlea, writing about the powerful forces that witchcraft and magic exerted on the scientific revolution of the sixteenth and seventeenth centuries, offers his study for the very reason that histories of science all too frequently ignore such matters in accounting for the rise of science, making the revolution "appear far too straightforward a triumph of 'reason' over 'prejudice' and 'superstition,'" and ignoring the "often passionately advocated or defended 'extrascientific' commitments" of scientists.[37]

Perhaps, then, we should not only enlarge our notion of the ideas, values, desires, and passions that accounted for the construction of the "Newtonian" revolution, but also begin to pay more attention to the fact that both Newton himself and his scientific community were responding to more than a quest for intellectual mastery. They were also responding, I would suggest, to a pleasurable encounter with "other" material, a desire they felt compelled to repress. In being attentive to this response, we can begin to see the mechanical spirit of the age as a reaction to that which it suppressed—an attempt to halt the progression of desire that turns away from systematic definition and toward pleasurable indulgences. The *Principia,* when seen from this perspective, is just what both Newton and modern scientists needed to turn away from these indulgences and set science forth on its straight path toward mastery. And it is just what they needed to prevent them from pursuing any other paths, especially those that led to something other than order and light—that took them instead into the realms of darkness, fluidity, color. Indulging in these other spaces, the scientist gives way to otherness, becoming almost enamored of those phenomena that excite pleasure rather than facilitate conquest and dominion. So it was that Newton's interest in mathematical laws and a systematic universe took precedence over his interests in alchemy and his fascination with religious mysteries. And so it was that the new science celebrated a mechanical philosophy and classical physics, while it dismissed almost entirely the hermetic tradition associated with the alchemical and occult worlds. The suppression of the "other" interests of science made it possible for the men of science to halt their drift into these pleasurable realms, and to turn instead toward the articulation of universal principles.

Could this world suppressed by science be feminine? We might begin to imagine this possibility by exploring the other side of Newton—a side that we might conceptualize by imagining an "other" scientific paradigm altogether. Or perhaps it would be better to discard such structuralist models, and conceptualize this other world in terms of Serres's figurations. Perhaps we should envision the suppressed side of science not so much as an other island composed of different intellectual material, but as the very waters that lie around the island of the *Principia*, that "rare summit" surrounded "by a slow conquest of the surf's randomness along the coast."[38] Once we begin to see Newton's *Principia* as surrounded by waters that threaten to invade its symmetry, we can begin to speak once again about Newton's Lady—this time as a figuration of his mother and her own figuration as woman, as the feminine material displaced throughout scientific systems. We can also begin to speak about Newton's father—not, of course, his real father who died before the child was born, but his father God—the figure with whom Newton powerfully identified, and in whose name he inscribed his "System of the World." Manuel believes that in Newton there was "simultaneously a longing for the abstract, for the ineffable, for what he never cast his eyes upon, and an astonishing sense of the real, experimentally wrested from nature by physical actions and controlled by mathematical notations." What I find most suggestive about Manuel's identification of these two "longings," however, is the way in which he connects them with the idea of father and mother: "One is almost tempted to recognize in his genius a union of two experiences, his relations with the father whom he never saw and with his mother whom he possessed with such intense emotion, whom he saw with his own eyes and always longed to see again as he has in the early years of his infancy—a fantasy he pursued in vain throughout his life, looking for the image through peepholes and in 'chymical glasses.'"[39] If Newton was loyal to the system of the father, he strikes me as being far more intrigued with the fantasy not so much of returning to the mother, but of turning his attention toward phenomena that he associated with the pleasures of his mother. Along with Newton's God and Newton's Lady, both the father and mother he "longed" for take their place in the story of the *Principia*.

THE FATHER AND THE MOTHER

It is well known that Newton was a profoundly religious man. What is perhaps less often noticed is that his religious devotion was intimately linked to his loyalty to God the Father. A person who did not believe in the trinity but who nonetheless kept his Arianism secret throughout his life, Newton allowed no place in his "System of the World" for any son other than himself. And the system itself, of course, allowed no place for woman. Well before Newton wrote in the General Scholium attached to the second edition of the *Principia* that this "most beautiful system of the sun, planets, and comets, could only proceed from the counsel and dominion of an intelligent and powerful Being" (p. 544), he had already had the opportunity to profess the religious dimensions of the *Principia* to the world. He allowed Richard Bentley to expound on the ways in which his mathematical principles, as Newton put it, "might work with considering Men, for the Belief of a Deity; and nothing," Newton went on, "can rejoice me more than to find it useful for that Purpose."[40] And after the publication of the second edition of the *Principia* and its new General Scholium, Newton allowed Samuel Clarke to engage in a lively defense of the religious grounds of his mathematical principles—in a famous exchange of correspondence between Clarke and Leibniz. Once again Leibniz had charged that gravity must be "a miraculous thing, since it cannot be explained by the nature of bodies." This time Newton let Clarke fight for him—not only defending himself through the agency of a theologian, but implicitly warding off the occult through refuge to his Father God.[41]

Clearly the *Principia* did not simply explain *a* "System of the World." It explained *the* system set in motion by God the Father, the figure who embodied for Newton what he called "the dominion of One" (p. 544). If the absence of Newton's mother, as Manuel suggests, fueled his desire to engage in the world of the unknown, it was the presence of God the Father that Newton relied on to halt the progression of desire—to fix him and his science in the world of certainty. Perhaps that is why, though the *Principia* went through three editions, Newton never made any substantive changes in his basic theory about the motion of bodies and planets—a situation that contrasts, for instance, with his increasing attention to new matters and queries in his revisions of the *Opticks*.[42] Once the mathematical system was set in place, it only required fine tuning. The puzzle had been solved. Nothing remained that would necessitate further queries.

The only nagging problem, of course, was the nature of gravity itself, and Newton had taken care of this matter not simply by dismissing it from the proper realm of experimental science, but by associating it with the powers of God the Father. We have every reason to think that Newton truly believed gravity to be a divine power. It was for this very reason that he felt compelled to align such a supernatural force, one that exceeded any attempt to be explained by science, with the power of God. For Newton, to suggest anything otherwise would leave open the possibility that gravity could be part of the occult and magical worlds that the mechanical science had so insistently rejected. If gravity could not be accounted for within the the domain of scientific principles, Newton was not going to give it up to anything outside that domain—at least not anything other than the very divine powers of the Father. It was not so easy for Newton to come to grips with alchemy that, as he surely sensed, had little to do with the laws of the Father.

We know that Newton spent many years studying the chemical world, and produced "a vast accumulation of papers" on the subject.[43] In these pursuits, he both stayed within and stepped outside the domain of experimental science. On the one hand, chemistry had come to define itself as a reputable scientific undertaking, as the work of Robert Boyle and others would easily testify. Magic had largely been extracted from the alchemical process, and the alchemist who was once portrayed as the stock figure in search of gold and chemical elixirs was transformed into the respected man of science who studied objectively the chemical changes that occur in physical phenomena. On the other hand, however, something of the mysterious and unknown still permeated the world of alchemy. The hermetic tradition in philosophy, long associated with alchemy and the occult—not to mention witchcraft—was diametrically opposed to the mechanical tradition in which scientists viewed the universe as composed of inert bodies that move according to mathematical laws.[44] If the new "chemists" of the scientific revolution formally dissociated themselves from this hermetic tradition, it was nonetheless difficult to purge chemistry entirely of its connections with the live and transmutable universe of alchemy.

Despite Newton's extensive readings in alchemy, and despite his own experiments in chemistry, he never pursued his interest as a science. Far from taking his alchemical studies toward the goal of certainty, he instead kept them secret—sharing only bits of information with select individuals.[45] If Manuel is correct in suggesting that much in Newton's scientific pursuits derived from a "desire to enjoy once more the pleasures of intimate visual exchange" that Newton associated with his mother, then what Newton has recorded about his alchemical studies would lead us to believe that it was pleasure, rather than the quest for scientific certainty, that lay behind his interest in alchemy. At one time, recording his experiments with mercury, he described a process that "makes gold to swell, to be swollen, and to putrefy, and also to spring forth into sprouts and branches, changing colours daily, the appearances of which fascinate me every day."[46] And in a letter to Oldenburg—dated 1675, well before the publication of both the first edition of the *Principia* and the second to which he added the General Scholium, Newton wrote: "For nature is a perpetuall circulatory worker, generating fluids out of solids, and solids out of fluids, fixed things out of volatile, & volatile out of fixed, subtile out of gross & gross out of subtile, Some things to ascend & make the upper terrestriall juices, Rivers and Atmosphere; & by consequence others to descend for a Recquitall to the former."[47] Are these the words of a mechanical scientist who believed in inert matter and fixed laws of motion?

No doubt that alchemy, like optics and the reflections of color, dealt with phenomena more unwieldy, more fluid, than the fixed domain of the *Principia* and its hard "bodies." Yet even in the General Scholium to the *Principia*, Newton betrayed his interest in a universe that was very alive, vibrating with a certain "spirit." In the very last paragraph, he wrote: "And now we might add something concerning a most subtle spirit which pervades and lies hid in all gross bodies; by the force and action of such spirit the particles of bodies attract one another at near distances, and cohere, if contiguous; and electric bodies operate to greater distances, as well repelling as attracting the neighboring corpuscles; and light is emitted, reflected, refracted, inflected, and heats bodies; and all sensation is excited, and the members of animal bodies move at the command of the will, namely, by the vibrations of this spirit, mutually propagated along the solid filaments of the nerves, from the outward organs of sense to the brain, and from the brain into the muscles" (p. 547). Such vibrating motion, which "lies hid" in bodies and through which "sensation is excited," seems out of place in the fixed world of the *Principia*. But then, it was not the Newton of the *Principia* who engaged in hidden and secret studies. This was a different Newton, the one who hovered on the edge of his own scientific paradigm, on the very last "added" comment of his mathematical treatise.

It almost seems as if, once having described the domain of the Father, Newton was now free to move into new territory, free to "add something" to ensure the progress of desire. Newton himself was aware that this different world of "subtle spirit" did not belong in the *Principia*, and he made this quite clear in the final sentence of the Scholium that brings his grand treatise to a conclusion: "But these are things that cannot be explained in a few words, nor are we furnished with that sufficiency of experiments which is required to an accurate determination and demonstration of the laws by which this electric and elastic spirit operates" (p. 547). Would Newton now seek that "sufficiency," or was the goal of sufficiency and accuracy merely a means for him to pursue other worlds?

Historians of science and biographers of Newton can argue about such matters forever, and surely, few would want to align Newton strictly with either the fixed world of mechanics or the more fluid world of alchemy. Besides, there is still the rich territory of optics that he explored throughout his entire life, and that at times seems as mathematically designed as those fixed bodies in the *Principia*, and at other times as fluid and mobile as the fiery mutations of chemically fused substances. Perhaps it is enough to say, as Newton himself had said of the mysterious force of gravity, that it exists—that the fascination with alchemy and the moving, fluid world of "spirit" was very much there in Newton, though hidden and suppressed. Easlea records the story of Newton packing away his alchemical papers when he assumed the position of Warden of the Mint in 1696, suggesting that the chest of papers contained evidence of "disreputable intellectual interests." "*Very* disreputable interests," Easlea goes on, for "when the chest was opened after his death, an executor of his will wrote on one of the manuscripts that it was 'loose and foul' and 'not fit to be printed.'"[48]

Perhaps it is time that we start asking some questions of science, questions—as Luce Irigaray would say—about its "lag" in accounting for fluid phenomena, as if even to acknowledge such phenomena would "jam" the systems of science.[49] Why is it that a mathematical physics functioned as the dominant model at this crucial stage in the "rise of modern science"? Why is it that grand systems of design and the principles that kept them in perfect motion were accounted for as the productions of a Father? Why were speculations about fluid, moving, transmutable phenomena not given any prominent place in the ruling paradigm, and in fact often kept hidden and suppressed? The history of science might offer several explanations for the way science developed in certain directions. What I am more interested in, however—and what is implied in Irigaray's question— is the possibility that the directions taken by Enlightenment science reflect its response to phenomena associated with specific genders. When Manuel, for instance, suggests that Newton's desire to indulge in mysterious phenomena was related to his desire to engage once again in the pleasures of visual exchange that he associated with his mother, he is building his speculations on certain facts about Newton's childhood: the fact that his father died before he was born, that his mother became a central and consuming figure in his early years, that she left the young boy and their home to remarry, that his mother's absence prompted Newton's hatred of his stepfather and a longing for a reunion with his mother.[50] Such factual details about Newton's life, as they tend to cluster around the image of the mother, become material for the biographer to use in constructing a psychological portrait of Newton. And so would the details about Newton's scientific interests, as they tend in various ways to cluster around the images of the Lady and the mother, become material that we might use to construct a psychological portrait of Newtonian science. I use the term *psychological* not only because I am trying to recover phenomena that were the subject of repression, but because this repression was specifically related to feminine ideas and associations, and was therefore inextricably linked to a sexual ideology.

It is time that we inquire not only about the influence of Newton's mother in his own science, but about the place of scientific pursuits that, instead of inscribing themselves within a father's system, reflect maternal longings—such as Newton's alchemical experiments and optical gazings, or reflect anxieties about engagements with impertinent Ladies—such as Newton's troubling encounters with hypotheses. In some ways, Newton's Lady and his mother assume their place in cultural configurations of the "madwoman" and the "angel." Yet as Nina Auerbach tells us, we need to "circle back to these 'images'" so that we can recover their energy as a source of "perpetual metamorphosis."[51] If, as Joseph Glanvill warned in the seventeenth century, scientists should beware of the *"Woman* in us" who "prosecutes a deceit," and to whom scientific knowledge is connected as if "wedded to an *Eve,* as fatal as the *Mother* of our *miseries,"*[52] then we should ask why this maternal connection became the cause of such anxiety and suppression. We need to ask science some questions about its response to maternal and feminine phenomena—to all the fluid, transmutable material excluded from its "System of the World"—so that we can recover their energy and begin to imagine what science might be like when it breaks from its moorings in a paternalistic universe.

Hidden and secret, alive and transmutable, a realm acknowledged only in the very final words of the *Principia,* on its edge where Newton seems to want to step out, and into somewhere else—what is this absent realm? Why would Newton keep his distance from it? Is it, as Manuel speculates, somehow embodied in the very force of gravity itself that Newton ostensibly associated with the system of the Father, but that may also have revealed a powerful and personal longing for "distant and absent ones"— for his mother, for the pleasure beyond system that his mother recalled?[53] We might well regard Newton's preoccupation with distance, the very absence of space between two bodies, as figuring both in the production of his perfect mathematical systems and the desire to immerse himself in phenomena that would never have a place in that system—that would always, inevitably, purposefully remain absent.

The words of our own contemporary writers, in search of what has been "left out" of our historical and scientific accounts, seem to have curious relevance to the enigma of Isaac Newton. "A woman seduces from a distance. In fact, distance is the very element of her power. Yet one must beware to keep one's own distance from her beguiling song of enchantment. A distance from distance must be maintained."[54] "Somewhere every culture has an imaginary zone for what it excludes, and it is that zone we must try to remember *today*."[55] "So we shall have to turn back to 'science' in order to ask it some questions. Ask, for example, about its *historical lag in elaborating a 'theory' of fluids,* and about the ensuing aporia in mathematical formalization."[56]

The story of Isaac Newton and his *Principia* has become one of the "grand narratives" of Western civilization. It was written and orchestrated by a group of men who sought out a "System of the World," and who explained the symmetry of that system in terms of the Father's law. Newton gave them that system. But he also left them, and us, a chest of absent material. He never fully opened that Pandora's box, but it needed to be there in order for him to place everything else neatly inside his box of mathematical principles. This absent material—was it feminine?

When Jonathan Swift satirized the scientists of the Royal Society, he placed them on an island where—distant and detached from the concerns of the real world—they engaged in their notably unrealistic experiments. Curiously enough, the women doomed to live on this floating island hated their confinement there, and would often sneak away to the "Diversions of the Metropolis." One woman, in particular, "hid her self" there for several months, and even after being discovered, "contrived to steal down again . . . and hath not been heard of since." Like Newton, Swift was a man who believed powerfully in systems, notwithstanding the satire he leveled against empirical scientists. Yet his sense that women somehow were not to share the island of the scientists was by no means peculiar to his exclusion of women from this imperfect scientific world. Swift's sense of woman as displaced, as outside the systems of men, was powerful and explicit throughout his writings.

Newton's absent material—was it feminine? In his "other" great scientific treatise, the *Opticks,* color proved to be a phenomenon that, though it fascinated Newton throughout his life, he could not effectively contain within a fixed theory. Curiously enough, Alexander Pope, who was also fascinated with color, repeatedly associated it with women. Do the scientist and satirist share a representation of the feminine, figuring through woman the material that would have no place in the systems of men? We will return to Swift's scientific island, where women are conspicuously absent, after considering the fluid and mingling properties of color that proved so disturbing to both Newton and Pope.

3

Newton, Pope, and the Problem of Color

Neither black on white nor white on black . . . not in this opposition of colors that stand out against each other. . . . Feminine light doesn't come from above, doesn't fall, doesn't strike, doesn't go through. . . . Her rising: is not erection. But diffusion. Not the shaft. The vessel . . . a turbulent compound of flying colors, leafy spaces, and rivers flowing to the sea we feed.

HÉLÈNE CIXOUS

And therefore if the reason of any Colour whatever be required, we have nothing else to do than to consider how the Rays in the Sun's Light have by Reflexions or Refractions, or other causes, been parted from one another, or mixed together. . . . I speak here of Colours so far as they arise from Light. For they appear sometimes by other Causes, as when by the power of Phantasy we see Colours in a Dream, or a Mad-man sees things before him which are not there; or when we see Fire by striking the Eye, or see Colours like the Eye of a Peacock's Feather, by pressing our Eyes in either corner whilst we look the other way.

ISAAC NEWTON

> Come then, the colours and the ground prepare!
> Dip in the Rainbow, trick her off in Air,
> Chuse a firm Cloud, before it fall, and in it
> Catch, ere she change, the Cynthia of this minute.

ALEXANDER POPE

FEW READERS of Alexander Pope would question his allegiance to those systems of order and design he celebrated everywhere in his poetry. Nor is it surprising that when we look for connections between the scientific world of mathematical principles and the literary world of classic design, Isaac Newton and Pope immediately come to mind. Pope's own famous comment summarizes their shared worldview well enough: "God said, *Let Newton be!* and All was *Light.*"[1]

That Pope should praise universal systems in terms of the Biblical inscription "Let there be light" only confirms the long-standing associations of light and order. Things are confused and often threatening in darkness, but in light, they can be clarified, defined, and controlled. The very idea of system, in other words, is dependent on the effects of light—or, as both Pope and Newton would have it, on the effects of the sun. In his *Essay on Man,* Pope explained "how System into System runs, / What other Planets circle other Suns" (123), and in the General Scholium of the *Principia,* Newton spoke of the "sun" and "fixed stars" as "centres" of systems, "especially since the light of the fixed stars is of the same nature with the light of the sun, and from every system light passes into all other systems" (544).[2]

The phenomenon of light, we might say, became inextricably linked to the very idea of system, almost as if one could not exist without the other. It was in this sense that light provided science and literature with a grand metaphor through which they could figure their common pursuits. Through the light of Enlightenment, men would come to know the grand system of things and understand their place in the system. We might very well think of light as defining the territory of the Enlightenment—a territory whose borders are all the more conspicuous because they demarcate the illuminated space of Enlightenment systems. Beyond this clean, well-lighted place was not only darkness and disorder, but also the phenomenon that both Newton and Pope could never fully accommodate in their enlightened systems. That fluid substance was color, associated in Newton's optical theory with material that resisted definition, and in Pope's poetry with the inconstancy and discontinuities of woman.

If we can envision Enlightenment systems, in Michel Serres's terms, as islands surrounded by the disordered waters of the sea,[3] we might regard Pope's enlightened territory as the domain of light itself, surrounded everywhere by the glimmerings and fusions of color that threatened to consume it in darkness. And if we can think of scientists journeying through what Serres envisioned as waters of the unknown, we might regard Pope as making his way through the fusions of color and the obscurity of darkness as he sought the desired domain of light. In this search for light, Pope was at one with Newton who continually placed himself in a "dark Chamber," observing the reflections and refractions of light, which he attempted to fix within a system "as truly mathematical as any other part of Opticks" (244).[4] The problem that confronted both men, however, was that they finally could not place color within their systems. Color was a kind of light that resisted definition and exceeded boundaries. Neither scientist nor poet could quite grasp it. But in trying to contain its protean form, both men would—if only for brief moments and in suppressed ways—indulge in its fluid mergings. It is in this sense that Newton's science and Pope's poetry became tinted, or perhaps we might say irredeemably tainted, by the fusions of color. Newton and Pope could no more resist indulging in its fusions than could Swift, as we will see, resist the fluidity of madness and water. Color assumed its place among all the feminine material that the Enlightenment found at once so threatening and so irresistible.

THE JOURNEY TO LIGHT

The archetypal journey, traditionally portrayed as a sea journey, inevitably involves a descent into darkness and ascent to light. We may hear this age-old story related specifically in these terms—as in the biblical account of Jonah and the whale, or somewhat more metaphorically—as in the account of Christ's death and resurrection. Pope and Newton had their own versions to tell—stories that are all the more fascinating not only because they are products of the age we now regard as the Enlightenment, but because they expressly concern quests for light and illumination. To understand their desire for light in terms of such a journey is to begin to understand the web of metaphoric associations that made light into more than merely an object of scientific scrutiny or a subject of poetic celebration. The journey to light was a journey to everything that light represented, and for the men of the Enlightenment, those representations had a rich background not only in the mythic journeys from darkness to light, but in the way that such mythic accounts were reshaped in philosophy and literature. In her study *Newton Demands the Muse*, Marjorie Hope Nicolson described the "light" of eighteenth-century poetry as going back to "remote ancestors . . . Hebraic, Christian, Pythagorean, Neo-Platonic":

> The first miracle of God was the creation of light in nature, the miracle of the last day the creation of the light of man's reason, the *lumen animae*, as St. Augustine called it. To the Pythagoreans and the Neo-Platonists light was a mystical symbol; so, too, it was to St. John. God is light; the Logos, the Son, is also light. . . . The symbolism of light was persistent in the period of the Renaissance, which delighted in the fusion of Hebraic, Christian, Platonic elements. Light is everywhere in Bacon. . . . It was a favorite figure of the seventeenth century philosophers, whether the Cartesian *Lumiere naturelle* or the Galilean *lumen naturale*. Newton's own recognized religious and mystical tendencies made it easy for the poets to read into

his austere intellectual theories emotional responses which, indeed, he shared with such mystic-scientists as Kepler.[5]

We need not look much before Newton's time to find poets who not only sang the praises of light, but made light the inspiration of their poetry. Milton's famous invocation of light in Book III of *Paradise Lost* offers a prime example, and Nicolson appropriately quotes the "Hail holy Light" passage in which the "Bright effluence of bright essence" orders the "waters dark and deep" and the "void and formless infinite."[6]

In telling the archetypal death-rebirth story, Milton also tells the archetypal man's story—one that would have special meaning for Newton and Pope. Simone de Beauvoir long ago explained this myth by connecting the hero's descent to darkness with the "cult of germination" and the "cult of death." Since both cults are dominated by female figures—the earth mother and the woman as death—feminine dark becomes "the chaos whence all have come and whither all must one day return." Because the man, she explains, is frightened by the woman's threat "to swallow him up," he "aspires to the sky, to the light, to the sunny summits, to the pure and crystalline frigidity of the blue sky. . . ."[7] Seen from this perspective, then, the descent to a dark feminine territory can fulfill two different desires: the longing for rebirth and inspiration, and the longing for sleep, repose, even death. One journey takes man through feminine darkness on his way to light; another takes him only to permanent darkness.

Newton and Pope, I believe, were caught somewhere between these two destinations. Newton in his "dark Chamber," and Pope in his underground grotto, both derived inspiration from the shadowy muse as they made their way to light. But it was also here, in this dark feminine territory, that they became fascinated with color—the dispersive force that shattered the rigid dichotomy of darkness and light, and that brought both men within a kaleidoscope of gender difference. Their responses to this experience provide grounds for an intriguing study of the desire to create order and hierarchy out of phenomena that continually resist containment. In order to understand the dynamics that set this desire in motion, we need to understand the place of color in a dualistic system of values that was bent on preserving distinctions not only between light and dark, but within the sexual economy that fostered the construction of this dualism. The desire to preserve sexual difference, as I will later elaborate, forced each of these men to a different accommodation of color. Newton attempted to structure its fusions and bring color under the patriarchal dominion of light—the dominion of the Father God to whom he ascribed the "System of the World" in his General Scholium. Pope associated the dispersions of color with feminine inconstancy, and ultimately placed color in the dominion of the "Mighty Mother" of darkness. In associating and placing color within these realms, both men gave it a sexual identification, a specific gender. In each case, color became a configuration of the woman outside man's systems—a feminine phenomenon whose absence was necessary for the very construction of Enlightenment scientific and literary systems, and yet whose stunning presence was seen and felt everywhere in this well-ordered, classical world.

We know that Newton's lectures on light and optics go back to the 1660s, almost two decades before the *Principia* and some thirty years before he finally published the *Opticks* in 1704. His "design," as he stated in the *Opticks,* was "not to explain the Properties of Light by Hypotheses, but to propose and prove them by Reason and Experiments" (1). This design necessitated a twofold approach to the subject: an attempt to understand the nature of light (which involved Newton in the debate about light theory), and an attempt to systematize the effects of light (which led him to the study of color). Neither of these approaches, however, easily accommodated itself to the kind of system that Newton desired. Bernard Cohen claims that the appeal of the *Opticks* derives from our watching "that stage of creation when the greatest and clearest of minds is baffled by the observed data and cannot reduce them to a simple, clear, straightforward conceptual scheme." [8] Newton, for instance, had to proceed on the assumptions of the corpuscular theory—that light moves as particles—in order to calculate and diagram its refractions; yet in his response to Robert Hooke's criticisms of his theory, he was quick to point out that he accepted the "Corporeity" of light "without any absolute positiveness," and that he would prefer to decline any theory and instead "speak of *Light* in *general* terms." [9] The very fact that Newton based his ideas on the "corporeity" of light shows his tendency to rely on a fixed, atomistic system rather than a more random, fluid state of phenomena. In such a system, particles of light might be explained in a way similar to that which Newton used to account for the ordered movement of physical bodies, and the prism could therefore become a centering force similar to the force of gravity that kept the universe in a fixed position.

But the process of explaining central forces requires that the scientist first center his own hypotheses as he strives to prove a parallel between experimental models and universal forces. "In a very dark Chamber," Newton wrote in his *Opticks* as he described his centering of the prism,

at a round Hole, about one third Part of an Inch broad, made in the Shut of a Window, I placed a Glass Prism, whereby the Beam of the

Sun's Light, which came in at that Hole, might be refracted upwards toward the opposite Wall of the Chamber, and there form a colour'd Image of the Sun. . . . About this Axis I turned the Prism slowly, and saw the refracted Light on the Wall, or coloured Image of the Sun, first to descend, and then to ascend. Between the Descent and Ascent, when the Image seemed Stationary, I stopp'd the Prism, and fix'd it in that Posture, that it should be moved no more. (26–28)

Newton's language, at once describing scientific method and imaginative design, relies on all the metaphors that he himself, in his *Observations Upon the Prophecies of Daniel,* associated with a patriarchal order. In the language of prophecy, he explained, the heavens are identified with power, dignity, and light, and the lower regions with darkness and misery: "Whence ascending toward heaven, and descending toward the earth, are put for rising and falling in power and honour. . . ."[10] More revealing, however, are the analogical relationships Newton described: "the Sun is put for the whole species and race of Kings . . . shining with regal power and glory; the Moon for the body of the common people, considered as the King's wife . . . the Sun is Christ; light for the glory, truth, and knowledge, wherewith great and good men shine and illuminate others; darkness for obscurity of condition, and for error, blindness and ignorance. . . ."[11] While science may not be prophecy, the language of each keeps them comfortably united, especially for the devout believer that Newton was. And while the "Image of the Sun" in *Opticks* may not be the same "Sun" that, in the *Observations,* Newton identified with "Christ," or the light in *Opticks* the same as the light that in prophetic language signifies "glory, truth, and knowledge," the man who described both phenomena could hardly escape bringing the metaphoric implications of one to bear on the other.[12] We might regard Newton as a sort of scientific prophet in the *Opticks,* announcing his theory of light and color, journeying to the light of illumination and the power and dignity of the heavens. He controls the prism of light and truth, controls as well its colorful refractions and the description of the very system he has created. In centering his prism, Newton's scientific theory found its own center, and that center was the same force of light that throughout history and legend had brought the dark void of chaos under the clarification of a patriarchal, crystalline emanation.

Pope, who as a poet could draw on a rich literary tradition in which light is equated with order, illumination, and wisdom, used light as a fixed standard against which moral, social, and literary deviations could be measured. In this sense, his poetic tribute "God said, *Let Newton be!* and All was *Light*" not only merged scientific knowledge and theological order, but brought scientific truth, conveniently associated with the phenomenon of light, inside an even grander system of light and order. The system, however, was both grand and fragile for Pope; it always seemed on the verge of giving way to darkness, the "Universal Darkness" that eventually did obliterate order and light in *The Dunciad*. The very desire to maintain the light of the system was a desire Pope shared with the scientists of the age who were preoccupied with a "theory" of light that would explain its ordered movement as particles or waves, and thereby systematize its properties. There is every reason to believe that the demand for a theory of light and the demand for a poetry of light derived from the same urge for ordered and systematic principles—what we now know as the mechanized universe. In the *Essay on Criticism,* Pope relied on "One *clear, unchang'd,* and *Universal* Light" (71) as his standard of judgment, in the same way that Newton in his *Opticks* used the prism as his "Image of the Sun" (26). For both men, the sun assumed its primary position within a patriarchal order structured by light, and continually restructured through man's attempt to comprehend its grand design through his enlightenment.

As if mimicking the patriarchal command "Let there be light," both Newton and Pope desired a neatly structured universe. But this desire for order was doomed to failure. Newton's attempt to produce a theory of color, following lifelong experimentation and speculation on the subject, culminated in his treatise on *Opticks* that, as he explained, was finally "interrupted" (338), and that he only provisionally ended by amending a set of queries to the treatise, rather than by concluding with the proof he initially desired. And Pope, always seeking clarity and light, finally surrendered his world to a colorful "Mighty Mother" who issued in a world of darkness. Newton brought into the mechanistic universe the very colorful phenomenon it could not contain; Pope brought into his ordered verse a feminine inconstancy that even his rigid couplets could not control. Like Milton, the men of the Enlightenment tell us that they are journeying through darkness to light. But unlike Milton, they somehow wandered into another dimension altogether. While Milton journeyed to light, the men of the Enlightenment journeyed elsewhere.

Yet even Milton's story was, to some extent, the story of "that strange / Desire of wand'ring," [13] the desire that Adam blamed for Eve's transgression. Northrop Frye speaks of two myths governing what he calls the analogical structure of *Paradise Lost* : the "male father-god" who "stresses the rational order of nature," and the "mother-goddess" who is "perennially renewing the mystery of birth in the act of love." [14] Nature, according to Frye, is a sort of double nature, divided by sexual differences, among them the difference between light and dark: "the male principle in nature is associated with the sky, the sun, the wind, or the rain. The specifically female part of nature is the earth, and the imagery of caves, labyrinths, and water issuing from underground recall the process of birth from a womb" (pp. 22–23). As mankind relies on the sun and system for his redemption, there emerges in Eve, Frye tells us, a different response altogether: instead of taking her place in the father's system, Eve wanders off, following an "unconditioned desire" (pp. 46–47).

And so did Newton and Pope as they were lured beyond the limits of a system defined by neat polarities of light and dark. Their wandering excursions into the realm of color put them in a precarious position on the edge of the very systems they defended. Both men desired light, order, and design. But it was color—not darkness—that confused that desire, and produced those fusions that made it impossible to attain the clear illumination that allows for definition and hierarchy. Color always demanded more than either Newton or Pope wanted to permit in a system constructed according to precise mathematical principles and in which everything that existed was somehow "right." Color demanded an accommodation of the feminine that neither man was either willing or able to offer.

COLOR AND FEMININE RESISTANCE

I have all along been speaking of color as a phenomenon not only outside Enlightenment systems, but as *necessarily* outside their parameters. In this sense, color takes on a feminine demeanor, becoming another configuration of the woman who functions as an object of desire and appropriation. To locate color within such a sexual economy requires that we view it not simply as material for scientific study and poetic metaphor, but in terms of what Julia Kristeva calls a "complex economy" that effects, among other things, "'ideological values' germane to a given culture," and that also explains "why metaphysical speculations on light and its variations go back to the very oldest of beliefs." [15] Kristeva's speculations about the ways in which light and color figure in late medieval art provide a context for my own understanding of light and color in the Enlightenment. In an essay entitled "Giotto's Joy," she argues that color becomes for Giotto a means of disrupting the ordered space and narrative design of his frescoes. Even as it functions as a component of controlled painting, color violates its "symbolic order": "It achieves the momentary dialectic of law—the laying down of One Meaning so that it might at once be pulverized, multiplied into plural meanings. Color is the shattering of unity" (p. 221). The important observation here, both for Kristeva's understanding of the effects of color in art and my own sense of their configurations in Enlightenment discourse, is not that color annihilates meaning—"Color is not zero meaning," but that it shatters meaning—"maintains it through multiplication" (p. 221). Violating and exceeding the code of "One Meaning," color belongs not to the realm of law, but of pleasure, "jouissance"—Giotto's joy.

Can we think of this shattering of unity as a feminine phenomenon? For Kristeva, the link in medieval art is the figure of the mother. "That this chromatic experience could take place under the aegis of the Order of Merry Knights commemorating the Virgin is, perhaps, more than a coincidence (sublimated jouissance finds its basis in the forbidden mother, next to the Name-of-the-Father)" (p. 224). Color, joy, and the shattering of unity, in other words, are to be associated with maternal pleasure rather than paternal law. From this perspective it becomes easy to understand why the dominion of the Father God is typically figured in terms of light—the thunderbolt of Zeus, the shining emanation of the God of Genesis who proclaims "Let there be light," the various mythic and legendary accounts, as de Beauvoir explains, of the "sun god."[16] It also becomes easy to understand why the mother—and this is especially true in the case of Newton and Pope—must be repressed if her colorful lures are to be contained within a unified order, and why color must be prevented from shattering the design and structure of the system. In a related essay on Medieval art, "Motherhood According to Giovanni Bellini," Kristeva associates the "objectless goal of painting" with the artist's desire to experience—through the intensity of color—maternal joy. Yet that joy can only be the result of a profound repression of the mother whose body the artist now seeks to recover.[17] We will find a very similar kind of repression at work in Newton and Pope, though for them, even the very joy of recovery is repressed. Unlike the painter who can at least accord motherhood a "symbolic status" (p. 249), these Enlightenment men would either place her, as Newton tried to do, under patriarchal control, or dismiss her entirely, as Pope did, from the ordered universe. Perhaps when we keep in mind Kristeva's association of color with phenomena "traditionally considered feminine,"[18] we can begin to have some sense of why there was little place for color in the systems of the Enlightenment.

It is from this perspective that I think we might properly view the different yet related responses to color that we find in Newton and Pope. In doing this, I am not dismissing the fact that their engagement with color derived from other sources as well and might be viewed in a variety of contexts—particularly, as I will elaborate later, the context of political and economic ideology, not to mention the scientific and literary traditions that had already made color the subject of their discourse. But I would argue that unless we come to terms with the sexual economy in which color functioned, our understanding of its role in different traditions and contexts can only be partial at best, and often grossly misleading. As a way of beginning, we might consider two passages: the first is from Newton's early optical lectures, the second from Pope's *Essay on Criticism*.

First, I find that to differently refrangible rays there correspond different colors. To the most refrangible ones there corresponds purple or violet, to the least refrangible red, and to the intermediate ones green, or rather the boundary of green and greenish blue. Blue, however, falls between purple and green, and yellow between green and red. Hence as the rays are more and more refrangible, they are disposed to generate these colors in order: red, yellow, green, blue, and violet, together with all of their successive gradations and intermediate colors.[19]

> *False Eloquence*, like the *Prismatic Glass*,
> Its gawdy *Colours* spreads on *ev'ry place*;
> The Face of Nature we no more Survey,
> All glares *alike*, without *Distinction* gay:
> But true *Expression*, like th' unchanging *Sun*,
> *Clears*, and *improves* whate'er it shines upon,
> It *gilds* all Objects, but it *alters* none.
>
> (311–17)

Both passages date early in each man's career. Yet although Newton seems to have made no substantial changes in his optical theory during the years between the 1660s and his publication of the *Opticks* in 1704, Pope came to rely more and more on color to express the distortions and deviations that fill his satires—just as he continued to rely less on light and increasingly on both color and the dark realm in which he placed color for his poetic metaphor. But what did color mean to Pope? What values did it enforce, and just as important, what ideological assumptions have we, as critics and readers, brought to our understanding of these values?

Let me address these questions by first briefly considering the question of what color meant for Newton, since his accommodation of its fusions are at once different from and relevant to Pope's predicament. For Newton, color was neither an essence nor a changeable mixture of light and shadow. It nonetheless derived from "some regular Cause" that he explained in terms of "Refrangibility," that is, the consistent "Disposition" of certain rays to correspond to different colors. The importance of this refrangibility principle to Newton's theory of color can hardly be over-estimated, since it allowed him to systematize both light and its various colorful "Dispositions" and therefore create a "Science of Colours" that became "a Speculation as truly mathematical as any other part of Opticks" (244). We see this propensity for definition and system in the passage I have cited from Newton's *Optical Papers,* where he strives to fix even "successive gradations and intermediate colors" in his mechanistic universe. In this sense, we might conceive of color as shaping Newton's imagination, rather than conceive of Newton explaining some heretofore imaginative phenomenon according to the new rules of a mechanistic science.

Richard Westfall, Newton's biographer, suggests as much when he reminds us that Newton had long been interested in color, from his grammar school days when he read John Bates's *The Mysteries of Nature and Art* to his Cambridge days when he read color theories advanced by Descartes, Boyle, and Hooke.[20] As mystery gave way to theory, Newton's fascination turned into a science, and scientific method became a way to explore a natural mystery. If the realm of nature, especially mysterious nature, is a feminine realm, it is possible to see Newton's science of light as a sort of science of the feminine dispersions that color metaphorically represents. Frank Manuel even suggests that Newton's lifelong fascination with color revealed his "desire to enjoy once more the pleasures of intimate visual exchange which he had experienced when alone with his mother during infancy. . . ."[21] Such a psychoanalytic explanation would seem to have much in common with Kristeva's view that color is not only linked with a feminine sense of fusion and joy, but specifically with the mother's body, which the artist, and, we might add, the scientist, seeks to recover. Newton's *Opticks,* understood in this context, may well have allowed him to produce a systematic discourse on light—albeit an unfinished one, and at the same time experience the "joy" of color and all its maternal stirrings.

Pope's aspirations for light, however, took him deep into the realm where Newton feared to tread. The scientist tried to systematize light's "Dispositions"; the poet, even as he paid tribute to the fathers of light, was lured into the spectrum of color that led him not to enlightenment but to a deadly darkness that he associated with the "Mighty Mother." Newton could at least take joy in his deception that feminine color might be brought under the dominion of masculine light; Pope would be tormented by the possibility that his system of "Universal Light" was fast slipping away through color into darkness.

The passage I cited earlier from Pope's *Essay on Criticism* is also the first cited by Marjorie Hope Nicolson in her study of "Color and Light" in

Pope. She describes it as "Pope's first lines on Newtonian light and color," and views the lines as the beginning of Pope's "struggling for a figure of light" that showed his interest in "the refraction of light into colors and the return of colors to light. . . ."[22] These last remarks identify the core of Nicolson's argument, since what both she and Pope seem most interested in—perhaps for similar reasons—is the "return of color to light." Assuming that color does always, or at least nearly always, return to light, she reads Pope's indulgence in color as homage to Newtonian light, a tribute that took its place in a long tradition of light symbolism. Thus the sylphs in *The Rape,* who fling their "transient Colours" that "change whene'er they wave their Wings," are viewed by Nicolson as "charming" creatures; and the ominous red Dog Star that appears in Pope's *Epistle to Arbuthnot, Fourth Dunciad,* and his translation of the *Iliad* shows the delight he took in the intensity of color (293, 276–81). Admitting that Pope's colors can be ethically pejorative—as in his *Epistle to a Lady*—Nicolson nonetheless insists that such color "is contrasted with the light of empyrean, the pure light of Reason." Only when darkness encroaches, she argues, does color begin to disappear from Pope's poetry, making *The Dunciad* a Miltonic rather than Newtonian poem because it brings with it all the chaotic associations of darkness that we find in Milton's satanic verse.[23] The notion of Miltonic darkness, however, also recalls the ambivalent nature of Milton's dark muse, and is therefore a notion I want to use to question Nicolson's ideological assumptions about light, color, and darkness in Pope.

A primary assumption, for instance, is that Pope, already an admirer of color and already responsive to the traditional metaphoric implications of light, also shared a scientific and particularly Newtonian interest in both light and color. It would follow, then, that since light and color are closely related in Newtonian theory, they are also connected in Pope's "Newtonian" verse. Thus the darkness of the *Fourth Dunciad* cannot possibly be Newtonian, and might therefore be conveniently explained as Miltonic— even though Milton's darkness led to light, while Pope's resulted from light's extinction. Yet if the Pope of *The Dunciad* does identify with a Miltonic darkness, perhaps Pope's darkness led him in the same directions that, according to Frye, it led Milton—to the earth, to its caverns and labyrinths, to the realm of the feminine. Nicolson has given us Pope as the "man of light," and has argued that his use of color pays tribute to the illumination that he associated with both scientific and literary truth. In doing so, she has also given us Pope as the "man," as the masculine voice of order, the sun god who seeks the light of the skies.

Yet throughout Pope's verse we also find color—ostensibly a systematic,

Newtonian disposition of light—associated with a feminine dispersion of Pope's clean, well-lighted place. The "transient Colours" of the sylphs, which Nicolson regards as "charming" in *The Rape,* only begin to show Pope's continual depiction of women as colorfully inconstant: the sylphs, themselves ghostlike remains of former coquettes, transform Belinda into a "painted Vessel," a container that will ultimately be shattered when Belinda experiences her own fall. The colorful portraits in the *Epistle to a Lady* not only expose Pope's attempt to paint, frame, and control elusive feminine qualities, but actually define feminine inconstancy in terms of color: since "'Most Women have no Characters at all,'" they are "best distinguish'd by black, brown, or fair" (1–4). The *Epistle to Arbuthnot,* which Douglas Atkins suggests is steeped in confusions of sexual difference, gives us the colorful portrait of Sporus—a "Butterfly," a "Bug with gilded wings," a "painted Child" (309–10)—in short, a disturbingly flamboyant and feminine creature.[24] Although the *Fourth Dunciad* is ultimately eclipsed in darkness, one cannot miss the colorful "gay embroider'd race" that swarms around the goddess of dulness, or the dispute between two young men who are infatuated with colorful objects—flower and butterfly (275, 401–36).

Even in the early *Essay on Criticism* Pope was quick to associate color not with fine art but with flawed painting: he speaks of "ill *Colouring*" and "unskill'd" painters, equating them with the "gawdy Colours" of the prism (24, 293, 312), and establishing the painting metaphor that he will later use for his feminine portraits. Only Clarissa, as her name suggests, can share the masculine light of the unchanging sun. Yet after she recites the moral that Pope tacked onto *The Rape* in the 1717 edition, Belinda and Thalestris immediately reject any illumination to be found either in her plea for "good Sense" or her caution that "painted, or not painted, all shall fade" (5. 1–36). Dark Eloisa ends her sad story with the maxim "He can paint 'em best, who shall feel 'em most" (366). There lurks in her statement much of the torment Pope must have felt about painting: on the one hand, it was a beautiful and precise art; on the other, it necessitated indulging in the very opposite of a systematic, masculine effort. Kristeva cites Henri Matisse's belief that pictures become "refinements, subtle gradations, dissolutions without energy" as they call for "beautiful blues, reds, yellows—matters to stir the sensual depths in men." To Matisse's notion of "dissolutions," she adds her own Newtonian-sounding observation that color "does not suppress light but segments it by breaking its undifferentiated unicity into spectral multiplicity."[25]

Did Pope seek that spectral multiplicity? If so, he was at the same time thwarting his masculine aspirations for light. This inconsistency might very well explain not only Pope's associations of color with the inconstancy of women (the male poet dissociating himself from the feminine as he seeks the light of the sky) but also his equally fascinating descents into the dark realm where he placed color (the male poet unable to resist the shadowy abode of the feminine). Because it is so conventional to regard Pope as the poet of order and light who was eventually overpowered by a dark and chaotic vision, we tend to forget that darkness for him was more than something that simply obliterated light. Two of Pope's early poems, *Windsor-Forest* and *Eloisa to Abelard*, show his conflicting desires for light and dark, and his ambivalent response to color within this light/dark economy. Even as he celebrates Granville's verse, which brings "the Scenes of opening Fate to Light" (426), or himself identifies with the control of Abelard who will smooth Eloisa's "passage to the realms of day" (322), Pope at the same time indulges in the colorful shades of Windsor Forest that seem to exceed the boundaries of order, and descends with Eloisa to the dark abode of desire that separates both her and Pope from the salvation of God and light.[26] This ambivalence, however, ultimately transformed itself into a fixed celebration of light and a firm association linking color, darkness, and woman. By the time of *The Fourth Dunciad*, Pope had both created and allowed himself to be "swallowed" by the dark mother who had disturbed and finally eclipsed his world of light.

It should actually come as no surprise that the poet of Newtonian light and truth should devise such a scenario for his career, draping the gown of the mother around his neatly designed and well-ordered universe. This finale resulted from a long seduction that Pope himself perpetuated, from a lifetime love affair with the shadows he at once created and tried to annihilate. Some of the most provocative biographical speculations about Pope can be found in Maynard Mack's study of Pope's "landscape"—particularly his grotto and gardens.[27] Mack, describing Pope's creative architecture as "an act of the mythopoeic imagination," cites Horace Walpole's description: "'The passing through the gloom from the grotto to the opening day, the retiring and again assembling shades, the dusky groves, the larger lawn, and the solemnity of the termination at the cypresses that lead up to his mother's tomb'—Walpole evidently means the obelisk erected in his mother's memory—'are managed with exquisite judgement.'"[28] Perhaps only a man who had followed his own dark retreat into gothic labyrinths could have called attention to just the right details: for the revealing part of Walpole's description is not, as Mack believes, his estimation of Pope's "exquisite judgement," but the earthly, shadowy, feminine features of the landscape—features that seem more deeply infused in an "act of the mythopoeic imagination." Pope's retreats to his grotto may have given him access to his muse, as Mack speculates. But if they did, the actual visual access his grotto permitted—of his garden on one side of the road dividing the property, and of the Thames river on the other side—offers a curious picture of the poet who centered himself in a dark grotto between the garden that led to his mother's obelisk and the waters of the river.

Pope's position here is a curious one, especially since it places him in the dark, shadowy realm that he ostensibly associated with the dispersions of light and with feminine cavelike enclosures. Newton, too, sat in a "dark Chamber," opening his window just enough to allow light to strike his prism in such a way that he could control its reflections and refractions. Pope, who we might expect to strive for such definition and control, actually indulged in the more fluid and random effects of light. He explained that when he shut the doors of the grotto, the room became "luminous" and on its walls formed "a moving picture" of the river, woods, and boats. He had also placed bits of mirrors throughout the grotto, explaining that "'when you have a mind to light it up . . . a thousand pointed Rays glitter and are reflected over the place.'" [29] Could it be that Pope in his dark grotto and Newton in his "dark Chamber" indulged in the spectral multiplicity that Kristeva associates with color, but that Pope and Newton would allow only in darkness? If the "gawdy Colours" of the prism became his metaphor for the feminine force of inconstancy—the same force that Frye discovers in Eve's wanderings and in her "unconditioned desire," the dark environs of Pope and Newton may well have become their metaphors to express the urge *not* to generate the "rising Light" of the sun, but instead to indulge in the glimmerings of reflections, the multiplicity that shatters the unifying force of light.

Perhaps, in this sense, there was a good deal of the "woman" in both of these Enlightenment men. Yet if this is so, we need to recover these feminine qualities from the dark realms into which they were repressed, and find in them a means to transform systematic thought. Luce Irigaray believes that we must reopen the "figures" of discourse "in order to pry out of them what they have borrowed that is feminine, from the feminine, to make them 'render up' and give back what they owe the feminine." [30] What Pope and Newton borrowed from the feminine were the glimmerings and fusions of color that they tried to appropriate for their dominion of light. They should give it back to "the feminine"—to a consciousness that might celebrate its excesses and shatterings instead of trying to confine them to systematic laws or exclude them entirely from a restrictive culture. They should give it back so that we can experience the "joy" that they denied themselves.

CAVES, NATURE, AND MUSES

Writing about the underground world of Pope's grotto, Mack suggests that we keep in mind the associations "between consciousness and caverns that are indicated in his own Cave of Spleen, Cave of Poetry, and Cave of Truth."[31] Yet like Nicolson, who traced the ancestors of light in literary, mythic, and philosophical tradition, Mack finds only male prototypes for these associations, suggesting that Pope followed Platonic and Lockean dark paths that ultimately led to light. Since I want to consider the implications of Pope's descent into caves from a very different perspective, it might be worthwhile to turn back to Plato's parable of the cave in *The Republic,* an account that pays more than enough attention to the metaphoric associations of light and dark, rising and descent, but that describes the glimmering world between these extremes only in terms of shadow and deception.

Plato's cave, of course, is itself a metaphor of ignorance. He tells the story of a group of men restrained within a dark cave, able only to see images and shadows of figures cast upon a wall by a fire that burns behind them. Trapped in this shadowy world of images, these men must learn to make their way slowly to light. Such also is the condition of the world above, Plato tells us. Here, too, men are in a prison where the sun, like the fire in the cave, casts only images of reality. Yet through education, the philosopher can achieve illumination and knowledge. The ascent from darkness to light becomes, in this way, a rising into the radiance of the world of the mind.

Two things are conspicuously absent in Plato's cave—women and color. Perhaps, considering the Greek subordination of woman, her omission from this narrative of man might only be expected. Yet it does seem surprising that Plato's description of the cave—a place partially illuminated by fire—would be devoid even of any reference to color. Colorful reflections and glimmerings, after all, could easily have found their way into the moral of the story as they might not only provide false images of reality, but lure man away from the truth of light.[32] Nonetheless, Plato's moral unfolds strictly in terms of light and dark—just as the archetypal story of the journey finds its principle metaphor in the ascent from the depths of darkness to the world of light. This exclusive focus on darkness and light, and particularly the omission of color, I believe, is very much connected to the exclusive focus on man in these narratives, and the notable omission of woman.

Recent feminist rereadings of literature and myth have questioned the absence of woman in such narratives, and particularly her confinement—

without the promise of escape—to the darkness of the underworld. Sandra Gilbert and Susan Gubar, for instance, believe that there are other "Parables of the Cave" that might give us a fuller account of the human experience. "Although Plato does not seem to have thought much about this point," they argue, "a cave is—as Freud pointed out—a female place, a womb-shaped enclosure, a house of earth, secret and often sacred." And throughout myth and literature, the cave is also a place where woman is imprisoned and abandoned, where woman's "cave-shaped anatomy" becomes her "destiny." The woman writer, they argue, is thus imprisoned in the very cave that might otherwise serve as a source of "female power"— a power deriving from "female depths," from the "Great Mother," the promise of rebirth. If the woman writer is to tap into this source of power, they suggest, she must "reconstruct" man's stories of the cave where she is abandoned, and find in them a "maternal creativity" that is the equivalent of "the male potential for literary paternity."[33]

Such a "parable of the cave" seems especially appropriate when discussing the predicament of women writers—and I will be returning to it in my own discussion of the peculiar anxieties confronting Anne Finch. But what I find particularly interesting about the parable recounted by Gilbert and Gubar is that it continues, despite its important account of woman's place in such stories, to retell the story in terms of darkness and light. I wonder if we are still not leaving something out. It is certainly important to realize the narrowness of myths such as Orpheus and Eurydice that abandon woman to the caves of the underworld. Yet other myths seem to hint at other scenarios. If Persephone, for instance, is doomed to darkness half the year, her return to the world above signals more than a resurrection to light. It brings with it all the colors and fusions of spring. Color, I would suggest, is the missing element in even these reconstructed parables of the cave—the phenomenon that shatters not only man's world of light, but pulverizes as well the darkness with which woman has been associated throughout our mythic, literary, and critical parables. And yet our tendency to focus only on the dichotomies of dark and light seems to prevail, even when color intrudes everywhere—within, around, and between these dichotomies. Such a fixation on the female underworld of darkness and the male summits of light, perhaps deriving—as some contemporary philosophers might say—from the fact that Western metaphysics is itself constructed according to such dualities, fails to take account of just that phenomenon that would "deconstruct" the order of things, fracture it into colorful multiplicity that cannot be appropriated either by the male in his search for light, or by the female in her search to escape the darkness in which she has been confined.

This failure to accommodate the fusions and multiplicity of color is strikingly apparent not only in the optical work of Newton—as he tried to control the reflections and refractions of color and define their orderly movement, or the verse of Pope—where he associated color with disorderly and feminine phenomena that exceeded the boundaries and decorum of classical systems. It is apparent as well in our estimate of their work which we continue to explain in terms of the light and illumination of Enlightenment, and the darkness that threatened its systems. From this perspective, we might well reconsider Mack's account of Pope's literary descent into caves that, like his grotto, are places of darkness *and* color. They are also the abodes of women—notably colorful women.

The Cave of Spleen particularly invites our speculation since Pope described it as a "Grotto . . . screen'd in Shades from Day's detested Glare" (4. 21–22). It is the seat of Belinda's passion, a place of darkness, flickering color, and sexual transformation and generation: among its "Strange Phantoms" are glaring fiends, rolling snakes, gaping tombs, purple fires, lakes of liquid gold, and crystal domes. The teapots, pipkin, and jar that come to life also bring with them, as Aubrey Williams has shown, all the feminine associations of chinaware.[34] Yet the final couplet of the passage captures the more disturbing sexual force: "Men prove with Child, as pow'rful Fancy works, / And Maids turn'd Bottels, call aloud for Corks" (53–54). This description of the confused, hallucinatory source of Belinda's emotions may well describe the same phenomena that lurked in Pope's own grotto, sources of his own poetic gender fusions. The Cave of Poetry in *The First Dunciad* is appropriately the home of the *"Mighty Mother,"* a "Chaos dark and deep." In her womblike cavern, things lie in embryo, are newborn, are half-formed maggots that crawl and meander. Presiding over this realm of "motley Images" and "Mob of Metaphors," the goddess, "tinsel'd o'er in robes of varying hues," watches her "wild creation"—and "with her own fools-colours gilds them all" (55–84). There is more than enough color in this feminine cave, and yet such color can hardly be viewed as a tribute to Newtonian light. For all her glimmerings, the goddess—the woman—remained for Pope a thing of darkness. Yet his own "Mob of Metaphors" betrays an ambivalent response to light and dark: while Pope speaks of encroaching darkness, he writes of color; while he aspires to light, he nestles himself in his shadowy grotto.

If Pope's Cave of Poetry generated the very moving, changing, colorful things that he feared he was unable to contain in his system, we might well think of Pope himself generating a poetry that always gave itself an object, as Kristeva might say, beyond its limits. In this sense, Pope's journey was a version of the archetypal male narrative of the journey to light.

But the object that Pope desired was neither pure light nor the dreadful dark that in desperation he associated with woman. It was a journey that brought him into a feminine territory that he might have enjoyed—if only he had not been so determined to preserve the domain of light in which, as Newton explained, "great and good men shine and illuminate others."

Yet Newton himself, even as he sought the illumination of God and system, was consumed with the prism—the object through which light was shattered and multiplied on the walls of his "dark Chamber." Commenting on the pleasure Newton took in his scientific probings into color, Frank Manuel cites his letter to Oldenburg in which Newton describes the effect of the prism as "'at first a very pleasing divertisement, to view the vivid and intense colours produced thereby. . . .'"[35] If Newton did take "joy" in color, his optical theory, which historians of science generally associate with the systematic Newton of the *Principia,* might better be associated with his alchemical interests, which he kept secret and hidden. The fusion and mingling of chemicals, after all, would seem to have much more in common with the fusions and shatterings of color—and both alchemical and optical experiments would seem, as well, to be pursuits quite different from mathematical calculation. Newton did strive, as he himself said, to produce a mathematical "Science of Colors," and it is this science of colors for which he is now remembered. Yet to dismiss the Newton who was fascinated with the very experience of color—who would stare straight into the sun and who would press tightly on his closed eyes just to create colorful sensations—is to surrender all that was feminine in his theories to the dominion of a systematic science. Unless we take account of this Newton who, like Pope, exceeded the system in his very attempts to observe its laws, we miss the opportunity to have him "'render up' and give back" what he has "borrowed that is feminine."

To speak about caves and colors, and especially about the feminine aspect of their fusions and mergings, puts us in the realm of another feminine configuration—the muse. Traditionally associated with shady haunts and the waters of inspiration, the muse finds her home in the natural world that became, as we have seen, the object of scientific domination during this period that marks the "rise of science." Nature was also, of course, the subject of poetry, though the major poetic spokesmen of the late seventeenth and early eighteenth centuries would, like their scientific counterparts, be enamored with an ordered and controlled natural world that we find portrayed again and again in their perfectly designed gardens. The Enlightenment home of the muse, we might say, became a tidy place. And the muse herself, instead of luring men to shady retreats from which they might derive inspiration, seems to take them through carefully designed and properly illuminated gardens. When Nicolson writes that Newton "demanded the muse" and influenced a group of eighteenth-century English poets who celebrated light and its colorful reflections in their verse, she was clearly speaking about a muse who had already been mastered by science, a muse who inspired verses that were ostensibly as controlled and regulated as Newton's own "Science of Colors." Or was science, perhaps, lured on by a poetic muse? Julia Epstein and Mark Greenberg suggest that Newton's language in the *Opticks*, far from purging itself of any imagistic intonations, was characterized by "its power to evoke images and metaphors" as it became involved in its own "poetic—or image-laden—undertaking."[36] If Newton himself, not to mention the poets who wrote about light and color, can be seen as following the calling of a muse, we might inquire further about the shady natural realm into which the muse led him.

We can begin by considering the possible connections between the muse's natural haunt and the actual world of nature studied by science. Carolyn Merchant tells us that Newton had a deep interest in the transmutable processes of nature, especially processes of organic transformation and fermentation—an interest that was ultimately subsumed by his work in mathematics and physics.[37] Nature, like alchemy, was both fascinating and yet somehow forbidden for this systematic scientist. Color, however—which was just as fascinating but also strongly linked to the domain of the physical sciences—was a legitimate and respectable subject of scientific inquiry. The science of optics, in other words, made the mechanical study of color possible, while biological and alchemical processes remained to a large extent associated with a taboo hermetic tradition and its links with magic, spirit, and witchcraft.[38] If science, particularly physics, could explain the systematic dispositions of color, it could find a way to control phenomena that might otherwise be surrendered to a natural world outside its dominion. But science could also find a way to enter that natural world, to submit to what Epstein and Greenberg call a "poetic—or image-laden—undertaking." Keeping in mind the feminine associations that, as I have been suggesting all along, plagued the Enlightenment mind, we might view color as a kind of feminine force, like the muse, leading science away from its strictly principled pursuits and into a realm far more pleasurable than that of mechanical physics. Color, in this way, became a feminine configuration of nature, a kind of muse beckoning the scientist into the very natural world that he wanted at once to appropriate and to enjoy.

Although Pope, unlike Newton, ultimately associated color with the "chaos" of a "Dark Mother," he had also, especially earlier in his career, tried to claim it for the cause of order and Enlightenment. We can sense this disposition in his expressed fondness for controlled colors—gardens and paintings, artistic attempts to maintain color within proper boundaries. In a strong sense, as I suggested earlier, this appropriation of color—especially in paintings and portraits—was an attempt to appropriate woman, to secure her otherwise inconstant nature within the kind of "frames" that Pope relied on in his *Epistle to a Lady.* Perhaps the most striking instance of this desired appropriation of color, particularly the color that Pope associated with nature and, through nature, with the muse and all her feminine lurings, can be found in *Windsor-Forest,* a poem that provides a fascinating context for perceiving the sexual economy in which woman and nature functioned in both Enlightenment science and literature.

The colors described throughout *Windsor-Forest* are intense and rich, reflecting "Order in Variety" (15)—the "Pheasant" with its "Purple Crest," "Scarlet-circled Eyes," and "vivid Green" plumes (111–18), "the bright-ey'd Perch with Fins of *Tyrian* Dye," the "yellow Carp," and "Trouts, diversify'd with Crimson Stains" (141–46), "Lillies blazing" on the shields of kings (306). Trees, reflected in silver streams, become "floating Forests" that "paint the Waves with Green." (216) Pope asks Granville, to whom the poem is dedicated, to "call the Muses" and "paint anew the flow'ry Sylvan Scenes." (284–85) And Pope himself, invoking his own muse, calls upon the "sacred Nine" to bear him "to sequester'd Scenes, / The Bow'ry Mazes and surrounding Greens" (259–62). Such connections between color and nature, nature and the muse, might all, of course, be viewed as Pope's own artful mastery of literary conventions. And yet it seems that conventions are not the only things that Pope is mastering. Nature is both colorful and "to Advantage dress'd," splendidly ordered within this garden in which no one is tempted into transgression. Even the young Nymph, pursued by a lustful Pan, retains her virginity and is transformed into a cold, silver stream. Her watery nature, far from disrupting the order of the forest, provides it with a "Glass" mirror in which its beauty and symmetry are reflected. Nature, color, woman—they are all fixed in place in this perfect garden, mastered by a poet who would put them all in the service of his art. And the muses, who take Pope exactly where he wants to go, have assumed their proper place in his poetic system. Pope appropriately concludes his poem with "Father *Thames*" flowing into the sea where all "Regions" of the world join together (330, 397–400), presumably under England's imperial rule. If *Windsor-Forest* is a poem that indulges in natural description, it also celebrates the mastery of nature and, through that mastery, universal domination.

Domination may, in a sense, seem too strong a term for describing Pope's desire for mastery and control, and yet recently Laura Brown, in her revisionist reading of Pope, argues that his very poetic form and subjects constitute a kind of imperial claim on the world. Describing the "neoclassical movement" as finding its "apotheosis and its coda" in a convergence of "imperialist ideologies," she explains that "never before was classicism so deeply in tune with the dynamic ideological structures of English literature, and never again would it play the same role in enabling and elaborating the primary expressions of English culture."[39] Brown finds evidence everywhere in Pope's poetry of his "elaborating" imperialist ideology—in his enumeration of commodities, his mercantilist discourse, his visions of capitalist prosperity, even in his wrestling with the "commodification of literature" and "problematic of capitalism" in *The Dunciad* (p. 156). Yet what I find most interesting about Brown's argument, especially as she develops it with reference to *The Rape of the Lock* and *Windsor-Forest*, is the way in which color serves this imperial poetry. In *The Rape*, for instance, Brown finds Pope's "commodity catalogues," especially those that are aimed "for female consumption," as "characterized by descriptive profusion, colour, light and an indiscriminate glowing vista of products" (pp. 11, 29). In a similar way, she calls attention to the creatures described in *Windsor-Forest* as "coloured—'crimson', 'gold', 'silver', 'vivid' and 'glossie'—like the commodities in Pope's trade catalogues—the reddening coral, the glowing ruby and the ripening gold. They are, in fact, gold, silver, and jewels displaced into the natural world and disguised as natural creatures. And they are also explicitly 'painted', decorated, dressed in these colours, as Belinda dresses herself in *The Rape of the Lock*" (p. 31).

Although Brown does not elaborate on the connections between these colorful products and the women who use them for adornment, the evidence would seem strongly to indicate that a sexual economy is here aligning itself with the workings of an imperial economy—and that woman is co-opted into each system so that she can facilitate man's profit and his return to himself. Just as Pope, in other words, would have nature, color, and woman conform to his garden of order and design—confirming his own sense of "rightness" and harmony in the universe, so he would have them play their part in an economic structure that seeks universal peace through imperial domination. The artistic ornamentation of woman, as Ellen Pollak explains in her reading of *The Rape of the Lock*, not only has the effect of shaping woman into "an object of male desire and ownership," but describes as well her social status in eighteenth-century culture: woman is put on display so that she can become the object of man's control.[40] In both her figurative representation and social predicament, woman must at once be colorfully adorned and yet firmly fixed in place. This is exactly the fate of Pope's Belinda, that "painted Vessel" who becomes emblematic of the beautiful young woman who will be kept neatly in place—like a carefully polished object—within the social order.

Belinda is a finely "painted" creature, just as carefully painted as the natural landscape Pope describes in *Windsor-Forest*. It is only when she becomes disordered, when the "painted Vessel" falls and, to use Kristeva's terms, "shatters" into a kind of "multiplicity," that Belinda poses a threat—a distinctly feminine threat—to the social order. Her colors do not stay in place, but instead threaten the systematic design of an imperial world that would keep its women and its colonies in line. Sheila Delany elaborates on just this issue when she suggests that Belinda is not so much a portrayal of imperial order as she is a threat to that order. Belinda's colors, Delany says, are "imperial colors" that represent a bourgeois desire for power—a desire threatening to the sexist system of both Pope and his aristocratic counterparts.[41] I would add to Delany's argument that it is not so much Belinda's colors as such, but their shattered effects that threaten *both* the aristocratic and bourgeois order. Describing the rape in metaphoric terms, Pope compares the scene to "when rich *China* Vessels, fal'n from high, / In glittring Dust and painted Fragments lie!" (3. 159–60). The shattering of color becomes a kind of feminine excess that the social order will not tolerate. If Belinda is not finally to become one of the "female monsters" that Susan Gubar describes as haunting eighteenth-century satire,[42] her excess—and her colors—must be contained. Pope, I would suggest, wanted to control Belinda's colors just as much as Newton wanted to control the colorful effects of the prism. For what is at stake here is not simply the possibility that fused and shattered colors will fail to conform to a systematic theory of light, but that colorful, feminine objects will refuse to assume their passive position in the ruling sexual ideology.

Such a feminine and colorful threat brings us back, once again, to the "Dark Mother" of *The Dunciad,* whose colorful following eventually destroyed universal order and replaced it with chaos and darkness. But it also brings us, I believe, to Pope's other muse, not the "sacred Nine" in *Windsor-Forest* who take him only where he wants to go, but the desire in Pope to go elsewhere, down into his grotto, into feminine caves, places that seemed far away from the world of Enlightenment. If there was another muse pulling Pope away from light and into the shattered spectrum of color, then perhaps this same muse—figured as the repressed desire to transgress systems—was the woman responsible for Newton's lifelong fascination with color. If Newton did "demand the muse," we might say that the muse demanded much more of both Newton and Pope. She took them away from, and at times entirely outside, the systems—scientific and literary—over which they sought mastery.

In her "demanding" nature, this muse reminds me of Robert Graves's "White Goddess," the female deity who is muse and mother of all living things, and who serves as the ultimate source of poetic inspiration. Associated with wildness, fury, and even destruction, she embodies the chaotic powers of the natural world that exceed any of "man's" attempts to control them. Yet though she inspires all "true poetry," Graves argues, she has very little effect on the "Classical poet" who "claims to be the Goddess's master." [43] In his attempt to master the goddess, the classical poet shares much with the scientist who, as Graves explains, inherits the law of philosophy, the legacy of Apollo now wielding "the atomic bomb as if it were a thunderbolt . . ." (p. 476). Perhaps we might well think of the absent woman of the Enlightenment as a figure of this goddess, as a configuration of feminine excess threatening the law and light of men—scientists and poets—who usurped maternal nature through their myths of domination.

In her whiteness, as Graves often noticed, this woman shimmered with color, though her principle color was the white linking her to the moon. But through the very reflected light of the moon, as some accounts record, she changed colors daily—from white to red to black to blue. She is variously described as "bright and mounting out of the sea," her hair decked in flowers, her "vestments" yielding "diverse colours." [44] Keeping in mind the colors that glimmer everywhere throughout Enlightenment systems, we might perceive the muse who led Newton and Pope into the shatterings of color as white only when we envision her as absent, ghostlike, haunting their systems—just as Graves sees her haunting the patriarchal systems of the warrior god who usurped her world. But when she excites in us a sense of joy instead of fear or disgust, when she is not the subject of someone's scientific or literary mastery—we might see her in all her colorful glimmerings. Neither dark nor light, she would become the propensity to experience a world "other" than the dualistic, systematic universe that we continue to valorize.

If Pope and Newton could not envision such a world, it was because they could not reach out to woman and nature without also trying to claim mastery. Their failure is an especially sad one, for they helped define and secure the associations that link classicism with mastery instead of joy, with control instead of pleasure. To take back from Pope and Newton "what they have borrowed that is feminine" will give us not only the fusions and glimmerings of color, but the means of discovering through color a world that exceeds the dualistic strictures of light and dark, right and wrong, order and disorder, male and female. Shattering these fixed oppositions, color becomes the material of multiplicity. And woman, long figured in terms of chaos and darkness, becomes the prism that shatters Enlightenment.

4

Swift's Disruptive Woman

They say that they [the women] foster disorder in all its forms. Confusion troubles violent debates disarray upsets disturbances incoherencies irregularities divergences complications disagreements discords clashes polemics discussions contentions brawls disputes conflicts routs debacles cataclysms disturbances quarrels agitation turbulence conflagrations chaos anarchy.

MONIQUE WITTIG

Fluid has to remain that secret *remainder,* of the one. . . . All threaten to deform, propagate, evaporate, consume him, to flow out of him and into another who cannot easily be held on to. The "subject" identifies himself with/in an almost material consistency that finds everything flowing abhorrent.

LUCE IRIGARAY

> Here Gallypots and Vials plac'd,
> Some fill'd with Washes, some with Paste,
> Some with Pomatum, Paints and Slops,
> And Ointments good for scabby Chops.
> Hard by a filthy Bason stands,
> Fowl'd with the Scouring of her Hands;
> The Bason takes whatever comes
> The Scrapings of her Teeth and Gums,
> A nasty Compound of all Hues,
> For here she spits, and here she spues.

JONATHAN SWIFT

SWIFT'S ISLAND

THE ISLAND of scientists described in Book III of *Gulliver's Travels* differs from all the other islands Gulliver visits in one particularly notable way— it floats in the air. More like a planet than an island, its motions are determined by the magnetic force of a "Load-stone" that functions according to precisely calculated mathematical principles. We are told, in fact, that the mathematicians of this island can explain these principles according to the laws of attraction and repulsion, and are given an example of their calculations that bear a striking resemblance not only to those published in the transactions of the Royal Society, but specifically in Newton's *Principia*.[1]

What is so curious about Swift's satire of such a mathematically precise system is that it also bears a striking resemblance to his own satiric system that, in one sense, we might also envision as an island—a moral system ideally untouched by the fluid phenomena that informed so much of Swift's writing. Yet the very fact that the contortions and flux characteristic of Swift's style were so fluid might, in another sense, entice us to see his satire resembling not an island, but instead the disordered waters that surround it. Or, in the case of this particular island that floats in air, we might regard Swift's satire as having less in common with the systematic scientists who inhabit the island, and more in common with the women—the wives and daughters of the scientists—who flee the island in search of "Diversions."

The question of exactly what this scientific island represented for Swift is a crucial one because, instead of clarifying the nature of the satire, it generates further questions that all seem to center on Swift's own ambivalence about his writing. When Gulliver describes the women who flee the island, for instance, he goes out of his way to distinguish their feelings about the island from his own. "The Wives and Daughters lament their Confinement to the Island, although I think it the most delicious Spot of Ground in the World . . ." (165). What seems like a paradise to Gulliver is more like a prison to these women—placing Gulliver with the foolish scientists whom Swift clearly seems to be satirizing, and placing Swift, strangely enough, with the women who not only find this island repressive of their "Vivacity," but who would do almost anything to escape and seek "Diversions" elsewhere. And yet to identify Swift with these particular women seems a terribly un-Swiftian thing to do—especially when we keep in mind that women rarely figured positively in Swift's prose satires, and often figured grotesquely in his poetry.

The question I am discussing here—which in a specific sense concerns whether Swift himself can be said to identify with Gulliver and the scientists or with a group of vivacious women in search of diversions, and in a larger sense concerns whether Swift identified with the men of systems or with the women fleeing those systems—can also be viewed in terms of a controversy about Swift that has attracted a good deal of attention from literary critics. This controversy, which I make no effort to resolve and want instead to exploit, centers on Swift's dubious position in and adherence to an Augustan worldview. Traditionally, literary critics have regarded Swift as one of several figures who shaped a distinctly Augustan outlook founded on principles of order and design.[2] No matter how disorderly and frenzied Swift's style may be, these critics would argue, there is ultimately a firm center in Swiftian satire—explicit or implied—that he uses as a touchstone against which all forms of deviance might be measured. Especially in recent years, however, several critics have questioned such assumptions about Swift and his satire. They suggest, in various ways and anticipating varied arguments, that disorder rather than order, disruption rather than systematic design, characterize Swift's world, and that he exceeds any attempt to place him within the confines of an orderly Augustan framework.[3]

I would argue that both observations need to be taken into account, that both a desire for order and an indulgence in disorder inform Swift's writing. But to understand the dynamics of their coexistence, we need to place these different perspectives within a sexual economy that accounts for such opposing tendencies in Swift—the tendency to work within and rally around ordered systems, and the tendency to divert his attention altogether from these systems and engage in what Edward Said would call Swiftian "anarchy."[4] To put the matter in its most specific terms, I suggest that we regard the Swift who creates and defends systems as the "man" of classical satiric structure, and that we regard the Swift who writes so vivaciously and disruptively as the "woman" who always seems to be hovering around his satiric systems. If this pseudo-biographical account of Swift sounds similar to what I have already suggested about Isaac Newton, it is because the two men, I believe, responded to remarkably similar desires, which their classical environment fostered. Just as the Newton of the *Principia* gave us a grand "System of the World" in all its mathematical precision, so the Augustan satirist Swift gave us a glimpse of an ideal ordered world against which human shortcomings—the subject of his satire—might be seen in some meaningful perspective. At the same time, however, there was always lurking in the background another Newton, and another Swift—men who were drawn to phenomena that defied systematic enclosure, phenomena that each associated in peculiar ways with woman. Swift's accounts of disruptive women were almost invariably derogatory, so that any argument suggesting that Swift himself unconsciously identified with these women will have to recover their energy from its disparaging Swiftian context. In attempting to do this, I not only want to expose an "other" side of Swift and his satire, but retrieve the feminine energies whose repression made the classical writer and his systematic satire possible.

Swift, like Newton, was powerfully drawn to what Gulliver described as that "most delicious Spot of Ground"—the island of scientists—where the world is unaffected by disorder and diversion. But Swift—like the women of the island and like the "Lady" in Newton—was just as powerfully drawn to a very different world that existed at the edge of his islands, to the shores where the shipwrecked Gulliver would always confront strange worlds, and the waters to which he would return again and again. Swift's islands, seen from this perspective, were at once a refuge from the disordered sea and a continual reminder of its disorder. They offered both Gulliver and Swift a home that was finally just as filled with tumult as the chaotic sea. Perpetually escaping from the perils of the sea to the promise of an island, Gulliver eventually finds himself having to escape from the perils of each island back to the sea—never enjoying the "homecoming" promised to most epic travelers. The journeys on which Swift embarked—figured through Gulliver's travels, through accounts of political and religious turmoil, tales of madness, and a poetry fixated on the body of woman—took him into the disturbing world of the unknown that he, like Newton, could not resist.

In attempting to account for Swift's engagement with this other world, literary critics have generally focused on Swift's language, which inverts meanings only to invert them again, continually digresses from the main subject, and endlessly diverts a reader. Perhaps such chaotic linguistic tendencies derived from Swift's sense of loss about traditions—as Edward Said suggests, from his own personal and psychological temperament—as C. J. Rawson would have it, from a phobia about language—as Terry Castle argues, or from a profound political engagement in the real world—as Carole Fabricant claims.[5] But whatever their specific manifestations and possible sources, they all seem to derive their force from unknown and unfixed phenomena that perpetually disturb neatly structured worlds and foster Swift's distrust of systems—scientific, political, religious, linguistic.

The crucial question I would pose, and one that literary critics have only begun to address, is this: can we understand the other side of Swift—the Swift of anarchy, flux, and disruption—as peculiarly feminine? Can we understand this other side of Swift as reflecting his own uncontrollable desire to be like the women he described, to write the kind of disruption they embodied? When Gulliver describes the women who escape from the floating island, he explains that they feel confined there, that they cannot bear to stay put in this staid world of speculation. In a curious way, these women resemble Gulliver himself who cannot seem to stay at home on his own island, and who begins each book of his travels describing a desire to voyage elsewhere—"condemned by Nature and Fortune to an active and restless life" (83), unable to quench "the Thirst I had of seeing the World" (153). And, in an even more curious way, they seem to resemble Swift himself—whose own career took him through the tempestuous worlds of political, religious, and literary controversy. What I am suggesting, in other words, is that even as he wrote his most disparaging and disgusting accounts of "women," there was something of the "woman" in Swift himself—something of that tendency to flee the systematic and sedate world and be tossed around in the waves, the unknown world of the sea. If we are to recover this woman in Swift, we will have to look for traces of what Hélène Cixous calls "bisexual" writing—not the androgynous merging of male and female, but "the location within oneself of the presence of both sexes," a writing "which does not annihilate differences but cheers them on, pursues them, adds more. . . ."[6] I find this "bisexuality" permeating Swift's writing—but not reflecting, as Cixous would have it, a "feminine" writing that breaks with the "phallic authority" of a discourse long controlled by men (p. 86). Instead, Swift's "bisexual" writing is caught up in the dynamics of a sexual economy in which the energies of woman are derogated and repressed. Recovering the "woman" in Swift means recovering the positive potential of fluid phenomena that he figured only in disparaging terms.

In order to understand Swift's complex response to fluid phenomena, let me recall Michel Foucault's ideas about the "ship of fools" that appeared on the Renaissance scene, ships containing "highly symbolic cargoes of madmen in search of their reason."[7] If we can think, as Foucault does, of the massive confinement of the mad during the "Age of Reason" as an attempt to fix and place madness, to secure madmen from their "wandering existence," perhaps we have grounds for viewing Swift—a writer who was preoccupied with tales of madness and who left "the little Wealth he had, / To build a House for Fools and Mad"—in similar terms. Compelled, as his age was, to confine the watery world of madness within the framed world of Augustan order, Swift nonetheless took his place in that other realm—on a ship of fools that brought his most famous narrator from island to island. "He has his truth," Foucault says of the madman, "and his homeland only in that fruitless expanse between two countries that cannot belong to him" (pp. 8, 11). The description might all too easily explain not only Gulliver's predicament, but that of a homeless author who seemed caught between England and Ireland, who would describe his own voyage across the sea as perilous and illfated, and who once described Ireland itself as a *"Poor floating Isle, tost on ill Fortune's Waves."*[8]

Swift's continual immersion of himself into fluid territory—most explicitly recorded through Gulliver's sea travels and through the infamous "tub" thrown out to sea to act as a diversion enabling a mad writer to tell his "Tale"—becomes a fascinating kind of ritual when we view it not only in terms of what Foucault called the connection between "water and madness," but what I have been speaking of as the connections that link water, madness, and woman. If it is possible to envision woman embodying fluidity—it "speaks 'fluid,'" Irigaray says of woman, "she belongs to the race of waves," Cixous writes[9]—is it possible to envision Swift as somehow embodying woman, taking on her dispersive and disruptive nature as he enters his fluid territory? There can, of course, be no simple answer to this question. Swift's ideas *about* women are sufficiently controversial to make any argument claiming that he may write *as* woman highly problematic, to say the least. Nor would it be accurate, I think, to describe Swift as a kind of "feminine" writer, though I am convinced that he has a good deal of the chaotic and disruptive woman in him—that he wrestled with her just as Newton wrestled with his "Lady" and his yearning for the absent "mother." With Swift, however, we can trace the details of this inner struggle more clearly since, unlike Newton, he directly portrayed women in his satire—he gave them a figuration, in other words, that we can explicitly identify and talk about.

I suggested earlier that, in coming to terms with the two sides of Swift that seem to inform his writing, we might see the man in Swift producing an orderly, cohesive satire, and the woman in Swift constantly diverting attention from the main satire—hovering on the edges and margins of his systems. Locating Swift's figurations of this woman, perpetually on the edge of his systems, will take us to the woman in Swift who accounts for the disruptive quality of his satire, and who gives us a particularly startling glimpse of the world that existed outside Enlightened systems.

GULLIVER AMONG THE WOMEN

When Gulliver distinguishes himself from the women who flee the island of scientists, he focuses particularly on their sexual "Vivacity" and "Diversions," which estrange them from their husbands. Taking up with "Gallants," they become mistresses who "may proceed to the greatest Familiarities" while their husbands remain "so rapt in Speculation" that they hardly notice the transgression. Deriving the moral from this story, Gulliver concludes his account of the episode: "This may perhaps pass with the Reader rather for an *European* or *English* Story, than for one of a Country so remote. But he may please to consider, that the Caprices of Womankind are not limited by any Climate or Nation; and that they are much more uniform than can be easily imagined" (166).

There is something about Gulliver's comment that is typical of Swift not only in *Gulliver's Travels,* but throughout much of his writing. When persons, events, and ideas become most disruptive and chaotic, and especially when that disruption is charged with sexual and bodily energy, they also tend to become feminine—and are often directly portrayed as females. It should not at all be surprising to hear Gulliver, for instance, characterize himself as different from the women of the floating island, especially women associated with sexual transgression and diversion. After all, he seems to be thrown in with such women throughout his travels—the Lady in Lilliput with whom he is accused of having an affair, the young maids in Brobdingnag who strip the tiny man and play with him on their breasts, the lustful female Yahoo who attacks him as he bathes in Houyhnhnmland. These women never figure prominently in the main parts of Swift's satire—in the discussions of politics, religion, language, and the social order. In these discussions, Gulliver actively exchanges ideas with prominent men. His encounters with women, on the other hand, typically ensue when Gulliver becomes the subject of some action—the subject of rumors about illicit sexual behavior, the subject of a playful rape by the maids in Brobdingnag, or of a lustful attack by a female yahoo. While Gulliver never talks about philosophical matters or governmental systems with such women, they are the ones who seem always to effect his fate in those systems. We might say, then, that while these women never figure directly in Gulliver's main encounters with new systems and worlds, they hover all around the islands he visits. And they seem always to be implicated in necessitating his departure from each island.

We might look more closely, for instance, at the circumstances surrounding Gulliver's relations with the "great Lady" in Lilliput with whom he is accused of having an affair. The political and social satire here is obvious enough. Mean spirited and suspicious, the Lilliputians show all their littleness in believing this gossip about Gulliver and a famous politician's wife. In appreciating the satire, however, we might overlook the fact that this gossip concerning the lady is what facilitates Gulliver's downfall in Lilliput. It disrupts, in other words, all his systematic strategems there: his mastery of their language, his education in their laws and customs, his efforts to aid them in building and construction, his role in their military pursuits. In Lilliput, as in Brobdingnag, Gulliver strives to build sys-

tems—linguistic and material—that will allow him to accommodate a social order in which he is so obviously out of place and proportion. It is a
woman who gets in the way of his best plans, preventing him from successfully entering into the system. We might even view Gulliver's maleness
as directly blocking, through his encounters with the female, his efforts at
accommodation. All the gossip about the affair only serves to call attention
to what one psychoanalytic critic described as Gulliver's sense of "sexual
aggrandizement," something our hero enjoys throughout his stay in Lilliput, perhaps most notably when the troops march between his widespread
legs and glance up at his "Breeches" that were "in so ill a Condition, that
they afforded some Opportunities for Laughter and Admiration" (42).
Such a passive display of male prowess, however, becomes far more dam-
aging to Gulliver when he actively uses his masculine equipment. Putting
out a fire by urinating on the Empress' apartment, for instance, is an action
that allows Gulliver to make use of his "admirable" male machinery, but
that also places him at odds with another woman who will figure prominently in his fall from grace in Lilliput. This "affair" ends up providing no
less than grounds for the first of the "Articles of Impeachment" against
Gulliver. In Lilliput, it would seem, women get Gulliver in trouble. Or is
it that Swift figures Gulliver's trouble in terms of women? To begin to
read *Gulliver's Travels* in this way will, I think, expose the peculiar feminine
configuration of Swiftian disruption that appears again and again in his
writing. The women in Lilliput are the first signs of this disruptive "thing"
at work in Swift's text, upsetting Gulliver's stratagems and threatening the
order of Swift's satire.

As we trace the figurations of this woman throughout *Gulliver's Travels,*
her effects assume a kind of pattern all their own in terms of Swift's tendency to associate woman with disruption. The same feminine force that
was responsible for Gulliver's downfall in Lilliput, for instance, makes a
mere plaything out of Gulliver's sexuality in Brobdingnag—that vast
space where the woman appears on her own terrain. Under the care of the
farmer's daughter and ultimately of the Queen herself, Gulliver is forced
by circumstances to enter into a profoundly feminine world in which he
must submit to feminine control. Without this maternal care, he would be
as helpless as an infant. We might read Gulliver's predicament here from
the perspective of Freudian Oedipal theory, and see him as the son desiring the mother, desiring the union with mother that the father would
threaten. Such an explanation seems even more convincing when we keep
in mind that many of the dangers Gulliver confronts are posed by males—
the farmer, the dwarf, the young prankish boy, even the boyish monkey.
Yet the most disturbing event in Brobdingnag comes not from any man,

but from feminine diversions. The male may take him away from mother and into the world of separation and alienation, but the female takes him into the even more threatening sphere of feminine sexuality. I am speaking, of course, about Gulliver's encounters with the "Maids of Honour," the women who make him into the toy of their playful antics. Since I want to offer several observations about this particular episode, let me quote the major part of it.

> The Maids of Honour often invited *Glumdalclitch* to their Apartments, and desired she would bring me along with her, on Purpose to have the Pleasure of seeing and touching me. They would often strip me naked from Top to Toe, and lay me at full Length in their Bosoms; wherewith I was much disgusted; because, to say the Truth, a very offensive Smell came from their Skins. . . .
>
> That which gave me the most Uneasiness among these Maids of Honour, when my Nurse carried me to visit them, was to see them use me without any Manner of Ceremony, like a Creature who had no Sort of Consequence. For, they would strip themselves to the Skin, and put on their Smocks in my Presence, while I was placed on their Toylet directly before their naked Bodies; which, I am sure, to me was very far from being a tempting Sight, or from giving me any other Motions than those of Horror and Disgust. . . . The handsomest among these Maids of Honour, a pleasant frolicksome Girl of sixteen, would sometimes set me astride upon one of her Nipples; with many other Tricks, wherein the Reader will excuse me for not being over particular. But, I was so much displeased, that I entreated *Glumdalclitch* to contrive some excuse for not seeing that young Lady any more. (118–19)

Why, we might wonder, did Swift place this particular passage in Brobdingnag? If he had brought women so forcefully to the forefront in Lilliput, he might have been able to engage in a more typical male fantasy: the large man toying with the small woman, the myth of the female as man's doll, the father's seduction of the daughter. Yet this is clearly not the case in the land of giants, especially here where the giants are also women. Assuming that Swift did have a choice—and one assumes that writers do make conscious decisions and also follow unconscious urges—we can at least say that he chose to deal with women as large and overpowering rather than small and submissive. But why? What was the feminine force he found so overpowering?

In her source study, "The Rape of Gulliver," Sheila Shaw relates the tale of "Hassan-al-Bassri" found in *The Thousand and One Nights,* a tale once thought to be a source for Swift's Maids of Honour episode but that, according to Shaw, is an English translation more likely indebted to Swift for its source.[10] In this tale we also have a female giant "manhandling" a tiny human, but this man, instead of recoiling in disgust as Gulliver had, actually enjoys the pleasure—to the point of exhaustion. Yet since the giantess cannot quite get enough of him, Hassan becomes weaker and weaker, and finally manages to escape. Gulliver's escape, if we can call it that, involves a very different scenario. Instead of running *away* from woman, he runs toward her—seeking safety in the protection of his young female caretaker.

If this episode of *Gulliver's Travels* was in fact a source for the tale of Hassan, as Shaw argues, we might use it for the purpose of contrasting the two stories and focusing on the distinctive aspects of Gulliver's response to woman. What, then—to repeat my earlier question—was the feminine force which Gulliver, and Swift, found so overpowering? It was, I believe, the chaotic and sexually charged woman whom he feared, and yet who, in her more maternal guise, always promised to take him away from his fears. In this sense, woman is like the waters of the sea that can be at once threatening and soothing, that can take the journeyer into a world of chaos, and also promise him islands of order, system, and stasis. Continually seeking a return to the sea was one way of seeking a return to maternal comfort and safety—away from complete chaos and disorder, but also away from the rigid systems that, on every island Gulliver visits, eventually imprison him as soundly as he was confined in his small "Box" of a home in Brobdingnag.[11] It makes sense to me, in more ways than the plot of this episode might dictate, that Gulliver's escape from his imprisonment in Brobdingnag is facilitated by a bird who drops him into the ocean—into the maternal but also potentially mad waters to which he continually returns. There is something about Gulliver that rejects the systems of man for the fluidity of woman, even as he fears the excess and chaos of her feminine force. And there is something in Swift, as there was in Newton, that continually sought a return to the world of the mother.

Whenever Swift speaks of women he speaks of diversion, of frolic, of some disturbing "thing" that disrupts his male systems. If, as I have been trying to argue, we can get hold of this "thing" by looking for the wanderings of the female in *Gulliver's Travels,* the search may finally show us only signs of something that is not there, just as the feminine in this narrative becomes most forceful when she inhabits the realm of the negative—"*the Thing which was not.*" Her elusive presence in Book IV, the thwarted resolution of the narrative, is what makes this book the most problematic and disturbing of Gulliver's voyages. Just at the point when our hero becomes most systematic and pristine, he turns against himself, rejects everything but the purely systematic and rational pursuits of a society of enlightened horses. These horses, of course, are notably unhorselike, their manners resembling the polite demeanor of gentlemen more than the uncontrolled power of the stud with which we might associate them. In an effort to understand exactly what they do represent, I would suggest that we play with the significance and sound of the word *Houyhnhnm,* as so many readers of *Gulliver* have done. If the word signifies "horse," since that is obviously the creature Gulliver is describing, what does the word sound like? Is it a homonym, a word whose sound refers us to another word of different significance? Yes, the story goes, it sounds like *human,* so that Houyhnhnms and Humans share a strange, and much disputed, character. But if we do play the homonym game, then perhaps we can find a word that sounds more like Houyhnhnm—perhaps *women,* an even closer correspondence since only a shift in two letters indicates any difference at all. Playful as this reading might seem, I find irresistible the suspicion that somewhere in the recesses of Swift's mind, a mind so accustomed to the process of inversion and opposition, he caught the similarity in sound connecting these opposite creatures—the One and the Other who both shape and disrupt his satiric systems.

But I am not sure that the matter can rest so easily, since I suspect that what lurks within the homonym game is that Houyhnhnm is a homonym for *homonym,* and that to play the homonym game is to play a game of endless repetition and referral—endless "diversion." That *Houyhnhnm* may actually be a homonym for *homonym* makes it possible for us to see these ostensibly rational and controlled creatures as themselves inscribed by a language that—through its endless referrals and deferrals—moves beyond their control. If, from one perspective, the Houyhnhnms cannot say "the Thing which was not," from another perspective their very name signifies the inevitably of speaking this negativity. *Houyhnhnm* as "homonym" may well be what subverts Gulliver's ideal existence among these rational creatures. And if this is so, then *Houyhnhnm* as "woman" may well be the disruptive feminine force within this subversion.

Several critics, as I have already observed, located Swift's discontinuities in the flux of his language—its diversions, inversions, and endless referentiality. We might, keeping the "Houyhnhnm" and "woman" connection in mind, entertain the possibility that Swift's very engagement with a language of flux was also his way of engaging with woman. In her essay "Why the Houyhnhnms Don't Write," Terry Castle suggests that Swift actually feared the written word, that he was plagued by a kind of "grammaphobia" that we can detect throughout his works and especially in *A Tale of a*

Tub and *Gulliver*. Her analysis of *A Tale* is particularly relevant to my own suspicion that what Swift feared about language is rooted in his partial fear of the feminine. Describing Swift's vision of the text as "a radically unstable object," "one disrupted at all points by obscurities, typographical ellipses, holes," Castle notices that Swift "figures its monstrosity by way of an imagery of fertility, of breeding. The Text, for the satirist, is womb-like (might we say female?): it gives birth, in a process at once out of control and horrifying, to replicas of itself . . . it invites commentary, it seeks to generate new texts." [12] In response to her question "might we say female?" I would suggest that we might indeed. The very terms of the argument would bear this out. If *A Tale,* Castle goes on, shows Swift actually writing the text of his fears, *Gulliver* shows him writing about his "grammapho-bia." In each of the voyages, we encounter a variation of this fear: the Lilliputian compulsion to textualize everything, the Brobdingnagian de-nigration of the text, the Laputan "text-breeding machine," and finally the absence of any written text in Houyhnhnmland (pp. 39–41). Following Castle's observations, we have a basis for reading *A Tale* as Swift's bizarre submission of himself into the language of the feminine, a submission that we find repeated in the Maids of Honour episode in *Gulliver* where sexual repression becomes another version of linguistic repression. We also have grounds for speculating that the real reason "why the Houyhnhnms don't write" is that, despite their pretensions to say only "the Thing which is," they themselves constitute another version of the woman who always disrupts this truth, another version of an unacknowledged propensity to defer and refer meaning elsewhere—a propensity in their very "hom-onym"-like name.

Yet for all these connections that might on an unconscious level link Houyhnhnm with woman with homonym, it was not the rational horses that Swift so directly and so often described in feminine terms. It was, of course, the Yahoos. Associated with filth, excrement, and bodily deform-ity, the Yahoos represented everything that Gulliver feared in himself. If we can say that the Houyhnhnm's shunning of writing betrays Swift's fear of the ceaselessly generative capacity of language, it is the Yahoo's associa-tion with a debased human form that betrays Swift's related fear of the body—specifically a body that is unmasked and uncontrolled. That Swift harbored such anxieties about the body is something we can find not only in Gulliver's disgust especially with the female Yahoos in Houyhnhnm-land, but with his account of those overpowering feminine forces he con-fronts in Brobdingnag, and finally with the shunning of his own wife when he returns home at the end of his travels. The special message that the Yahoos offer, however, is not simply that Gulliver was disgusted with

his own human body and hence with "mankind." In describing the Yahoos, Gulliver shows us that he is far more disgusted with "womankind,"
since woman has come to figure all that he finds so disruptive of the paradise he seeks on each island, and ultimately on the island to which he will
go home. It was woman's body that disturbed Gulliver and made this
homecoming impossible, just as powerfully as this body would disturb
Swift in his poems on women, and just as powerfully as it disturbed Enlightenment medicine and its fascination with the diseases of women.

In describing the "Female-*Yahoo*,"—a creature who is always wallowing,
with her male counterparts, in filth and excrement, and who distinguishes
herself from them by also lusting after something or someone—Gulliver
laments that "the Rudiments of *Lewdness, Coquetry, Censure*, and *Scandal*,
should have a Place by Instinct in Womankind" (264). If Swift, as we
might like to believe, satirized women in this way ultimately for the purpose of showing them, along with "mankind," the extent to which they
deviate from ideals and even from commonsense norms, he also nonetheless betrayed his suspicion that woman embodied this deviance. Like Eve,
her prototype, this woman is not simply the person who violates the law
of order and system, but who represents the very notion of transgression
itself. So Swift's woman is more than a mere image that functions within
his satiric contexts. Instead of portraying the foibles of "womankind," she
has *in her* the very "Rudiments" of violation. She exceeds by her very
definition, becoming the material and the body of that excess.

If Gulliver was ashamed of his own body, keeping it hidden from the
larger Houyhnhnm population so they would not identify him with
the Yahoos, he did so because he was afraid that they would discover
the woman in him—the body whose unwieldy nature might generate and
degenerate beyond control, beyond the confines of any system that Gulliver continually sought in his passage from island to island. Ultimately
banished from Houyhnhnmland because of his body, Gulliver returns
once again to the fluid world of the sea—his "other" home, his "no-man's
land." [13] But Gulliver does not entirely give up some desire for stasis. Hop-
ing to "discover some small Island uninhabited" that might allow him to
spend the rest of his days reflecting on the "Virtues of those inimitable
Houyhnhnms" (283), he encounters instead an island inhabited by savages,
"stark naked" humans who run after him as he once again takes refuge
"into the Sea." They discharge an arrow that wounds Gulliver in his
knee—"(I shall carry the Mark to my Grave)" he says (284). Perhaps the
wound marks, as it had for Achilles, Gulliver's one vulnerable spot. And
perhaps that vulnerability is the desire—despite his search for systems—
to return again and again to the disorder of the sea.

Yet Gulliver, like Swift, knew that he must eventually leave the realm of disruption and disorder, and finally come home. He did so with a tremendous sense of dissatisfaction. He could not stand the sight and smell of his wife, dreading the fact that "by copulating with one of the *Yahoo*-Species, I had become a Parent of more . . ." (289). What Gulliver dreads is not only the inevitable connection between his wife's body and his own, but that through his connection with her, he has reproduced, generated, engaged in the activity that is itself a process—bodily, sexual, linguistic—that exceeds the confines of a controlled system. Among the women, Gulliver can never find the systems he seeks, since the woman who hovers around these systems represents the very force that disrupts and transgresses systematic closure and enclosure. Swift told this tale again and again. The lonely figure of Gulliver epitomizes the fate of a man who ostensibly sought the solidity and firmness of land, but who—on an unconscious level—might say with Hélène Cixous: "I really do prefer swimming. I prefer being in the water and openly in the water. . . ."[14] Swift's desire for the very fluid phenomena that he shunned and at times abhorred was figured through his desire to be like a woman—a desire that he continually indulged and continually repressed.

Mad Tales and Poems about Women

Throughout my discussion of *Gulliver's Travels,* I have been suggesting that Swift was both drawn toward and away from the systems that were so much a part of his age. Seeking new systems on each new island, Gulliver finds that they all somehow prove inadequate. And Swift, like Gulliver, ultimately finds more of a home in the disordered sea—to which both he and his storyteller have always been drawn. In my own search for connections between the waters that were so appealing to Swift, and the woman who seemed so disturbing to him, I began by recalling Foucault's association of water and madness and suggested that woman—through her configurations and embodiments of madness and hysteria—was also necessarily to be associated with water and fluidity. In this way, it is possible to view Swift's own immersion in chaotic and fluid matters, especially the world of language, as an immersion into a distinctly feminine domain.

Madness, fluidity, and woman, in fact, are repeatedly linked in Swift's writing—either in the direct portrayal of actual females, or in the feminine configuration of ideas and individuals who are, through their disruptive capacity, always close to becoming feminine. We might consider, for instance, the similarities between the Goddess of Criticism described in *The Battel of the Books* and the mad and modern narrator of *A Tale of a Tub.*

One is a monstrous female creature whose "Diet was the overflowing of her own *Gall*," and whose motherly body—nursing the modern writers of the age—is eventually transformed into a text on which her parents and children "strowed a Black Juice, or Decoction of Gall and Soot, in the Form of Letters . . ." (154–55).[15] The other is a mad storyteller, ceaselessly generating texts long after "the Subject is utterly exhausted . . ." (133). As the monstrous female "overflows," so the mad storyteller digresses on and on until his digressions entirely overtake the main narrative of the three brothers. As the monstrous female, Goddess of Criticism, generates more and more commentary that diverts us from ancient and primary texts, so the mad storyteller—like the "tub" set afloat for the very purpose of diversion—generates commentaries like seed that "will multiply far beyond either the Hopes or Imagination of the Sower" (118). In their ceaselessly flowing and generative capacity, both the woman and the madman violate the principles of order and system that might otherwise supply Swift with the fixed center of his satire.

But is there a fixed center to be found? The question brings us back again to the two sides of Swift that both seemed to play a part in his writing. Describing Swift's "two best-known fictive identities" as "marginal men who dramatize an anarchic dispersion of energies through their respective peregrinations and digressions," Carole Fabricant argues that although *A Tale of a Tub* has "a center of sorts," it exists "as little more than a hypothetical construct, an implied antithesis to what *is,* so that all of the most appealing, vital energies seem to be located on the fringes"[16]—or, we might say, in the "tub" drifting around on the waters, continually diverting our attention from the principal and central subjects. These "marginal men," I would suggest, are in fact more like women than men, more caught up in the process of diversion and disruption than in the construction and defense of systems. Like the actual female portrayals who appear throughout Swift's writing, they are notably fluid characters, often directly associated with water and the sea. And like Swift's digressive and chaotic language, they bring us to the edge of his systems, to its "fringes," where boundaries never seem capable of holding.

I have already discussed some of the ways in which recent feminist theory speaks of woman in fluid terms. For Irigaray, the feminine associations of fluidity compel us to ask science some questions, specifically about its *"historical lag in elaborating a 'theory' of fluids."* Instead of taking account of fluid phenomena, she claims, science tries to achieve dominance over whatever resists its structures, a process that inevitably entails subordinating the fluid to the solid.[17] For Cixous, the nature of feminine fluidity has everything to do with the "body"—"with its thousand and one thresholds of ardor . . . she lets it articulate the profusion of meanings that run through it in every direction. . . ."[18] I find both of these responses to fluidity—the attempt, on the one hand, to subordinate it to firm and solid matter, and on the other to celebrate its generation and profusion—descriptive of Swift's own response to the feminine elements in his writing. And that response, it seems to me, is most clearly and directly voiced in his poems about women. I want to inquire into these curious poems, which have understandably been the subject of a good deal of critical commentary, before returning to the mad storyteller of Swift's *Tale,* and finally, once again, to Gulliver's tale, where a particularly important absent woman needs to be confronted, and accounted for.

Interpret them as you will, Swift's poems about women focus almost exclusively on their bodies, specifically on their bodily fluids. Whether he is describing the "Vapors and Steams" surrounding Diana's face or his beloved Stella's "doubled" size, whether his subject is the frailty of feminine beauty or the emptiness of a woman's mind,[19] Swift seems to zero in on the body—as if it were the perfect metaphor of whatever it was he tried to say. But what exactly was he trying to say? And why was woman's body with all its fluid effusions so apt a metaphor?

Critics and readers can argue about such matters forever, placing Swift in classical, Christian, even in antifeminist traditions that might account for his choice of subject and method of satire.[20] In discussing such matters, the assumption would seem to be that Swift held certain attitudes about satire, and about women, that account for his notably unromantic portrayals. The assumption, in other words, is that Swift's poetry takes woman as its subject—that Swift himself chose to write about women in this way—for reasons that we might discover and explain in terms of certain literary and historical contexts.

I would suggest that we need to reverse the terms governing this assumption. Instead of assuming that Swift chose to write about women, we should ask why this particular fluid configuration of woman captured his poetic imagination. Why is it that woman embodied Swift's poetry, or to put the matter more directly, why did her body actually become the subject and material of his poems? Was there a woman haunting Swift's imagination, just as a "Lady" had haunted Newton's? I think that there was, and that Swift's poems about "women" portray this "woman" most clearly. Elsewhere in his writing, she may take the form of madness, or of watery and wandering phenomena that always exceed systems of containment and closure—and that appear most pervasively throughout Swift's writing in his very fluid and disruptive language. But in the poems on women, this "woman" assumes a distinct feminine aspect. She takes on the body of the female. It was not Swift, then, who chose to write about women or to use them metaphorically for certain satiric purposes. It was the woman *in* Swift—the force that was so disruptive of his systems and that nonetheless provided the very energy of his writing—that produced these poems. It was not women and their unwieldy bodies that horrified Swift. It was the womanly part of Swift himself.

In trying to see this woman as another configuration of what I have been calling Enlightened Absence, we need to see a large part of Swift himself as being absent from England's classical age—as occupying a place on its "fringes," and often stepping outside its systems altogether. Viewed from this perspective, his poetic portrayal of woman as constantly in a state of decomposition provides a perfect means for Swift to voice his anxieties about the possibility that his own writing failed to achieve coherence and firmness, and that it was somehow uncontrollably feminine. Woman's disruptive body represented for Swift his own disruptions of a classical order that he knew he should be defending. In writing about the decomposition of her body and making her into a ghostlike, absent creature, I think that Swift was configuring that part of himself that was absent from classical systems, that hovered on its margins and at times stepped outside entirely. Woman decays into absence just as Swift feared that his own writing would decay into nothingness. "The Progress of Beauty" is ultimately the progress of such decay as Diana, figured through the changing moon and all its feminine associations, dismantles herself until there is no "Matter" left of her body. "The Furniture of a Woman's Mind" is its vacancy. "A Beautiful Young Nymph Going To Bed" is literally the account of a woman deconstituting herself as she removes both her clothes and various bodily parts. Even the so-called scatological poems, where a young man is shocked to discover that women actually "shit," focuses its attention on waste.

We might understand more clearly Swift's fear of his own feminine and decomposing self by considering the specific effects of woman's fluidity in these poems. It is fluid matter that accompanies and often facilitates this process of decomposition and annihilation. In "The Progress of Beauty," Diana's hair is a "mingled Mass of Dirt and Sweat" (20), and what "Mercury" has taken away from her, "Oyl" and "Soot" restore (109–10). In "The Lady's Dressing Room," Celia not only "shits," but "spits" and "spues" (118, 42), and her handkerchiefs are "varnish'd o'er with Snuff and Snot" (50). The young lady in "Strephon and Chloe," having consumed twelve cups of tea, shocks Strephon by producing a "noysom Steam / Which oft attends that luke-warm Stream" (179–80). And in "A Beautiful Young Nymph Going to Bed," Corinna explores her "running

Sores" before going to sleep, and dreams of standing "near *Fleet-Ditch's* oozy Brinks" (47). As this woman, embodying Swift's own ambiguous response to fluidity, wastes away to nothingness, his ideal woman remains as fixed and firm as the stars. Stella's "Form" not only shows no evidence of "decline," but is "doubled" in size ("On Stella's Birth-day, 1718–19"). Even as she ages, Swift tells us, her "Body" continues to "thrive and grow / By Food of twenty Years ago" ("Stella's Birth-day, 1727, 55–56). Yet while her "Mind" becomes an emblem of that which remains untouched by bodily changes and decay, "Woman's Mind" is constantly in a state of flux, "all she prates has nothing in it" ("The Furniture of a Woman's Mind," 6). Just as water in Swift's "Description of a City Shower" mingles all the filth and smells of the city—which takes on its own feminine form as the Trojan horse "Pregnant with *Greeks,* impatient to be freed" (48)— so woman becomes that pregnant monster threatening to flood Swift's world.

Woman, body, waste, absence—they are all configurations of the phenomenon other than that which was solid, firm, and fixed within systems, the phenomenon whose fluid properties exceeded the boundaries of those systems. If we can entertain the possibility, as I have been developing it, that Swift himself had much of this absent, fluid woman in him, how are we to understand his attachment to the systems of his age? Has modern criticism created the Swift who we see defending systematic worlds in the same way that histories of science have created the Newton who explained and defended a systematic universe? To a large extent, I believe, this has happened—though to deny that Newton and Swift felt a strong allegiance to the systems of their age would be misleading. Yet we need to recognize an important difference between Newton and Swift. While Newton, even as he was lured into the realm of fluid and "vibrating" phenomena, did succeed in producing the mathematical calculations that accounted for a perfectly systematic universe, Swift continually failed to produce literary material that confirmed the order and design of a systematic Augustan worldview.

Although critics have offered varied explanations that might account for Swift's disruptive and chaotic tendencies, only recently has anyone entertained the idea that they are directly related to his portrayals of women. Ellen Pollak, describing a "Poetics of Sexual Myth" that constituted a kind of "sexual ideology" in the verse of Swift and Pope, argues that both poets responded, but in different ways, to a "myth of passive womanhood." This myth, the creation of male writers, postulated an ideal woman as one who was obedient, submissive, and passive—a woman who was not an individual self at all, but rather "an extension of male desire."[21] Pope, she claims, successfully accommodates women to this myth, portraying them as the submissive complement to man. But with Swift, she says, "no such unifying equilibrium is ever comfortably achieved" (p. 160). Describing Swift as "mastering his disappointment by becoming its very agent, basking in the condition that he hates," Pollak concludes: "if Swift's savagely reactionary response to modern discourse reflects an aversion to an all-absorbing textuality for which woman is a central metaphor, it is also—paradoxically—the grounds for his own production of a mode of writing that ultimately embraces the ontological and epistemological premises of modern discourse . . ." (pp. 171–72).

What Pollak argues here is nothing less than that the "vexing" woman in Swift's poetry not only refuses to conform to the ruling "sexual ideology," but is representative of the "active principle of difference itself" that "becomes the motivating structure of Swift's art" (p. 160). Such an argument locates the very activity of difference within woman. It is woman who becomes the generative process that Barbara Johnson has described as the "difference within," differences that instead of establishing firm hierarchies—such as male and female—continually defer within and thereby maintain the process of deferral and decomposition.[22] This notion of difference, when we understand it in terms of its feminine context, situates woman in that ill-defined and ceaselessly active territory in which texts "deconstruct," in which and through which the endless play of difference makes any systematic cohesion and closure impossible.

That literary deconstruction can provide a fruitful context for understanding the flux and instability of Swift's language has already been suggested by critics, such as Douglas Atkins who sees *A Tale of a Tub* as a text that constantly questions the authority of the word, and in which "freeplay reigns,"[23] and Terry Castle who explores Swift's fear of the written text in terms of Jacques Derrida's critique of "writing."[24] What I have in mind in speaking of Swift's woman as disruptive, however, is not only that Swift's "deconstructive" energies prevent him from achieving the closure and structure that classical systems celebrated, but that these energies are distinctly feminine. Viewed from this perspective, his poems on women are not only failed attempts to accommodate a "sexual myth," but also Swift's attempt to purge himself of this disruptive woman by continually and consistently portraying her as a monstrous and decomposing creature. Just as Gayatri Spivak would argue that woman occupies the "place" of deconstruction—"the place of a general critique of the history of Western thought,"[25] so I would argue that the woman in Swift, who appears conspicuously in his poems *as* the very process of becoming an absent thing, occupies the place of his own deconstruction—the place where Swift located his fear that what was disturbingly feminine in his writing would destroy his systematic pursuits.

It should not be surprising, then, that Swift's phobia about the female body—its ability to decompose into a horrid nothingness—figures prominently in his writing as early as *A Tale of a Tub*, and culminates late in his career with *Gulliver's Travels*. What makes the mad tale teller so feminine is not only the fact that Swift associated him with madness, but that in his diversions, disruptions, and digressions he is doomed to write on forever. As the tale teller explains in his own "Conclusion": "I am now trying an Experiment very frequent among Modern Authors; which is, to *write upon Nothing*; When the Subject is utterly exhausted, to let the Pen still move on; by some called, the Ghost of Wit, delighting to walk after the Death of its Body" (133). The "nothingness" of this mad discourse, figured most expressly in Swift's poems where the fluidity of woman's body becomes the material through which she decomposes into absence, is also figured in the fluid and excremental substance of Gulliver's own body in Houyhnhnmland. Not only does his bodily resemblance to the Yahoos necessitate his banishment from the island, but it is the very part of himself that he must banish from himself. On his return to England, he cannot bear the sight, touch, and smell of his wife and children. Their bodies are now seen by him as presenting those very propensities that he wants to banish from his own. Even in his partial "Reconcilement" to the human "*Yahoo*-kind," Gulliver continues to be repulsed whenever he beholds a "Lump of Deformity, and Diseases both in Body and Mind" (296). To the very end, he continues to figure his dissatisfaction with and alienation from the world in terms of the body. But now it is no longer simply the body of woman that disturbs him, and from which he insistently distinguishes himself. Now it is his own body as well, his own physical link to the world of decay, waste, and decomposing material that takes him to "nothingness" and absence.

Seen from this perspective, we can view much of Swift's phobia about a peculiar feminine disruptive force in terms of his expressed anxieties about fluid matter. When Irigaray accuses science of harboring a similar anxiety about fluids, she describes this threatening fluid matter in terms that seem especially relevant to Swift's figurations of feminine fluidity: "Milk, luminous flow, acoustic waves, . . . not to mention the gases inhaled, emitted, variously perfumed, of urine, saliva, blood, even plasma, and so on."[26] The correspondence between Irigaray's embodiment of fluid and Swift's fascination with the fluid dimensions of woman's body becomes even more intriguing when she speaks in specific bodily terms about the scientific attempt to subordinate fluids to solids. Since women, she argues, "diffuse themselves" in ways that are not compatible with the "ruling symbolics" (p. 106), their fluid nature is suppressed by being transformed into that which can be accounted for—the solid matter over which science can claim dominion. Irigaray's explanation of this transformation has a curious bearing on what Norman O. Brown calls Swift's "excremental vision."[27] Describing the primary concerns and assumptions of science as "object *a*," she wonders why fluid matter is never enumerated in scientific theory as this "object *a*." Her response is in the form of a question that might well be taken up by psychoanalytic critics of Swift: ". . . will feces—variously disguised—have the privilege of serving as the paradigm for the object *a*? Must we then understand this modeling function—more or less hidden from view—of the object of desire as resulting from the passage, a successful one, from the fluid to the solid state? *The object of desire itself . . . would be the transformation of fluid to solid?* Which seals—this is well worth repeating—*the triumph of rationality*" (p. 113). Following Irigaray's observations, I would suggest that we read what many consider Swift's fixation on excrement as a desire to transform feminine fluidity—toward which he himself was powerfully drawn—into solid matter over which he could maintain dominion. Such a desire would not only explain why a woman "shitting" becomes such a crucial, if ludicrous, subject in Swift's scatological poems on women, but also why Gulliver pays so much attention to the subject of his own excrement, and why he becomes so horrified and victimized when the Yahoos assume control over him as they "discharge their Excrements" on his head. All of this attention devoted to excrement seems to reveal the workings of a sexual economy in which solid matter becomes, in the case of Swift's poems, the desired object of fluid and feminine decomposition, and, in the case of Gulliver, the means to achieve positions of accommodation and power within given systems.

The consequence of not being able to control and contain such disruptive fluidity is madness itself, at least as Swift had figured his account of madness in *A Tale of a Tub*. In the famous "Digression on Madness," the tale teller describes the origin of madness as a "Vapor . . . got up into the Brain." His elaboration of this description is no less than an elaboration of that Swiftian anxiety about fluids. "Mists arise from the Earth, Steams from Dunghils, Exhalations from the Sea, and Smoak from Fire; yet all Clouds are the same in Composition, as well as Consequences . . . and then it will follow, that as the Face of Nature never produces Rain, but when it is overcast and disturbed, so Human Understanding, seated in the Brain, must be troubled and overspread by Vapours, ascending from the lower Faculties, to water the Invention, and render it fruitful" (102–3).

To support his claim, the tale teller offers two examples of the ways in which this vapor has generated tumult and confusion on a grand scale. In one case, the vapor manifested itself in the "*Semen*" of a "Great Prince," and in the second case, settled in the "Anus" of a "mighty King." Swift's scatological humor, as many psychoanalytic critics have noted, may often reveal more than his satire would seem to intend. Yet I find the case of the "Great Prince" particularly revealing of a sexual economy in which Swift accounts for threats to man's systems by figuring these threats as fluid.

I explore the story further because it supplies the crucial missing link between fluidity and madness—namely, woman. The tale teller identifies the source of the problem in none other than an "absent *Female*." It was discovered, he explains, that "this *Vapour* took its Rise" from the direction of an "absent *Female*, whose Eyes had raised a Proturberancy, and before Emission, she was removed into an Enemy's Country" (103). The vapor, whose mad effects are instigated by the very woman whose absence will only ensure frenzy, proceeds to disrupt the body of the Prince and, through him, threaten to unleash chaos in his kingdom. "Having to no purpose used all peaceable Endeavours, the collected part of the *Semen*, raised and enflamed, became adust, converted to Choler, turned head upon the spinal Duct, and ascended to the Brain" (104). Extrapolating on this situation, the tale teller concludes: "The very same Principle that influences a *Bully* to break the Windows of a Whore, who has jilted him, naturally stirs up a Great Prince to raise mighty Armies, and dream of nothing but Sieges, Battles, and Victories" (104).[28]

This "Principle," it seems to me, is the very feminine force that "stirs up" Swift's own writing, whose fluidity always seeks to be contained and yet moves on beyond containment—outside the borders of systems and into the world of madness. Commenting on the moral to be drawn from the story of the Prince, the tale teller quotes Horace: "*Cunnus teterrima belli / Causa* _____," loosely translated "Woman is the most terrible cause of war."[29] A more precise translation, however, would call attention to Swift's specific emphasis on the female body, since "*Cunnus*" is literally "the female genitals."[30] The "absent *Female*" may ultimately be the sexually generative and disruptive capacities that Swift specifically associated with the female body, and that the age associated with the hysterical woman's body and its dangerous fluid mobility. Not only was the prince affected by an imbalance of humors, which might explain his predicament in terms of conventional medical and cultural assumptions governing humors theory. The very imbalance itself is effected and directs its effects within the context of sexual desire: man's desire for woman, thwarted because of her absence, generates madness and violence.

If Swift forged this association linking woman's body and madness some-what indirectly and playfully in *A Tale,* he later made it quite explicit in his portrayal of the "Maids of Honour" in Brobdingnag whose bodily sexual exuberance proved overpowering to Gulliver—the man who finally could not bring himself to tolerate the body of his wife.

GULLIVER'S WIFE

The account of this "absent *Female*" who figures as a source of madness in *A Tale* bears a strong resemblance to an absent woman in *Gulliver's Travels.* Gulliver's wife, hovering on the very edges of each of the four books de-scribing his voyages, seems the epitome of the "passive woman" who, as Pollak explained, provided the age with its ruling sexual ideology. But this woman shows us that in addition to harboring a "myth of passive wom-anhood," England's classical age also harbored a myth of disruptive wom-anhood. The failed reunion of Gulliver and his wife explodes the very idea of the epic homecoming, and through this explosion, the absent woman again figures powerfully in the disruption of classical systems.

What is distinctive about feminine fluidity, as I have been discussing this phenomenon throughout my reading of Swift, is that it seeps beyond boundaries, exposing, as Catherine Clément would say, "the cracks in an overall system."[31] The absence of Gulliver's wife reveals a different kind of fissure in the structure of Swift's narrative. She exposes a "crack" in the very parameters of epic structure by *not* serving as that other element that the man will finally appropriate. The great literary epics, from Homer through James Joyce, all tell the story of the homecoming—Odysseus re-turns to Penelope, Leopold Bloom comes home to Molly. Even Cole-ridge's ancient mariner is compelled to tell his story to the wedding guest, as if the union of sexual difference is crucial to the successful closure of the epic journey. But not so with Gulliver. In rejecting his wife, he rejects epic closure and conclusion, refusing to accommodate the demands of the lit-erary system. Something is not only missing, but its absence is what pre-vents Gulliver from bringing his narrative to a resolution—just as it had prevented the mad tale teller from ending his digressions. Gulliver's wife is forced out of the system at the very moment when her appropriation would have justified the grand system after all. Her absence at this crucial moment is Swift's final and ultimate refusal to be placed within systems. Like the women on the floating island, Swift wants to escape, to go else-where and seek "Diversions."

Edward Said suggests that "the active content of Swift's mind" is its "essential resistance to any fixed boundaries."[32] I sense this resistance in

Swift's ambivalent response to endings, a response that shows how profoundly the very woman he repressed—figured as excessive and disruptive throughout his writing—came to inhabit his own literary mind. During Gulliver's travels in Book Three, he visits the island of Luggnagg where he hears about people who are immortal, the Struldbruggs. Initially crying out in "Rapture" at the very notion that such people actually exist, Gulliver boasts that if he were immortal he would devise a "whole System" of studies and activities to improve his own life as well as the general lot of "Mankind" (207–10). But after receiving a more realistic account of these immortals, he changes his mind entirely, concluding that "no Tyrant could invent a Death into which I would not run with Pleasure from such a Life" (214). The Struldbruggs, it seems, are doomed to a meaningless existence without end. Aged, forgetful, and altogether miserable, they are, Gulliver tells us, "the most mortifying Sight I ever beheld; and the Women more horrible than the Men" (214). What once struck Gulliver as the grand prospect of eternal life now impresses him as the "dreadful Prospect of never dying" (212).

Although Gulliver seems to learn the lesson that a life concluded is far preferable to a life that only goes on and on forever, I am not sure that Swift adequately dealt—through this episode—with his own fear of endings. As Gulliver is about to depart from Luggnagg, the king of the island jokingly offers to give him a couple of Struldbruggs to take back to his own country, "to arm our people," Gulliver says, "against the Fear of Death" (214). It would seem as though Swift were trying to arm himself against such a fear of closure in having Gulliver relate this story. Like the Goddess of Criticism in his *Battel of the Books,* these Struldbruggs are monstrous creatures who exceed the very boundaries of the human form—the women, Gulliver reminding us, more horrible than the men. Their expanding dimensions mark their transgression of limits, just as the "Maids of Honour" in Brobdingnag were emblematic of both bodily and sexual excess, and as the women in Swift's poems were characterized by the fluid mingling of decomposing forms. None of these creatures is contained, enclosed, fixed in place. They are not the stable and cohesive material of which systems are made. Swift, it seems to me, relied on these portrayals of feminine transgression to figure his own "restless" writing that had the propensity to go on and on. His portrayals were monstrous because, as the defender of Augustan systems, he knew that this form of excess violated the principles of classical decorum. Yet the insistence with which he kept returning to these varied portrayals shows us a writer who was fascinated with the idea of transgressing boundaries—those of the body, of language, of literary structure.

Gulliver's wife, monstrous perhaps only to Gulliver, was that feminine element in Swift that once again allowed him to escape closure within a structure. If Gulliver had only accepted her, come home to her, he would have played out his part in the sexual economy of classical systems. He might finally have appropriated her otherness, as Cixous would say, and given "himself the pleasure of enjoying, without too many obstacles, the return to himself. . . ."[33] But that does not happen. Instead, Swift kept the woman outside of his system, refusing his hero the opportunity to return home and to himself. While Gulliver is left locked within a system after all—returning "to enjoy my own Speculations in my little Garden at *Redriff*" and thinking of ways to instruct humankind in "those excellent Lessons of Virtue which I learned among the *Houyhnhnms*" (295)—Swift seems to step outside his literary system entirely. In refusing to permit his hero a homecoming, Swift refuses to play his own part in the sexual economy. Like Gulliver, and like Gulliver's wife, he remains unaccommodated.

The exclusion of woman from classical systems, I have been suggesting, is what made the cohesion of those systems possible. In order to consolidate some forces, others need to be outside. This logic prompts Irigaray to inquire into "*the conditions under which systematicity itself is possible.*" We need to ask this question if we want to gain access to all the "other" phenomena that never seem to find a place in the systems of man and yet that are continually figured in their accounts—like the wife who hovers at the end of the epic, hardly ever appearing in its action, yet making its successful resolution possible. "Whence the necessity," Irigaray says, "of 'reopening' the figures of philosophical discourse . . . in order to pry out of them what they have borrowed that is feminine, from the feminine, to make them 'render up' and give back what they owe the feminine."[34]

It is time, I think, to reopen the figures of Swift's discourse, just as we have with Newton and Pope, to pry out of them what he has borrowed from the feminine. For he has borrowed much. And so have the two other grand spokesmen of classical order, Newton and Pope. Perhaps what distinguishes them from Swift in this regard is that his borrowing was so obvious, consuming as it did a good part of his own identity as a writer— both in spite of and to spite his own best intentions to speak for the systems of man. We can have him "render up" what Irigaray would call this "woman-thing" that "speaks" if we listen for the woman in Swift, much as I have suggested we listen for the fluid and continuous phenomena in Newton's science. But to do this, we "*must know how to listen otherwise than in good form(s) to hear what it says*" (p. 111).

Swift lets us know that to speak "otherwise than in good forms" is to annihilate those forms—just as woman and all that she figures in his writing not only inhabits a realm on the margins and outside man's systems but seeps through the cracks and, in the process, blurs the very boundaries that define those systems. And that is why, more than either Newton or Pope, he exposes the most disturbing and threatening omissions in the classical order—gaps that at once horrified and fascinated him. Unable to appropriate the woman outside, unable to claim her as his conquest and "return to himself," Swift was somehow appropriated and claimed by her. He fought her all the way, but the very intensity of the struggle shows how powerfully the discourse of the other permeated classical systems, and—in the case of Swift—took him into her waters.

III

Writing and Woman

5

Anne Finch Placed and Displaced

To be sure, we can only muse in the twilight byways of bad faith upon the positive reality of the Mystery; like certain marginal hallucinations, it dissolves under the attempt to view it fixedly.

SIMONE DE BEAUVOIR

Femininity . . . is not the opposite of masculinity but that which subverts the very opposition of masculinity and femininity.

SHOSHANA FELMAN

A Monarck he, and ruler of the day,
A fav'rite She, that in his beams does play.

ANNE FINCH

AS A WOMAN

ANNE FINCH had a special fondness for shade. We might even say that shady retreats were the landscape of her poetic imagination. Like Alexander Pope's grotto and Isaac Newton's "dark Chamber," these partially illuminated areas became the spaces in which the creative imagination generated its offspring. Nestling herself in these shady areas, Finch would seem to partake in the same kind of birthing process archetypally associated with the journeyer who seeks inspiration in deep, dark spaces.[1] And yet I sense something different happening with Finch, something distinct about the feminine retreat to shade. This difference, it seems to me, requires an entirely "other" reading of the mythic descent into darkness and resurrection to light. For Newton and Pope, I suggested that we use the terms of the dark-light duality to understand their inability to accommodate in their systems the fusions and minglings of color. For Finch, however, I want to suggest that we need to change the very terms of the dark-light myth. If the feminine associations of darkness and the masculine associations of light constitute a structure within which we can and have charted the *progress* of man, we are going to have to dismantle this structure if we want to begin to understand the *process* of woman.

I read Finch's desire for shade as both a shattering of light and Enlightenment, and a disruption of structures long associated with the systems of man. While Newton and Pope tried to force color to conform to the definition of their universal systems, Finch, rejecting the spaces of pure light and pure darkness, entered instead the vaguely defined space of shade. If, as I will be suggesting, this space is profoundly feminine, it does not simply oppose the light of man or the darkness associated with woman. It splits that duality from within. Shade is not the opposite of light. Instead, it is that which subverts the opposition of light and darkness. Like Newton's "Lady," Pope's colorful women, and Swift's disruptive woman, the shade that Anne Finch sought became a configuration of woman that could not be accommodated within the structures of Enlightenment systems. And in subverting the opposition of light and darkness, it also became, as Shoshana Felman might say, a process that subverted the opposition of the masculine and the feminine. For Finch, shade was not simply a retreat, but the process of a radical displacement that was hers both as a "woman" who wrote, and as a poet who wrote "woman."

The question of what it means to read and write "as a woman" has recently generated a good deal of commentary and controversy.[2] And the problem seems to hinge on the word *woman*. From one perspective, that adopted by many feminist critics in the United States, *woman* refers particularly and explicitly to the female human being: to read or write "as a woman" is to do so from the vantage point of a female whose biological and cultural identity shapes her responses as different from those of the male's. From another perspective, one more commonly associated with the French feminist writers, the term *woman* refers less to an individual person and more to a process, specifically those processes that disrupt the structures of male discourse and systems: to read or write "as a woman" is to subvert those structures and open man's systems to the space of the "other." Both of these feminist perspectives have generated radical changes within academic disciplines by fostering entirely new and different visions of our cultural past and its bearing on the future. Yet within the feminist movement, there is some tension between those who see themselves involved in two apparently different projects—a concern with the historical predicament of actual "women," and a concern with the disruptive and feminine processes of "woman."[3]

I write about Anne Finch in an attempt to capture the positive energies of that tension, and to seek in it the feminine potential for a writing that exceeds the dualistic oppositions fundamental to systematic thought, especially the opposition of "women/woman." In asking what it means for Finch to write "as a woman," I have found that it means to write simultaneously in the historical predicament of an actual woman, and through the process of disruption that was suppressed in the discourse of Newton, Pope, and Swift. Anne Finch, it seems to me, is one of many woman writers who challenge us to explore the connections between the largely feminist concern with recovering the lost women of history, and the largely theoretical concern with figuring loss and absence as feminine. And she is particularly challenging because she writes "as a woman" during that age that, as Alice Jardine explains, was bent on the consolidation and perfection of systems.[4] I try to read and write about Finch in response to that challenge—to speak at once about the concrete experience of a woman writer displaced among the major figures of the English Enlightenment, and about the process of displacement that is so alive in her poetry. Finch was a woman clearly displaced within and from her culture, but she was also a woman whose writing—in voicing and celebrating that displacement—became a feminine process that exceeded both Enlightenment systems and the larger classical structures that they epitomized.

The implications of this double displacement can tell us much both *about* and *beyond* the historical period we know as the English Enlightenment. Reading Finch within the context of England's classical age, for instance, makes it possible to understand her "displacement" during this age in the same ways that we have conventionally understood the firmly "placed" positions of Newton, Swift, and Pope. Just as I sought in these men the feminine configurations of absence that made their systems possible, I also seek in Finch the feminine identity and process that made her own absence from the Enlightenment world inevitable. But I also try to understand Finch's predicament in terms that exceed her historical context, in terms of the convergence of history and theory that I discussed in the opening chapter of this book. To "place" Anne Finch in the Enlightenment world is to add new material to a literary canon still dominated by Enlightenment men and their well-structured systems. To account for her "displacement" within those systems, however, is to account for those very omissions of history that make "man's story" possible. We cannot place Finch in a historical context when her womanly identity has already situated her among the material whose absence made that history possible. We cannot restore any woman to history when the system of history itself is constructed by and through the exclusion of woman—both the actual women of history, and the feminine configuration of otherness that she embodies.

And so my reading of Finch will take me beyond her historical place and displacement in the Enlightenment, and into many of our contemporary theoretical concerns with the process of reading and writing. That is to be expected, since Finch's virtual "absence" from literary history is directly related to the gaps between history and theory, between the actual "woman writer" and the process of "feminine writing." But I do not want to lose Finch to absence. In her descriptions of brightly colored tapestries, nocturnal reveries, and absolute retreats, I try to recover the discourse of the "other" that was suppressed by Enlightenment men. In attempting this, I do not want to place Finch within systems from which she was excluded and whose values she was continually questioning. What she shared with the notable men of the Enlightenment was a fascination with the "other" discourse which revealed itself in Newton's alchemy and optical fusions, in the problem that both Newton and Pope had with color, in Swift's fluid and disruptive writing. But what makes Finch different is that she did not suppress this discourse. Instead, she immersed herself in it—in much the same ways that Newton, Swift, and Pope celebrated systems of universal order. Occupying this seemingly impossible place of displacement, Finch is already outside the history to which we might return her. What's more, she has already questioned the terms of her return to that history. She has already made herself the subject of theories that seek to discover the material abandoned by history. She has moved into the shady realm where all the metaphoric associations of light and Enlightenment were eclipsed.

WANDERING THROUGH SHADE

In a poem addressed to her husband, Finch invites him to leave his studies in mathematics and painting, and accompany her on a walk through the fields. The specific terms that she uses almost make the invitation seem as though it were an appeal to abandon the orderly world of Enlightenment systems, especially as she asks him to leave his "busy compasses" that measure the ground, and the "Rich colors" that he carefully applies to his painting.[5] In walking away from the controlled world of measurement and art, Finch "strays," as she puts it, from two of the "*usual Employments*" of the age—two particular employments that we might easily associate with Newton's physics and Pope's controlled verse. She enters instead a natural world of "disorder'd beauty," one that is "Warm without Sun, and shady without rain" (1–5). Her preference for shade, or what we might more properly call her desire for shade, is directly related to her retreats *from* the masculine world that she associates with husband, science, and a poetry of men. It is also a desire that she expresses again and again throughout her verse. In the "Introduction" to the manuscript collection of her poems, for instance, she concludes by acknowledging her "fallen" abilities as a woman writer and accepts her position not in the light of men but in an obscure darkness: "For groves of Lawrell, thou wert never meant; / Be dark enough thy shades, and be thou there content" (63–64). Her poem "On Myselfe" concludes in a similar way, calling attention to her "slight" abilities and to her "retirement" from the "Sun" where she will "bless the shade." Often these areas of shade are juxtaposed to those places where Finch prefers not to be, where her absence is her own choice. In "Upon Ardelia's Return Home," Finch describes herself as having "stray'd" far from home and into a "secret shade" that she has difficulty leaving (24). When a friend invites her to the "Town," she replies, in "Ardelia's Answer to Ephelia" that she would prefer "some shade" for her "Pallace" (5). And in her "Petition for an Absolute Retreat," a world of "Windings" and "Shade" becomes a place entirely other than the world of "Crouds, and Noise"—a place where she wants to construct her own reality.

In coming to terms with the metaphoric implications of light both in Newton's science and Pope's poetry, I tried to discover just what light meant to these men, to understand what it means to be "enlightened" and "illuminated" during an age that was so caught up in the "Discourse of Light."[6] In the same way, I think we need to inquire into the implications of shade for Finch, especially shady retreats that were also associated with straying and wandering, with watery sounds and winding excursions, and with mingling colors. Finch's shady world is, of course, the world of nature, and her continual excursions into this green world have prompted several critics to read her in terms of Wordsworth's belief that she was one of the first great nature poets.[7] No doubt Finch did distinguish herself from contemporary poets by writing a *kind* of nature poetry that differed from descriptions of manicured gardens and neatly designed landscapes. And yet there is much in her verse that is distinctly non-Romantic, qualities easy to understand when we keep in mind that Finch lived during the time when Restoration wits and Augustan writers were dominating the literary scene, and that she inevitably expressed many of their values and desires in her poetry.[8] Her longing for shade, however, was clearly not one of these Augustan values. Perhaps we could say, then, that Finch's displacement as a writer resulted from her different literary subjects—that in retreating to a shady, natural world, Finch simply deviated from the subjects that normally preoccupied her contemporaries.

Perhaps. There is, however, another subject to which Finch returns again and again in her poetry—the subject of her being a woman, of her being *different* because she is a woman. If her interest in nature has prompted some readers to place Finch among the nature poets, her concern about being a woman has more recently prompted others to place her within a tradition of women writers. Distinguishing Finch from the "masculinist" writing of Wordsworth and Shelley, for instance, Sandra Gilbert and Susan Gubar have called attention to Finch as one of the first women writers to be painfully aware of her predicament as a woman. They recognize Finch as the woman who "struggles to escape the male designs in which she feels herself enmeshed," who was "imprisoned" by the very anxieties she felt about her ability to write at all.[9] And Katharine Rogers, who has put together the only edition of Finch's poems now readily available, distinguishes Finch in this same way, describing her as "a woman imprisoned in man-made conventions."[10] If Finch did feel trapped within man's world—the world not only of her contemporary writers but even of her husband and his "Employments" with mathematics and painting— it would seem that her retreats into a shady natural world were directly related to her retreats *from* the domain of man and *into* the space of woman. It was not simply that she happened to write poetry about nature, but that her retreats to the shady, natural world were poetic ways of figuring her displacement, as a woman, in and from the Enlightenment world of men. Nature, shade, and woman all become linked in their associations with displacement.

Finch herself confirmed these linkages in her own configuration of woman, as she figured herself wandering through shady natural haunts. In "The Appology," she explains her particular "weakesse" as that of the "Woman" who must "write tho' hopelesse to succeed," and reconciles herself to the fate of one who must "follow through the Groves a wand'ring Muse." This "wand'ring Muse" seems especially descriptive of Finch herself, who typically "strays" along "winding" paths, and whose shady world seems to complement her own feminine deviations from the fixed world of pure light or darkness. The very process of "wand'ring" and "wav'ring" is one that Finch directly associated with both her retreats into nature and the very notion of woman. In her poem "Adam Pos'd," she describes Eve as that elusive and perplexing "New Element" in Adam's world. While his "Skill" is that of fixing things in place, of assigning "Just Appellations to Each several Kind," Eve's "wav'ring Form" resists his attempts to give "this Thing a Name." This "thing" that wanders and strays, that eludes man's attempt to fix it in place, that figures in his "grand narrative" as Eve—could she be that fluid, continuous, diffusable "woman-thing" about whom contemporary feminist theorists are speaking?[11] If I am correct in suggesting that Finch's configuration of woman involved both a portrayal of herself and the winding, shady spaces to which she retreated, then the "woman-thing" in her poetry gives us a picture of both the "woman writer" that Finch was, and the "writing of woman" in which she engaged.

Two particular poems, I think, call attention to these concepts of woman that distinguish Finch not only as different from her contemporary male writers, but as herself a configuration of that which was necessarily absent from and displaced within their fixed systems. In her "Petition for an Absolute Retreat," she longs for a place "That the World may ne'er invade," a retreat through "Windings" and "Shade" (5–6). But what is especially interesting about this poem is its detailed vision of that other "World." She asks not for the "Patriarch's Board," but a table containing "Fruits" that "did in *Eden* grow," food that she describes as "plain," yet that seems to exceed its own containment: "Grapes, with Juice so crouded up, / As breaking thro' the native Cup; / Figs (yet growing) candy'd o'er, / By the Sun's attracting Pow'r" (30–47). For her garments, she wants something like the "dazling white" robe of Solomon, though, as she is quick to add, "not so Gay"—nor so stunningly light (64).[12] Instead of pure white, she would have color:

> Let me, when I must be fine,
> In such natural Colours shine;
> Wove, and painted by the Sun,
> Whose resplendent Rays to shun,
> When they do too fiercely beat,
> Let me find some close Retreat,
> Where they have no Passage made,
> Thro' those Windings, and that Shade.
>
> (96–103)

Such notions of excess, figured in these descriptions of Edenic fruit and woven colors, seem to reflect a desire to transgress and blur fixed boundaries—a desire that Enlightenment men found both fascinating and threatening, and that they continually associated with woman. Finch's colors, however, are not the colors of Newton and Pope. Nor is the sun, which threatens to beat "too fiercely," that source of light in which, as Newton put it, "great and good men shine and illuminate others."[13] Finch's retreat takes her away from the world of definition and light, and into a fluid time that she figures as "some River" that "slides away, / To encrease the boundless Sea" (130–31). What is perhaps most revealing of the feminine quality of her retreat is that she imagines transforming its shady space into a "wond'rous Cave," not simply any cave, but like the particular one that Crassus escaped to when he fled the rage of Marius. Yet while Crassus, Finch tells us, was hardly "content" with his cave, Finch would transform hers into a "wond'rous" dwelling only partially illuminated, and filled with "Rising Springs" that "stray" over the ground (202–33).

This "Absolute Retreat," this place of absence, was not simply some natural abode desired by the Romantic writer as he sought to discover his poetic voice in nature. Far from it, Finch's retreat took her away from man's poetic voice, absolutely away from his world, and into an other space that displays all the markings and configurations of woman. But I have suggested that it was not only Finch's descriptions of herself and her retreats that betrayed her "writing as a woman." It was also her very configuration of shade and wandering and wavering as feminine, as that elusive substance of a "woman-thing." In her poem "Clarinda's Indifference at Parting with Her Beauty," Finch describes the very process of being woman in terms of wandering airs, fading colors, restless time, and spreading shades. The space of these movements and minglings is the very face of a woman parting with her beauty. Like Eve's "wav'ring Form," Clarinda's cannot quite be captured and fixed by man. Finch configures this elusive quality in terms that might well remind us of Newton's inability to fix the minglings of light and color: her face is like "Those morning beams, that strongly warm, and shine, / Which men that feel and see, can ne're define" (7–8). As woman is transformed through the processes of "restless time," she leaves behind the light of morning for "ev'ning shades" that begin "to rise, and spread" (9–10).

What Finch describes as "Clarinda's Indifference" to this process, to the loss of "That youthfull air, that wanders ore the face" (5), is something we might well regard in terms of Finch's own acceptance of her process as woman—her identity as a "woman writer" and as a poet who "writes as a woman." She accepts change and transformation, welcomes the "shades" that take her away from man's world of light and into the process that is woman. Understanding Finch's longing for shade in terms of her own identity and writing as woman, we are perhaps in a better position to appreciate what shade meant to her, what her excursions into and figurations of shade tell us about a poet who wrote during a time when men were consumed with the "Discourse of Light." I would suggest that shade was the absent space in which Finch, as a woman writer, was displaced. At the same time it was also the feminine space that she desired. In both of these functions, it became a configuration of absence that was somewhere between the light that men desired and the darkness that they feared. It was in this displaced area between light and darkness that Anne

Finch's shade became the undoing of the light-dark duality through which Enlightenment men figured their pursuits. In saying this, I am suggesting that shade for Finch was much like color for both Newton and Pope, and like fluidity for Swift. Just as color and fluidity exceeded the definition of system, so shade exceeded the very definition of light and dark, of liquid and solid. It seeps, as Catherine Clément might say, through the "cracks in an overall system."[14] And what it produces is not the enlightened world of man, but a world of fusion and process that is, in the case of Finch, the identity and writing of a woman.

But the comparison with Newton, Swift, and Pope ends here. When color and fluid infiltrated their systems, they reacted by imposing strict controls, by trying to force it to serve as part of the definition of man's systems. Anne Finch had little reason to defend these systems. She rejected the age's literary preoccupation with satire just as soundly as she walked away from the "Employments" of her husband. "I never suffer'd my small talent, to be that way employ'd," she wrote when distinguishing her poetry from the "abusive verses" of her contemporaries, verses that could be produced, as she said, by anyone "who can but make two words rime. . . ."[15] That she should describe her dislike for the dominant literary forms in terms of a "facility" to "make two words rime" is curious in itself. The closed couplet, after all, epitomized the rage for order and structure that revealed itself in eighteenth-century literary form, and though Finch relied on this general structure in most of her poems, she clearly wanted to avoid being considered any kind of "Versifying Maid of Honour."[16] We might well regard her disparaging view of the ability to "make two words rime" as an indictment and rejection of the very compulsion to rally around structures, especially those structures in which she had no place and from which she desired to "retreat."

Her retreat into shade, then, was neither from light to dark nor from dark to light. It did not function within such a dualistic and "coupled" economy. Shade was the configuration of Finch's attempt, as a woman, to come to terms with her displacement by mingling light and dark, by fusing and confusing its dualistic construction. I suggested earlier that if we are to understand what shade meant to Finch, we will have to dismantle the terms of the light-dark myth, the myth in which a man descends into darkness only to recover his own image and ultimately ascend to the world of light and himself. This dismantling, it seems to me, is figured not only in Finch's retreat to shade, but also in the processes of wandering, straying, and wavering—processes that take us away from the myth of light and dark, and bring us once again into the realm of color. What distinguishes these colors, however, is that they are woven together by women.

Enlightened Absence

The Weaving Process

Finch approached her shady retreats through winding paths, by straying and wandering and, we might say, "weaving" herself through her own poetic imagination. If this meandering approach constitutes a feminine deviation from the Enlightenment preoccupation with structure and hierarchy, how are we to recover the values associated with such deviation? How are we to recover, in Finch's poetry, the writing "of a woman" and "as a woman" that was suppressed in Enlightenment discourse? I suggest that we do this not simply by turning our attention away from the fixed categories and structures in which Enlightenment men contained phenomena, but by seeking "other" metaphors of engagement with phenomena—metaphors that might allow us to recognize the values of both a "woman" and a "feminine writing" that strays and wanders.

And so I turn—with Finch herself, and with several feminist critics today—to the process of weaving and the myth of Arachne. This myth became for Finch a story about both herself as a writer and the more general plight of a woman "writing as woman." The story has also, perhaps not coincidentally, become the subject of recent commentary from literary critics who differ in their reading of Arachne's narrative—notably female critics interested in recovering the lost woman writer whom Arachne represents, and male theorists interested in using Arachne's feminine weaving as a kind of metaphor of textual "indeterminacy." I want to explore these different understandings of the Arachne story in terms of their bearing both on Finch herself and on the process of writing-as-weaving that becomes, through Finch, a feminine configuration of that which subverts classical systems.

Introducing a chapter in their study of *The Madwoman in the Attic,* Gilbert and Gubar cite these lines from Finch's poem "A Description of One of the Pieces of Tapestry at Long-Leat" where Finch speaks about Arachne.

> Thus *Tapestry* of old, the Walls adorn'd,
> Ere noblest Dames the artful *Shuttle* scorn'd:
> *Arachne,* then, with Pallas did contest,
> And scarce th'Immortal Work was judg'd the Best.
> Nor valorous Actions, then, in Books were fought;
> But all the Fame, that from the Field was brought,
> Employ'd the *Loom,* where the kind *Consort* wrought:
> Whilst sharing in the Toil, she shar'd the Fame,
> And with the *Heroes* mixt her interwoven Name.
> No longer, *Females* to such Praise aspire,

And serfdom now We rightly do admire.
So much, All Arts are by the *Men* engross'd,
And Our few Talents unimprov'd or cross'd.[17]

Finch's particular account of Arachne's weaving, as Gilbert and Gubar point out, is "closely associated with the female fall from authority."[18] Arachne, though the loser in the weaving contest with Pallas, was at least able *through* her weaving to mix "her interwoven Name" with that of heroes. For Finch, however, such a fate is "No longer" possible. "All Arts" are now dominated by "*Men*," she tells us, and the "few Talents" of women remain "unimprov'd or cross'd." Figuring her own fallen lot as a woman writer by contrasting it with Arachne's, Finch associates her writing with the process of weaving. But it is a process that seems to take her nowhere—or to take her, perhaps, into that space of nowhere that I have been describing as displacement and absence. In her poem "The Bird and the Arras," Finch relates a similar story. Mistaking a "well wrought Arras for a shade," a bird hopes to rest there in order to avoid "the scortchings of the sultry Noon." Once inside the room in which this tapestry is hung, the bird, described by Finch as "she," tries to fly into its skies—only to be "dash'd" to the ground, unable to escape the room in which she is an "imprison'd wretch" and left "Flutt'ring in endless cercles of dismay." The fall of the bird is perhaps akin to Finch's own fallen predicament as a woman writer, and as one whose weaving fails even to attain the recognition given to Arachne.

Yet in weaving a poetry that will go unrecognized, as caught within the very process of weaving itself—Finch would seem not so much to differ from Arachne, as she would seem to be exactly in her predicament. Her art, like Arachne's weaving, has found a place in the myths of man only to be eclipsed by a poetry that relates the exploits and victories of the gods. Pallas, the victor, weaves the story of those victories, while Arachne spins depictions of women who were their victims. Arachne loses the contest in the same way that Finch must necessarily lose: in writing and weaving about women, they are pitted against the very forces whose prominence and splendor have already been inscribed in our mythic and poetic consciousness. Not only fallen *from* authority, but also fallen *within* the very process of her weaving, the woman writer is doomed, like Arachne, to take on the shape of an insignificant creature who ceaselessly spins webs.

If she is afraid that her writing will not be able to compete in the poetic contests of men, Finch nonetheless continues to weave—to wander and stray through her shady retreats. She chooses, in other words, to write a poetry figured through weaving even though she knows that her fate as such a writer is not even as promising as Arachne's. To understand why Finch does this, and what compels her to reject fixed systems and structures in favor of weaving, we need to probe deeper into the associations between woman and weaving. We need to inquire into the nature of the process itself, and discover its peculiar feminine qualities. Gilbert and Gubar, who seek these associations in the work of several women writers, call attention to the myths of both Arachne and Ariadne—mythic women who weave their way through their own prisons, and who serve as the prototypes of women writers who must spin their way through the "problematic" nature of their narratives.[19] More recently, Nancy K. Miller has used the term *Arachnologies* to describe both "a figuration of woman's relation of production to the dominant culture" and "a possible parable . . . of a feminist poetics." If we are to recover women's writing, Miller argues, we need to "reappropriate" the story of Arachne—read it not in terms of a "web of indifferentiation," but as the construction of "a new object of reading, women's writing."[20]

As much as I agree that we need to "reappropriate" the story of Arachne for the woman writer, I wonder if we should not be just as concerned with the dangers of appropriation, an act that Hélène Cixous associates with the male's attempt to reach out and claim woman only so that he can finally "return to himself."[21] Nancy Miller, for instance, wants very much to distinguish between the poststructural appropriation of mythic stories about women weaving, and the feminist reappropriation of the woman artist. What she particularly has in mind are the "deconstructive" readings of Arachne and Ariadne by Geoffrey Hartman and J. Hillis Miller who, instead of recognizing the victimized women in these mythic stories, find in woman and her associations with textual weaving a metaphor of language.[22] Although I sense the urgency of Nancy Miller's caution that we "preserve women from the fate of woman" (p. 283), I also sense the urgency of recovering the indeterminate and subversive processes that have long been associated with woman, so that we can tap their energies in transforming a world that has been all too exclusively structured and hierarchized. The question is not so much whether we can "preserve women from the fate of woman," but why we should want to recover women writers at all if we cannot locate in their writing a profound critique of exclusive systems. If we are to seek in women's writing a poetics that is truly other than and different from that associated with masculine writing, and especially if we are discovering that difference in the process of weaving, it seems to me that we should acknowledge and celebrate the feminine process of textual indeterminacy that undoes the "grand narratives" of man, narratives largely responsible for the suppression of both women writers and a writing of the feminine. We need to be open to a reading of woman's texts not only as narrative tapestries different from those of men, but as processes of weaving that dismantle the structure of his narratives.

An important part of this effort is to read the story of Arachne as Nancy Miller reads Finch's description of her tapestry, in the "tradition of recognition that Gilbert and Gubar have described, in a gesture meant to restore woman to her text . . ." (p. 287). We need to acknowledge, in this way, the very different values attached to a literature that is spun by women—webs that, as Virginia Woolf said, "'are the work of suffering human beings, and are attached to grossly material things, like health and the houses we live in.'"²³ Following the urgings of such feminist critics as Gilbert, Gubar, and Miller, we can come to discover in Finch the actual woman who wrote, the female person who found her poetic voice through the process of weaving her way through shady retreats, wandering and straying within and away from the systems of her male contemporaries. Yet at the same time we also need to recognize in this weaving the process of subversion that undoes the "grand narratives," the process of "writing as a woman" that has already inscribed Finch as displaced within Enlightenment systems just as it had inscribed Arachne's woven narrative as "other" to Pallas's account of the conquests of the classical gods.

If Finch's retreats into shade, as I suggested earlier, do not simply oppose the light of Enlightenment, but shatter and subvert the very opposition of light and dark, I would suggest that her engagement with the process of weaving not only opposes the fixed systems of Enlightenment thought, but instead subverts the very construction of those systems. In her poem "The Prodigy," Finch cautions women not to be moved by men who proclaim their love for them: "Assert your pow'r in early days begun, / Born to undo, be not yourselves undone" (51–52). We might read her caution in terms of the myth of Arachne who also wove the story of women victimized by love. While Pallas weaves her depiction of the grand exploits of the gods, Arachne weaves a very different picture—of women who were loved and then betrayed by the gods. In one sense, Arachne constructs a definite narrative, a narrative about women. In another sense, however, her weaving undoes Pallas's account, questioning the magnitude of the gods' conquests by removing them from their grandiose context, and setting them next to portrayals of their abuse and betrayal of women. To weave as Arachne weaves, we might say, is both to construct and dismantle—to deconstruct the narratives of man through the agency of woman.

If Finch does desire to enjoy the fate of Arachne, her desire is not only to construct a poetry as respectable as that of her contemporary male writers, but to dismantle the assumptions that have been used to designate their subjects as primary and important, and hers as secondary and inferior. She would not, I believe, reverse this hierarchy, but rather dissolve it. Like Swift, she preferred the disorder of the waters to the definition of the land, though unlike Swift, she had no qualms about saying so. In one of her songs, "The Nymph, in vain, bestows her pains," Finch describes a nymph who tries to thrive in Bacchus's kingdom, but who ultimately finds herself drowned in "his torrent" of "Immages." Finding him "inaccessible, and cold," she says that he "makes an Island, of the heart." The very paradoxical idea of drowning on an island shows, I believe, Finch's own predicament as a weaver. She would weave a poetry that might be comparable to that of men—just as she herself would merge into the pleasures of Bacchus's kingdom. And yet she is overcome by the very pleasures she seeks—just as her identity and process as a woman makes that pleasure inaccessible, makes her heart into the "Island" that she would shun.

Yet though she felt overcome by the very waters she sought—the fluid, wandering processes so different from the fixed islands and systems of the Enlightenment—Finch was nonetheless able to celebrate the fluid world with all its mixings and mergings. In "The Bargain," she has Bacchus and Cupid engage in a dialog, debating whether Bacchus's reign over the "mighty punch bowl" or Cupid's reign over "hearts" and "tears" is absolute. In the end, Cupid suggests that the two "joyn" their realms, "To mix my waters, with thy wine." And in her Song "For my Br. Les: Finch. Upon a Punch Bowl," she imagines "the whole Universe floating" in a punch bowl that invites us to forget the "Titles" and "Places" of "History." All this is not to mention the flowing rivers and streams that figure in much of Finch's descriptions of nature, or the fluid and fusing colors of the natural world that mingle in her landscapes. These fusions blur the systematic distinctions that Enlightenment writers sought, just as shade shattered the light of pure emanation. No wonder Finch described poetry, in the final lines of "Enquiry After Peace," as "the feav'rish Fit, / Th' overflowing of unbounded Wit." It overflows and exceeds boundaries just as the juices of her Edenic fruits described in the "Petition for an Absolute Retreat" seem almost to burst their own forms, or as the river "slides away" to "the boundless sea."

The "woman-thing" described by Luce Irigaray as "fluid," as "continuous, compressible, dilatable, viscous, conductable, diffusable,"[24] has much in common with the poststructural configuration of "woman" as indeterminate and therefore subversive of enclosed structures. Yet this "thing" is also intimately connected to the writing *of* woman and *as* woman that defines both feminine identity and process. For Cixous, such writing is also intimately connected with the body, with inexhaustible processes that exceed the systems and stratagems of the head, and that "articulate the proliferation of meanings that runs through it in every direction."[25] If we can envision the mind as producing the clarity and definition of illumination, we might envision the body as a kind of prism, generating the "proliferation" of color. These colorful minglings and proliferations are also connected to the process of weaving, once again through the story of Arachne. Ovid describes the weaving contest as strikingly colorful. But what is perhaps more curious about his account is the way he describes the *fusions* of color. He speaks about those vague spaces where green becomes blue and blue becomes violet, the spaces between distinctions that Newton was so determined to define. The dyed threads woven by Pallas and Arachne are as richly fused as Newton's colors—like a rainbow, Ovid says, that casts a thousand different colors that merge into each other and remain dazzlingly indistinguishable.[26]

That Finch herself was far more enamored with the weaving of colors than the fixity of light is something we can sense in the distance she perceives between her own work and that of the sun god. In her poem "The Consolation," she describes Phoebus as a "Monark" who is "ruler of the day," and the "soaring Lark" as "A fav'rite She, that in his beams does play." Associating herself with what we might regard as the feminine play of light and color rather than the godlike control of the sun, her consolation—though she ostensibly identifies it with the coming of morning—may well be that as a woman she does not need to defend the light of the gods or, I might add, the systems of man. Nor does she rely on the service of Apollo and light. In her "Upon Ardelia's Return Home," she petitions Apollo for his "Chariot," only to be refused and assigned instead to a "water cart" that is transformed, through her own imaginative powers, into a "tryumphant Charret" (88–89). This cart, a far cry from Apollo's chariot of the sun, rested in a "Beeche's secret shade" (24)—the place to which Finch, as Ardelia, has "stray'd," and from which she will be transported, like water, to her home.

Weaving herself through the reflections of light, through its shadows and colors, Finch also wove a poetry that was remarkably different from the poems of men we now recognize as the "masters" of the age. Her different subjects made her, in a sense, opposite to them. But the process of her weaving was also a feminine subversion of the very structures—light and dark, solid and liquid, male and female—that they relied on to construct their "grand narratives." Finch reminds us that Arachne's story, told again and again throughout the centuries, is one that we must recover for the woman writer. But she also reminds us that the subversive force of Arachne's weaving is what makes her story worth recovering.

NATURE, SCIENCE, AND CAVES

All along I have been describing Finch's displacement as a literary displacement that was "en-gendered" by her identity "as a woman" writer and her process of writing "as a woman." Reading Finch in terms of her historical, literary context only shows how she did not fit in that context—how her feminine wanderings and strayings into shady, natural retreats marked her difference from the very contemporary writers among whom she wanted a place. She is like the "other," womanly side of Swift and Pope. She is the unconscious of Swift, the fluid Swift who would prefer to swim in the feminine waters that, as a proper Augustan satirist, he consciously had to shun. And she is like the dark Pope who preferred the colorful reflections of light in his subterranean grotto to the poetry of pure light that he ostensibly sought.

But what would happen if we were to read Finch's preoccupation for nature and straying and wandering in a scientific context, in terms of what I have been sketching out as the larger cultural context of Enlightenment systems that shaped both the classical structure of Augustan literature and the development of modern science? I pose this question because it seems to me that if we are to recover "woman" as both identity and process, or as Irigaray would put it, if we are to "(re)discover a possible space for the feminine imaginary,"[27] we need to envision her displacement within the larger spaces of the masculine world. It is not enough to say that Finch wrote nature poetry at a time when the vogue for nature poetry was not the literary fashion, or that she described herself as wandering away from fixed places and into shady retreats when her contemporary writers were seeking structure and illumination. Her *literary* preoccupations marked both her literary displacement and a profound *cultural* displacement through which she wrote as a woman. We need to remember that Finch wrote about wandering and wavering at a time when science was fixing the universe in place. We need to remember that she wrote about nature at a time when science had set out to dominate the natural world, which it had rendered again and again as feminine.

If it is possible to think of Finch as resembling the other, womanly side of Swift and Pope—embodying the very otherness of their classical demeanor, she also becomes the otherness of nature that science, on its way toward Enlightenment, sought to conquer. Francis Bacon, we should recall, encouraged the scientist "to follow and as it were hound nature in her wanderings," so that "you will be able when you like to lead and drive her afterward to the same place again."[28] He would seek, as Carolyn Merchant explained, to claim nature, and in so doing, to reclaim the dominion over nature that man lost through Eve in the garden.[29] In this scientific quest, Bacon was at one with a group of poets who reclaimed and celebrated the garden, and who made its neat design and perfect symmetry into a metaphor of their own sense of order. Pope's *Windsor-Forest,* as we have seen, not only epitomized a nature reflective of the designs of men, but one that provided a model of universal and imperial order—a world that England could clearly "lead and drive," and master.

It is hard to imagine Anne Finch leading or driving nature anywhere. It is hard to imagine her own immersion in natural retreats as reflective of such attempts to control and master. But what is most important to realize about Finch's wandering through nature is not simply that she views nature differently, but that in her wanderings and absolute retreats she actually embodies the very material of the scientific conquest. If her excursions through nature took her into a place other than that which was the object of scientific and literary mastery, this other place, I would suggest, *was* the displacement of her identity and process as woman.

When science figures nature as woman, the woman who wanders through and writes about nature becomes a configuration of that which science seeks to dominate. Woman is already part of a sexual economy in which she functions as the desired object of man's appropriation. I have discussed, especially in the first two chapters of this book, the ways in which the feminist critiques of science are questioning its implicit androcentric and masculine bias. And I have tried to show, through my readings of Newton, Swift, and Pope, that the new science was hardly alone in its desire to differentiate itself from and appropriate phenomena that it variously regarded as feminine—that it was in league with a classical literature that was bent on the same desire to consolidate its systems. The connections between literature and science, in other words, are not only implicated in matters of gender, but reflect hierarchies that have been socially constructed and ingrained in our minds—hierarchies that privilege culture over nature, system and definition over disorder and fusion, male over female.[30] For if Enlightenment literature and science not only shared in the effort to consolidate systems but actually figured all that was displaced from these systems in terms of "woman," it is impossible to view the exclusion of women from these systems as either a purely literary or distinctly scientific phenomenon. Woman's displacement—and we can see this all too directly in Finch's immersions in nature—was a necessary part of man's classical pursuits. A literary woman who wrote about nature, and who wrote about woman, figured as forcefully in the scientific quest for dominion as if she herself had been the metaphoric Lady whom Newton figured as the disturbing and problematic side of his otherwise fixed mathematical calculations.

When we hear Bacon speak of the scientist "entering and penetrating into those holes and corners when the inquisition of truth is his whole object,"[31] we might pause to think how profoundly the quest for truth has been figured in terms of the penetration of dark, isolated, and mysterious spaces. Alice Jardine even suggests that the exploration of such spaces is "the very essence of philosophy," something we can understand more clearly when we consider "the 'exemplary images' used by philosophers since antiquity to define the world: for example, Plato's 'cavern,' Descartes' 'closed room,' Kant's 'island,' or, in another register, Kierkegaard's 'finger in the mud.'"[32] If the philosophical purpose of this penetration is to fill the void, to think it into some shape and meaning, its sexual connotations are all too obvious. Jardine cites Michèle Montrelay's description of this philosophical quest in terms of a male fantasy: "'First,'" Montrelay writes, "'a central tube which cannot be the closed and satisfying container of an interior. . . . Intestine, pipe, image of cavern, of dark, deep, inner spaces, all that exists, but submitted to forces of suction that empty them in the most painful fashion. Or else, the void is already established . . . Or else, the fullness is such a tremendous threat that it must be parried at all costs'" (p. 70). We have already seen in Pope the threatening fullness of the feminine cave, and the cost of his suppressing this fullness—the cost to woman. Belinda's "Cave of Spleen" in his *Rape of the Lock,* the caves of Poetry and Truth in the *Dunciad,* Pope's own underground grotto—these are all feminine spaces in which he figured the void of thoughtlessness, whose fluid fullness so threatened him that he would have it suctioned out and replaced with the substance of thought, the material of the enlightened mind. His fantasy—like Bacon's, like that of philosophers since antiquity—is to penetrate the hole, claim dominion over the feminine cave, that darkest and deepest recess of nature.

And yet what of the woman in that cave? What of the woman who is the cave? In order to recover this woman and her subversive energies, we need to question not only the masculine assumptions inherent in any quest to "penetrate" nature—inherent in the act of thrusting, intruding, and dominating—but also the unacknowledged assumption that these spaces are feminine and therefore an appropriate object of the male quest. We need to deconstruct, in other words, the philosophical system—the entire metaphysic—whose meaning and closure are dependent on the "penetration" of cavelike spaces. Such a metaphysic is bent on a kind of excavation, a removal from the cave of that void which troubles the philosophical mind, so that it can claim dominion over the woman who occupies this space. Thus we find Orpheus making his way back to the world of light while Eurydice is abandoned to the caves of the underworld.[33] Then there is Echo, whose punishment—for falling in love with a man who was consumed with himself, and for warning vulnerable maidens of gods who would assault them—was to be imprisoned in caverns where her utterances would echo throughout the forests and hills. And there is the tradition of the gothic, particularly the gothic novel in the hands of many eighteenth-century women writers, where women encounter the horrors of their own sexuality by being sequestered in dark interior spaces, secret chambers, dungeons, locked staircases, and attics.[34]

Anne Finch also occupied caves, such as the one she described in her "Petition for an Absolute Retreat," one that she would transform from a "lonely" to a "wond'rous" space. This "wond'rous" cave that she seeks, I believe, is exactly that place of fullness not yet suctioned into thought, not yet conquered by the enlightened mind. It is, as she describes it, a "commodious ample Cave," with "Beds of Moss," "Rising Springs," and "Canopy'd with Ivy" (209–23). We might compare Finch's underground retreat with Pope's grotto, set with bits of mirror, where he enjoyed visual pleasures that he denied himself in the world of light. Or we might compare it to Newton's "dark Chamber," where he, too, indulged in a space of reflected light. Yet while Pope and Newton organized their dark retreats into artificial structures that ultimately reflected and refracted the light of Enlightenment—places where their systems of thought were at once the subject of analysis and definition, Finch's retreat is steeped in the material of nature—moss, ivy, water—material that conceals the demarcations that the Enlightenment mind so desperately wanted to uncover.

But Finch's caves were not always so comforting to the woman who was seeking this "Absolute Retreat," this space of "Peace and Rest"—"(Peace and Rest are under Ground)" she says (233). Just as Pope's Belinda was plagued by her "Cave of Spleen" with all its inversions, hallucinations, and distortions, so Anne Finch was plagued by "Spleen"—her own cave, the cave in which she figured her tormented femininity. Finch's poem, "The Spleen," perhaps her most famous,[35] shows not only the personal cost to the woman who writes, but the cost of writing "as a woman" during an age that often figured woman in terms of disease. The Enlightenment, as we have seen, was fascinated with hysteria and hypochondria, a fascination that shows the intricate connections that the age forged linking disease, madness, and woman.[36] It can hardly be coincidental that Anne Finch, the female poet now achieving recognition in the Augustan literary canon, should describe herself as infected with the hysteria that the age figured through woman. For as I have already suggested, she herself—as a woman—was the substance of that which science excluded from its systems and attempted to appropriate. With Newton, Swift, and Pope, we can watch the male dynamics of this appropriation in action: as the man seeks to establish his orderly system, he purges it of disorderly elements that he renders as woman. With Finch, however, we witness some very different dynamics in action. Hysteria begins to speak. But it is not an uncontrolled hysteria, not complete madness or otherness. It is the voice of a woman who wants to be able to speak in this world of men, and who finds herself imprisoned in a world that allows no space for the feminine.

In our own time, Luce Irigaray describes the world in terms of "masculine parameters" in which woman has always been defined, confined, and silenced. "And yet that woman-thing speaks," she tells us.[37] I have heard her speaking in the repressed utterances of Enlightenment men, where her voice truly sounds hysterical because it has been repressed. But I also hear her in the voice of a woman who wanted something other than that repression, who wanted herself to be something other than the voice of hysteria. Finch was confused by her gender, deeply perplexed by what it meant to be a woman during a time when the feminine was itself the substance of a dis-ease that plagued systems of order. "Spleen" becomes for her, I believe, the very perplexing substance of her femininity, toward which she felt simultaneously repulsed and drawn.

The subject of her poem is, of course, the ailment of woman, whose "secret" and "mysterious ways" only "baffle" the "Physicians" who try to control it (138–41). That Finch herself was tormented by this ailment, not simply as a woman, but as a woman writer, is all too obvious from her own admission: "O'er me alas! thou dost too much prevail: / I feel thy Force, whilst I against thee rail; / I feel my Verse decay, and my crampt Numbers fail" (74–76). In their reading of these lines, Gilbert and Gubar pose the question: "Is it crazy, neurotic, splenetic, to want to be a writer?" Their own feeling is that Finch, like so many women writers, fears that it is—and that she in particular is driven "into a Cave of Spleen in her own mind."[38] They are surely correct in suggesting that Finch is caught in the dis-ease of being a woman writer, the illness that dooms her to possess all the characteristics and desires of woman and yet to strive to write like a man. That disease, it seems to me, is the spleen that repulses her. Yet at the same time, Finch is also caught in the dis-ease of writing the feminine, the poetic expression of desires very different from those of her contemporary male writers—and that disease, I would suggest, is the spleen toward which she is implicitly drawn.

No doubt that Finch derogates her illness, portraying herself as victim to its powers. And yet the terms she uses to describe both spleen and its effects are remarkably similar to those that she uses elsewhere to describe her own poetic endeavor. She finds spleen, for instance, *"Proteus"* in form, something that she cannot "fix" into "one continued Shape"—like the calm of a "Dead Sea," or the rage of a "Storm," or like "Shadows" that intrude on "Sleep" (1–12). Its "varying" and "perplexing Form" seems very much like that "wav'ring Form" embodied in Eve, the woman who perplexed Adam with her "various Fashions, and more various Faces," the "New Element" that he was unable to fix in place by assigning it a "Name." ("Adam Pos'd") Eve, of course, enjoys Finch's poetic admiration, while spleen is the object of her fears. Yet both the woman and the disease are figured through the same metaphors. Something similar happens when we consider Finch's figurations of spleen as fluid—as both sea and storm, and when we consider her associations of spleen with shadows and sleep. We need to remember that water and fluid motions also expressed for Finch the unfixed and wandering quality of her own poetry. In her "Absolute Retreat," for instance, she compares her own "Windings" through nature and her progress toward "Eternity" to a "River" that "slides away, / To encrease the boundless Sea" (130–31). And the cave that she transforms into a "wond'rous" place is filled with "Rising Springs" that "stray'd" over the ground (222–23). If, in her poem "The Spleen," she feels her verse "decay," then we should consider the possibility that the idea of decay may only have been a disparaging reference to what Finch considered characteristic of her poetry all along—its *process* of moving away from the fixed forms of expression that we associate with Augustan verse, and that she herself associated with the poetry of those "who can but make two words rime."

Her associations of spleen with shadows and sleep are perhaps most revealing of the ways in which Finch was drawn to the very disease of woman that plagued her as a writer. Just at the moment when she speaks of those who are "to thy Shades inclin'd" (73), she proceeds with the description of her own illness as a poet who feels her verse decaying. The two images—of being inclined to shade and feeling unable to resist the decomposition of her verse—must have been at least as closely associated in Finch's mind as they are in these lines from her poem. The comfort that Finch experiences in the shades of nature, and the torment she experienced in the shades of spleen, may well be different versions of her fate as a woman writer. When she becomes the poet who writes through a certain metaphor—as that of shadow and shade—the metaphor becomes a poetic expression, the subject of her writing. Yet if we can envision shade, as I suggested at the beginning of this chapter, as a subversion of the dualities of light and dark through which the Enlightenment defined itself, Finch's poetic metaphor can also become much more than the subject of her poetic expression. It can become the very feminine thing that the Enlightenment mind feared—the absence of distinction between light and dark, the fluid annihilation of boundaries. It was this feminine shade, I believe, that became for Finch the disease of spleen. It was this feminine shade that was not the comforting subject of her nature poetry, but the tormenting substance of her own process of writing as a woman, writing the feminine, writing dis-ease.

In her poem "An Invocation to Sleep," Finch imagines herself "seal'd" in a space of "Silence" and "darknesse." She desires this space, and wonders how she may best "wooe" the "gentle rest" that will bring her this calm (1–14). In a different poem, "A Nocturnal Reverie," she imagines something similar—a *"Night"* when she can see the "waving Moon and trembling Leaves" in "some River, overhung with Green," when *"Glow-worms"* illuminate a fine "Twilight," when "darken'd Groves their softest Shadows wear, / And falling Waters we distinctly hear" (9–24). All nature is covered with shadow, and she imagines the creatures of the wood enjoying "Their shortliv'd Jubilee" while "Tyrant-*Man* do's sleep," and where there is "no fierce Light" to "disturb" the "Content" (37–40). Almost as if inverting the desires of Enlightenment man, she writes: "In such a *Night* let Me abroad remain, / Till Morning breaks, and All's confus'd again" (47–48).

Anne Finch's nocturnal reverie is like a dream, the space of a feminine imaginary that Enlightenment man figured as darkness, as the space within woman and of woman, as cave and spleen, womb and hysteria—the dis-ease that his systems could not tolerate. He wanted, as Francis Bacon had, to "penetrate" this space—excavate its fullness and establish there the definition of structure, system, and thought, the light of Enlightenment. But Anne Finch lived in this space. She wanted its fullness, because it was an excess that she could feel in her own femininity—a femininity that was not the opposite of enlightened masculine systems, but that became the substance of wandering, fluid processes that subverted the structure of those systems. In these processes, we find the feminine substance of Enlightened Absence. And it is this femininity that belongs to Finch as a woman who wrote, and as a poet who wrote woman.

Post-Scripting

Thus the society of the future falls less within the province of a Newtonian anthropology (such as structuralism or systems theory) than a pragmatics of language particles.

JEAN-FRANÇOIS LYOTARD

Women have almost everything to write about femininity: about their sexuality, that is to say, about the infinite and mobile complexity of their becoming erotic, about the lightning ignitions of such a minuscule-vast region of their body, not about destiny but about the adventure of such an urge, the voyages, crossings, advances, sudden and slow awakenings, discoveries of a formerly timid region that is just now springing up. Woman's body . . . she lets it articulate the proliferation of meanings that runs through it in every direction.

HÉLÈNE CIXOUS

IN WRITING a postscript, I want to conclude and also begin. I think of this process as "post-scripting"—a writing that comes after something has been concluded, a writing that continues.

Throughout this book, I have been arguing that Enlightenment England, in an attempt to consolidate its classical empire, excluded material that threatened the symmetry of its systems, and represented that material in various ways as feminine. This suppression of what the age itself configured as feminine inevitably imprisoned women within representational categories created by men. It shaped them into objects of discourse and desire, objects that were excluded, appropriated, and ultimately controlled. If the fate of woman in the Enlightenment was to function as the object of men's discourse, we might wonder, with Luce Irigaray, "what would become of the symbolic process that governs society" if women "were to become 'speaking subjects'. . . ."[1]

As I bring this book to an end, I also want to begin to explore a different discourse. There are signs all around us now that a "woman-thing," as Irigaray describes this subject, is speaking in these late years of the twentieth century, and speaking in ways that reveal a profound break with systems of thought and discourse that we have inherited from the Enlightenment. One of these ways, one that has particularly influenced me in this study, is through a discourse that we have come to regard as "poststructural," a discourse that writes itself *after* the rise and fall of structures.[2] In the opening chapter of this book, I spoke of these structures in terms of history and philosophy, and tried to show the ways in which a variety of poststructural writers were questioning the exclusivity of these structures. Michel Foucault, for instance—in stepping outside the domain that historians have used to map out their territory—found himself drawn instead to the omissions of history. As he looked back to the Age of Reason, he focused not on manifestations of enlightenment and rationality, but on madness, hysteria, and deviance.[3] And Jacques Derrida, the individual perhaps most recognized for the poststructural critique of language, has found himself drawn to the infinite play of "differences" that prevents the metaphysical closure that Western philosophy has always sought. Instead of writing about cohesive structures, he writes a language that constantly transgresses the boundaries in which meaning has traditionally been fixed.[4]

My own sense of the radical implications of poststructural writing is that they are intricately interwoven with those of the feminist critique of discursive systems long dominated by men. In its explorations of phenomena and processes that are absent from classical discourse, poststructural writing takes as its subject the very material that woman has all along represented. Woman, in other words, is providing poststructural discourse with its metaphor, its means of expressing itself. And so it is woman, conventionally the object of discourse, who has now become the subject of post-scripting.

Such an idea is implicit and at times explicit in a good deal of poststructural and feminist writing. Alice Jardine has even suggested that the connection between "feminist" thought and what she calls "postmodernism" constitutes a kind of "post-feminism." The emphasis here is not so much on the differences between male and female—traditionally a subject of "feminist" discourse—but instead on a "rethinking" of the very structures and narratives we have used to frame such dualistic oppositions. "In France," Jardine says, "such rethinking has involved, above all, a reincorporation and reconceptualization of that which has been the master narratives' own 'nonknowledge,' what has eluded them, what has engulfed them. This other-than-themselves is almost always a 'space' of some kind . . . and this space has been coded as *feminine,* as *woman*."[5] If the "nonknowledge" of the Enlightenment was rendered feminine, then its space of uncertainty—unidentified and absent—now seems to be generating a discourse other than man's, other than that produced by the men who have written our history, philosophy, literature, science.

But how is this "woman-thing" speaking? How can we hear what she says? Listening for her voice means listening, as Irigaray says, *"otherwise than in good form(s),"*[6] because woman is speaking in ways that exceed the closed forms of representation to which we are accustomed. She speaks as the unknowing, uncertain, unthinking, questioning, disturbing, threatening. And not surprisingly, the metaphors used by men to figure her discourse betray its unsettling quality. In Derridean terms, she may well be the very process of deferral that makes cohesion and closure impossible, the thing that always beckons from a distance, and yet will not allow that distance to be traversed and conquered.[7] At times she figures conspicuously in the writing of men who engage a poststructural discourse, as she does in Klaus Theweleit's exploration of *Male Fantasies* governing the fascist mind—fantasies in which women were imagined as threatening to dissolve ego boundaries, and in which they were figured as the object of conquest and domination.[8] For Freud, of course, woman was the "dark continent," and Jacques Lacan told us that she was the very thing that lured Freud on—what Lacan called "The Freudian Thing," and what became for Lacan himself the enigma of the unconscious.[9] More often in the writing of male theorists, however, it is not woman herself so much as ideas carrying feminine signification that figure in their accounts of what is unknown and uncertain—as they do in Jean-François Lyotard's description of *The Postmodern Condition,* especially "postmodern science," which concerns itself "with such things as undecidables, the limits of precise control, conflicts characterized by incomplete information, *"fracta,"* catastrophes, and pragmatic paradoxes. . . . " This postmodern science, Lyotard says, "is changing the meaning of the word *knowledge.* . . . It is producing not the known, but the unknown."[10] Is Lyotard's "unknown" another figuration of woman, and if so, what can she tell us about speaking "nonknowledge"? We might also ask this question of Georges Bataille, who writes about *Visions of Excess,* visions that have long-standing associations with woman and the feminine.[11] And we might ask it as well of Michel de Certeau who, in his *Heterologies: Discourse on the Other,* writes about the repressed, about savages and mystics, melancholy and death, the sea, language, silence—modes of existence and articulation profoundly "other" than those that have conventionally dominated more traditional "discourse," modes now increasingly associated with the identity of woman and processes of the feminine.[12]

Are these men of poststructural discourse the voice of a "woman-thing" now speaking something different, something other? We might have grounds for regarding their theories in this way, since it is in their writing that we can hear the suppressed discourse of Enlightenment man—of a

Newton, Swift, Pope—surfacing from within, revealing itself not in terms of disparaging configurations of woman that were the product of severe repression, but in terms of an "other" discourse that openly challenges traditional modes of thought bent on the exclusion of whatever does not fit into its system.[13] And yet I cannot help but wonder if these poststructural "visions of excess" also remain, on some level, manifestations of male desire—visions that Enlightenment man could not tolerate, and that poststructural man finds enticing and consuming. Are these two kinds of men only different suitors approaching the same woman? Does one seek her out as the man who wants finally to appropriate and conquer, while the other seeks her as the suitor who ceaselessly pursues the distant woman?

I leave such questions lingering because I find myself less drawn now to the dynamics of sexual desire implicit in man's discourse—his figurations of excess that may ultimately only constitute his vision of woman—and more intrigued with the potential voice of woman *as* excess. What happens as this "woman-thing" is beginning to speak? How is she speaking? In my own attempt to listen for the voice of Enlightened Absence, to hear the woman who figures and speaks that absence, I have felt compelled to read through the discourse of men and *their* configurations of woman. And yet I have also sensed a powerful undercurrent pulling me away from their systematic discourse, and pulling me toward the articulation of that womanly absence. My access to the speaking of these processes—through the discourse that was suppressed in Newton, Swift, and Pope, and through the unsettled and displaced quality of Finch's writing—has allowed me to hear the unstable voices of classical culture. And that kind of access, which makes it possible to seek the unstable *through* a reading of fixed discourse, itself constitutes an important point of departure—

A departure leading us into an other discourse. What led me to this different space were the theories of men, but what occupies that space is the writing of women who are now speaking not simply a discourse *of* the other, but *as* the other. Cixous, Kristeva, Irigaray—I have called attention to these women in particular because their writing challenges both the rigidity of systematic discourse and the comfort that feminists may themselves find within these fixed discursive systems. They write about women being outside and displaced. But they also remind us of the dangers of becoming part of a system that consolidates its empire and excludes "others" according to the principles of sexual difference. By listening to them as speaking subjects, I have gained access to those processes—long associated with woman and now coded in contemporary theory as feminine—that can *break* with structures rather than accommodate them, that can *diffuse* power rather than order it into systems that function at the expense of some excluded and suppressed other.

But how is it possible to write fluidity and diffusion, to write a discourse that celebrates something other than our long-standing cultural values of oneness, unity, closure? I suggested earlier that we can see signs all around us that a "woman-thing" is speaking. One of the most revolutionary and controversial ways in which this is happening is through the articulation of the female body—that body which, during the Enlightenment, became emblematic of disease, deviation, and excess. We are now, over two centuries later, listening to the voice of this body, a body that was once suppressed but is now effecting a "political reconstitution" of itself and all that it represents.[14] If enlightened culture could thrive only on the condition that woman's body be purged from the social order, our own intellectual culture seems to be thriving on the possibility of reconstituting that body.

This reconstitution has put woman in a paradoxical position, for she is being called upon to function as both an object and subject—an object about which and through which writing circulates, and a subject who is writing herself into her own existence. The effects of these two reconstitutive acts can hardly be ignored, since they are shaping both the representational and political status of women. The extent to which woman continues to be objectified—no matter how theoretically sophisticated this objectification—will be a reflection of the power of modes of thinking bent on the appropriation of disorderly bodies. That way lies the continued suppression of women.

The extent to which woman can be freed from her inscription in discursive categories will reflect the willingness of both women and men to open their discourse to the processes long associated with woman's body—to write "as a woman" while refusing to participate in discursive systems that, implicitly or explicitly, represent woman as an object of writing. If we can imagine woman as a process, as embodying those processes that she has all along represented for men—the seepage of fluidity, the excess of the hysterical body, the shatterings of color, the fusions of shade—then woman becomes not so much an oppressed entity to be given her proper place in systems, but the very possibility of breaking loose from those systems. And her speaking becomes a process that will not be placed—either within the domain of a systematic discourse, or within that other domain of absence that has been the source of her silence. "It is in writing," Cixous explains, "from woman and toward woman, and in accepting the challenge of the discourse controlled by the phallus, that woman will affirm woman somewhere other than in silence, the place reserved for her in and through the Symbolic. May she get out of booby-trapped silence! And not have the margin or the harem foisted on her as her domain!"[15] Writing other than a controlled discourse, writing other than absence and silence—this woman is becoming the agent of post-scripting, the subject of an other discourse.

Man's tragedy, which he speaks again and again in his grand tragedies, may well be that he is caught within the confines of his own discourse. Fearing that excess can only mean universal darkness, he brings his systems to a close, and insists that the rest is silence. The rest is *not* silence, for silence is only another of his figurations of that which does not fit his discourse, another configuration of the woman who remains unaccommodated.

The very notion that "the rest" is somehow beyond our grasp and vision—even beyond life itself—may be man's tragic vision, but it is woman's tragedy. For she has been represented as the absent material that fuels this vision. What we need is not simply to change that configuration, but to liquify configuration into process—those processes that have been there all along, and that are now proliferating through a writing of her "body." We need to do this not so that woman can find a better place in systems of discourse, but so that she can explode the dynamics of their representational schemes, which continue to function at the exclusion and expense of something "other," something feminine.

Notes

PREFACE

1. For a good discussion of the situation of this "classical period" in various theoretical conceptions of history, see Alice Jardine, *Gynesis: Configurations of Woman and Modernity* (Ithaca: Cornell University Press, 1985), pp. 84–85.

2. Luce Irigaray, *This Sex Which Is Not One,* trans. Catherine Porter (Ithaca: Cornell University Press, 1985), p. 164.

3. Ibid., p. 74.

1
HISTORIES, THEORIES, CONFIGURATIONS

Epigraphs: Simone de Beauvoir, *The Second Sex,* trans. H. M. Parshley (1953; rpt. New York: Vintage Books, 1974), p. 161; Kristeva, "Woman Can Never Be Defined," trans. Marilyn A. August, in *New French Feminisms,* ed. Elaine Marks and Isabelle de Courtivron (New York: Schocken Books, 1981), p. 137; Luce Irigaray, *This Sex Which Is Not One,* trans. Catherine Porter (Ithaca: Cornell University Press, 1985), p. 68; Hélène Cixous, "Sorties," *The Newly Born Woman,* trans. Betsy Wing, Theory and History of Literature, vol. 37 (Minneapolis: University of Minnesota Press, 1986), pp. 67–68.

1. See Barbara B. Schnorrenberg and Jean E. Hunter, "The Eighteenth-Century Englishwoman" in *The Women of England from Anglo-Saxon Times to the Present,* ed. Barbara Kanner (Hamden, Conn.: Archon Books, 1979), pp. 183–228, for a good summary of women's achievements, particularly in science and literature. For discussions of the problems inherent in the very project of writing women's history, see Berenice A. Carroll, ed., *Liberating Women's History: Theoretical and Critical Essays* (Urbana: University of Illinois Press, 1976). Recently, scholars have been devoting particular attention to feminist women writers who emerged during the years that I describe as Enlightenment. See, for example, Hilda L. Smith, *Reason's Disciples: Seventeenth-Century English Feminists* (Urbana: University of Illinois Press, 1982); Katharine M. Rogers, *Feminism in Eighteenth-Century England* (Urbana: University of Illinois Press, 1982); and Ruth

Perry, *The Celebrated Mary Astell: An Early English Feminist* (Chicago: University of Chicago Press, 1986).

2. Dominick LaCapra, *History and Criticism* (Ithaca: Cornell University Press, 1985), pp. 18–19.

3. Hayden White, *Tropics of Discourse: Essays in Cultural Criticism* (Baltimore: Johns Hopkins University Press, 1978), p. 2.

4. Paul Ricoeur, *The Reality of the Historical Past* (Milwaukee: Marquette University Press, 1984), p. 2. Also consider LaCapra's argument that historians need "a more interactive model of discourse that allows for the mutual—at times the mutually challenging—interchange of 'documentary' and 'rhetorical' dimensions of language" (p. 21).

5. Cynthia Ozick, The Moral Necessity of Metaphor: Rooting History in a Figure of Speech," *Harper's* 272 (May 1986): 62–68.

6. Carol Smith-Rosenberg, *Disorderly Conduct: Visions of Gender in Victorian America* (New York: Alfred A. Knopf, 1985), p. 19. Also consider historian Joan Kelly's comments on the ways in which our attempts "to add women to the fund of historical knowledge" have at once "revitalized theory" and "shaken the conceptual foundations of historical study." *Women, History, and Theory: The Essays of Joan Kelly* (Chicago: University of Chicago Press, 1984), p. 1.

7. David Vieth, "Introduction" to "A Symposium on Women in Swift's Poems: Vanessa, Stella, Lady Acheson, and Celia," *Papers on Language and Literature* 14 (1978): 115.

8. Susan Gubar, "The Female Monster in Augustan Satire," *Signs* 3, no. 2 (Winter 1977): 380–94. Such representations of woman as excessive and monstrous may also be related to the peculiar sense of liberation women enjoyed at eighteenth-century carnivals and masquerades, especially when we keep in mind Terry Castle's notion of the masquerade as an "organized infatuation with otherness. . . ." See Castle's discussion of these matters in *Masquerade and Civilization: The Carnivalesque in Eighteenth-Century English Culture and Fiction* (Stanford: Stanford University Press, 1986), pp. 41–46, 90–94, 99.

9. Felicity Nussbaum, *The Brink of All We Hate: English Satires on Women, 1660–1750* (Lexington: University Press of Kentucky, 1984).

10. Terry Eagleton, *The Rape of Clarissa: Writing, Sexuality, and Class Struggle in Samuel Richardson* (Minneapolis: University of Minnesota Press, 1982), pp. 14–16.

11. Terry Castle, *Clarissa's Ciphers: Meaning and Disruption in Richardson's "Clarissa"* (Ithaca: Cornell University Press, 1982), pp. 22–25. The "tyranny" of "sexual ideology" may have its own complement in contem-

porary criticism of Richardson. Consider, for example, William Warner's attempt to engage in a reading of *Clarissa*—a reading that curiously aims to defy mastery of the novel—by "Traversing the Body of *Clarissa*" and finding endless "pleasure" in that experience. See *Reading Clarissa: The Struggles of Interpretation* (New Haven: Yale University Press, 1979), pp. v, 258.

12. Ellen Pollak, *The Poetics of Sexual Myth: Gender and Ideology in the Verse of Swift and Pope* (Chicago: University of Chicago Press, 1985), pp. 2–5, 63.

13. Hélène Cixous, "Sorties," *The Newly Born Woman*, p. 79.

14. Catherine Clément, "The Guilty One," *The Newly Born Woman*, p. 6.

15. Michel Foucault, *The Archaeology of Knowledge*, trans. A. M. Sheridan Smith (New York: Pantheon Books, 1972), pp. 6–12.

16. Alice Jardine, *Gynesis: Configurations of Woman and Modernity* (Ithaca: Cornell University Press, 1985), p. 86.

17. Cited in Jardine, *Gynesis*, pp. 86–87.

18. See Thomas Kuhn, *The Structure of Scientific Revolutions*, 2d ed. (Chicago: University of Chicago Press, 1970), pp. 10–11 and 208–9; and Kuhn, "Comment [on the Relations of Science and Art]," *Comparative Studies in Philosophy and History*, 11 (1969): 403–12. For a theory of scientific epistemology that challenges Kuhn's, see Paul Feyerabend, *Against Method: Outline of an Anarchistic Theory of Knowledge* (Boston: Schocken Books, 1978).

19. Michel Serres, *Hermes: Literature, Science, Philosophy*, ed. Josué V. Harari and David F. Bell (Baltimore: Johns Hopkins University Press, 1982), p. xiii.

20. Irigaray, *This Sex Which Is Not One*, p. 164; and Jardine, *Gynesis*, p. 71.

21. Michel Foucault, *Madness and Civilization: A History of Insanity in the Age of Reason*, trans. Richard Howard (New York: Vintage Books, 1965). The specific dates of Foucault's study are 1656–1794, marking those years during which "classical" thought found expression throughout Europe, and coinciding with the general European preoccupation with defining and confining madness. These years also encompass the period during which Newton, Swift, Pope, and Finch were writing in England— the period I regard as manifesting the characteristics we commonly associate with classicism and enlightenment.

22. See E. P. Thompson's study of various exploited groups in eighteenth-century England in *The Making of the English Working Class* (New

York: Pantheon Books, 1964), especially pp. 55–61. Also see Foucault's discussion of the development of "workhouses" in England during these years in *Madness and Civilization,* pp. 43–44.

23. Clément, "The Guilty One," p. 7.

24. Sandra Gilbert and Susan Gubar, *The Madwoman in the Attic: The Woman Writer and the Nineteenth-Century Literary Imagination* (New Haven: Yale University Press, 1979), p. 17; Auerbach, *Woman and the Demon: The Life of a Victorian Myth* (Cambridge, Mass.: Harvard University Press, 1982), pp. 41, 64–66. The statement from Malebranche is cited by G. S. Rousseau, "Science and the Discovery of the Imagination in Enlightened England," *Eighteenth-Century Studies* 3 (Fall 1969): 118, who translates the statement without observing its gender implications. An interesting context for understanding Auerbach's views on the female corpse in the nineteenth-century imagination is Foucault's ideas on the importance of the corpse in eighteenth-century medicine, and especially the function of the corpse in intensifying the "gaze" and control of the physician. See *The Birth of the Clinic: An Archaeology of Medical Perception,* trans. A. M. Sheridan Smith (New York: Vintage Books, 1975), pp. 124–48. Also consider Foucault's notion of "sexuality" as a discourse of power and control, specifically control over the body. It was during the eighteenth century, he claims, that "strategies of knowledge and power" had marked sexuality as such a discourse, and that Freud, in confirming this discourse of sexuality, was "worthy of the greatest spiritual fathers and directors of the classical period." See *The History of Sexuality,* vol. 1, trans. Robert Hurley (New York: Vintage Books, 1978), p. 159.

25. Smith-Rosenberg, *Disorderly Conduct,* p. 23.

26. Mary Ann Doane, "The Clinical Eye: Medical Discourses in the 'Woman's Film' of the 1940s" in *The Female Body in Western Culture: Contemporary Perspectives,* ed. Susan Rubin Suleiman (Cambridge, Mass.: Harvard University Press, 1986), p. 152. For a good discussion of medical treatises devoted to various forms of madness, including treatises on hypochondria, hysteria, nymphomania, and the powers of "imagination" in pregnant women, see G. S. Rousseau, "Science and the Discovery of the Imagination," pp. 118–21. Also see Rousseau's essay on "Psychology" in *The Ferment of Knowledge: Studies in the Historiography of Eighteenth-Century Science,* ed. Rousseau and Roy Porter (Cambridge: Cambridge University Press, 1980), pp. 143–210. The role of women in medicine is a topic that has attracted much attention from feminist critics and historians. I would emphasize here what Carolyn Merchant describes as the "female's passive role in biological generation" which largely resulted from male physicians solidifying their replacement of female midwives in the

seventeenth and eighteenth centuries. See Merchant, *The Death of Nature: Women, Ecology, and the Scientific Revolution* (New York: Harper & Row, 1980), pp. 150–55. Also see Barbara Ehrenreich and Deirdre English, *Witches, Midwives, and Nurses: A History of Women Healers* (Old Westbury, New York: The Feminist Press, 1973).

Much of the recent interest in hysteria and other peculiar "female" disorders has informed the rich field of inquiry exploring connections between feminism and psychoanalysis. See, for instance, the collection of essays *In Dora's Case: Freud-Hysteria-Feminism,* ed. Charles Bernheimer and Claire Kahane (New York: Columbia University Press, 1985), and Dianne Hunter, "Hysteria, Psychoanalysis, and Feminism: The Case of Anna O," in *The (M)Other Tongue: Essays in Feminist Psychoanalytic Interpretation,* ed. Shirley Nelson Garner, Claire Kahane, and Madelon Sprengnether (Ithaca: Cornell University Press, 1985), pp. 89–115.

27. Clément, "The Guilty One," p. 34.

28. For a fascinating study of the connections between the physical body and the social body—especially the ways in which the health and disease of society are figured through the body—see Mary Douglas, *Natural Symbols: Explorations in Cosmology* (New York: Vintage Books, 1973).

29. This quotation from Bacon's *De Dignitate et Augmentis Scientiarum* is cited by both Merchant, *The Death of Nature,* p. 168, and Sandra Harding, *The Science Question in Feminism* (Ithaca: Cornell University Press, 1986), p. 237.

30. Evelyn Fox Keller, *Reflections on Gender and Science* (New Haven: Yale University Press, 1985), pp. 52–53.

31. Brian Easlea, *Witch Hunting, Magic and the New Philosophy,* p. x.

32. Cixous, "Sorties," p. 80.

33. Harding, *The Science Question in Feminism,* p. 245.

34. Jean-François Lyotard, *The Postmodern Condition: A Report on Knowledge,* trans. Geoff Bennington and Brian Massumi, Theory and History of Literature, vol. 10 (Minneapolis: University of Minnesota Press, 1984), pp. xxiii-xv.

35. For discussions of the convergence of feminist theory particularly as it is written in the United States and France, see Jardine's comments on a "new French-American connection," pp. 43–44, and Sandra Gilbert's "Forward" to *The Newly Born Woman,* pp. xvi-xviii.

36. Julia Kristeva, *About Chinese Women,* trans. Anita Barrows (New York: Marion Boyars, 1986), p. 19.

37. Claudine Herrmann, "Women in Space and Time," trans. Marilyn R. Schuster, in *New French Feminisms,* p. 169.

38. Jardine, *Gynesis,* p. 36.

39. Jardine, *Gynesis,* pp. 41–42. Jardine considers the emergence of this concept of "woman as process" as an event that we might well ponder: "Why," she asks, "at the end of the twentieth century, has 'the feminine' become a wide-ranging area of concern?" (p. 27) Just as the conspicuous appearance of this configuration of woman fuels her exploration of post-modern theory, so does it underlie my own search for the absent phenomena in Enlightenment discourse, the elusive "woman" whose displacement accounted for the construction of systems that are now proving to be the subject of a radical feminist critique of culture. Our projects, however, proceed according to very different assumptions. The connections that Jardine explores between postmodern configurations of woman and a wide-ranging concern with "the feminine" suppose that postmodernity and feminism are closely related movements, each informing the other with its peculiar perspectives. The connections I explore between Enlightenment configurations of woman and both the feminist and postmodern interest in woman suggest that Enlightenment discourse—far from re-garding women in any positive sense—suppressed her otherness, leaving us access to "the feminine" only through tracing the configurations of this suppression.

40. Kristeva, *About Chinese Women,* p. 21.

41. Irigaray, *This Sex Which Is Not One,* pp. 106, 75. The distinction I am making between "patriarchy" (a system that can be reconstructed and renamed, to account for the presence of women) and the "symbolic order" (a system from which women/woman have been excluded and should be wary of entering in any reconstructed condition) marks perhaps the most important difference between the Anglo-American and French versions of feminist theory. Sandra Harding, in *The Science Question in Feminism,* has also explored such differences in varying feminist approaches to science, identifying them with different epistemological perspectives, and suggest-ing that we "learn to live with" this "tension in feminist thought," pp. 194–96.

42. Irigaray, p. 74. This question underlies much of Irigaray's writing, as well as my own understanding of the systems of the Enlightenment. For a rich sense of the ways in which she poses such questions about major Western systems of thought, especially those perpetuated by Plato and Freud, see Irigaray's *Speculum of the Other Woman,* trans. Gillian C. Gill (Ithaca: Cornell University Press, 1985).

43. Jacques Lacan, "The Signification of the Phallus," *Écrits: A Selection,* trans. Alan Sheridan (New York: W. W. Norton, 1977), p. 284. For dis-cussions of the complex and controversial relations between Lacanian

theory and feminist theory, see Jane Gallop, *The Daughter's Seduction: Feminism and Psychoanalysis* (Ithaca: Cornell University Press, 1982); Gallop, *Reading Lacan* (Ithaca: Cornell University Press, 1985); and Ellie Ragland-Sullivan, *Jacques Lacan and the Philosophy of Psychoanalysis* (Urbana: University of Illinois Press, 1986).

44. For my reading of Derrida, I refer to his essay "Differance" in *Margins of Philosophy*, trans. Alan Bass (Chicago: University of Chicago Press, 1982), the interviews in *Positions*, trans. Alan Bass (Chicago: University of Chicago Press, 1982), and *Of Grammatology*, trans. Gayatri Chakravorty Spivak (Baltimore: Johns Hopkins University Press, 1974).

45. Gayatri Chakravorty Spivak, "Love Me, Love My Ombre, Elle," *Diacritics*, 14, 4 (1984): 21–22.

46. Toril Moi, *Sexual/Textual Politics: Feminist Literary Theory* (London: Methuen, 1985).pp. 150–73.

47. Gayle Greene and Coppelia Kahn, *Making a Difference: Feminist Literary Criticism* (London: Methuen, 1985), pp. 22, 26.

48. Elizabeth Meese, *Crossing the Double-Cross: The Practice of Feminist Criticism* (Chapel Hill: University of North Carolina Press, 1986), p. 86.

49. Jardine, *Gynesis*, p. 21.

50. Jacques Derrida, *Spurs*, trans. Barbara Harlow (Chicago: University of Chicago Press, 1978), pp. 51–55. Subsequent references to Derrida in this chapter are to *Spurs*.

51. Derrida, for instance, imagines himself caught up in the quest for this object that cannot be "pinned down." Though "she is certainly not to be found in any of the familiar modes of concept or knowledge," he says, "it is impossible to resist looking for her" (p. 71). Perhaps he, too, feels the desire. I explore the question of whether much postmodern discourse itself has appropriated woman in the final section on "Post-Scripting."

52. Kristeva, *About Chinese Women*, p. 14.

53. Kristeva, *Desire in Language: A Semiotic Approach to Literature and Art*. ed. Leon S. Roudiez, trans. Thomas Gora, Alice Jardine, and Leon S. Roudiez (New York: Columbia University Press, 1984), p. x. Women, of course, can and do participate, to a greater or lesser extent, in the dynamics of exclusion as they become affiliated with the symbolic order—an affiliation that seems inevitable in modern societies. The issue, for many feminists, is not whether any individual woman is "in" or "out" of men's systems, but whether women—historically, linguistically, and culturally—have already been excluded from the symbolic order. The involvement of individual women in the dynamics of exclusion, then, would not detract from the larger issues of power and subordination that have traditionally

been linked to the power of men and the subordination of women. See, for instance, Irigaray's "The Power of Discourse and the Subordination of the Feminine," *This Sex Which Is Not One*, pp. 68–85.

54. Quoted in Verena Conley, *Hélène Cixous: Writing the Feminine* (Lincoln: University of Nebraska Press, 1984), p. 151.

55. Cixous, "Sorties," p. 90.

56. Klaus Theweleit, *Male Fantasies, 1. Women, Floods, Bodies, History*, trans. Stephen Conway, Theory of History and Literature, vol. 22 (Minneapolis: University of Minnesota Press, 1987), pp. 229–300.

57. Foucault, *Madness and Civilization*, pp. 7–11. In discussing the function of liminality in ritual and symbol, Victor Turner observes that "liminality is frequently likened to death, to being in the womb, to invisibility, to darkness, to bisexuality. . . ." Much of the recent feminist theory I have been describing would associate these states with the symbolism of woman, supplying a sexual context for Turner's belief that "there is a certain homology between the 'weakness' and 'passivity' of liminality . . . and the 'structural' or synchronic inferiority of certain personae, groups, and social categories in political, legal, and economic systems." See *The Ritual Process: Structure and Anti-Structure* (Chicago: University of Chicago Press, 1969), pp. 95, 99–100. For a fascinating discussion of the ways that woman has figured in worlds of liminality and inversion, see Natalie Zemon Davis, "Women on Top: Symbolic Sexual Inversion and Political Disorder in Early Modern Europe" in *The Reversible World: Symbolic Inversion in Art and Society*, ed. Barbara A. Babcock (Ithaca: Cornell University Press, 1978), pp. 147–90.

2

NEWTON'S EXCLUSIVE PRINCIPLES

Epigraphs: Evelyn Fox Keller, *Reflections on Gender and Science* (New Haven: Yale University Press, 1985), p. 64; Michel Serres, *Hermes: Literature, Science, Philosophy*, ed. Josué V. Harari and David F. Bell (Baltimore: Johns Hopkins University Press, 1982), p. 27; Isaac Newton, "General Scholium" of the *Principia*, trans. Florian Cajori (Berkeley: University of California Press, 1934), p. 544; see note 15 below.

1. Cited in I. Bernard Cohen, *Introduction to Newton's "Principia"* (Cambridge, Mass.: Harvard University Press, 1971), p. 134.

2. Cited in Cohen, *Introduction to Newton's "Principia,"* p. 133.

3. Cited in Cohen, *Introduction to Newton's "Principia,"* p. 134.

4. See Frank Manuel's comments on Newton's language in *A Portrait of Isaac Newton* (Cambridge, Mass.: Harvard University Press, 1968), pp.

76–77. Also see J. M. Coetzee, "Newton and the Ideal of a Transparent Scientific Language," *Journal of Literary Semantics* 11 (April 1982): 3–13; and Geoffrey Cantor's exploration of different kinds of scientific language, particularly the straightforward and the metaphorical discourse on "light" in the mid-eighteenth century, in "Light and Enlightenment: An Exploration of Mid-Eighteenth-Century Modes of Discourse" in *The Discourse of Light from the Middle Ages to the Enlightenment* (Los Angeles: William Andrews Clark Memorial Library, 1985), pp. 67–106.

5. Henry Adams, *The Education of Henry Adams,* ed. D. W. Brogan (Boston: Houghton Mifflin, 1961), p. 458.

6. Adams, *Education,* p. 460. For an interesting comparison of Newton's view of the Catholic church as an "Adulteress" and Adams's very different ideas about the creative energies that the Virgin brought to Catholicism, see Gale E. Christianson, *In the Presence of the Creator: Isaac Newton and His Times* (New York: The Free Press, 1984), pp. 253–54.

7. See, for instance, I. Bernard Cohen, *The Birth of the New Physics* (New York: Doubleday, 1960); Thomas Kuhn, *The Structure of Scientific Revolutions,* 2d ed. (Chicago: University of Chicago Press, 1970); and Paul Feyerabend, *Against Method: Outline of an Anarchistic Theory of Knowledge* (Boston: Schocken Books, 1978).

8. Carolyn Merchant, *The Death of Nature: Women, Ecology, and The Scientific Revolution* (New York: Harper and Row, 1980).

9. Merchant, *The Death of Nature,* pp. 168–69.

10. Keller, *Reflections on Gender and Science,* p. 43.

11. Sandra Harding, *The Science Question in Feminism* (Ithaca: Cornell University Press, 1986), p. 112.

12. Harding, *Science Question,* p. 120.

13. Merchant, *The Death of Nature,* p. 172.

14. Serres, *Hermes: Literature, Science, Philosophy,* p. 28.

15. Newton, *Sir Isaac Newton's Mathematical Principles of Natural Philosophy and his System of the World,* trans. Florian Cajori (Berkeley: University of California Press, 1934), p. 397. Though there are some problems with Cajori's modernized text of Andrew Motte's 1729 translation (see Cohen's remarks in his *Introduction to Newton's "Principia,"* p. xvi), Cajori's revised translation remains widely accessible and is cited in commentary on Newton. My references are therefore to the Cajori translation, and are noted parenthetically in the text.

16. Newton spoke of "principles not philosophical but mathematical" as those that "we may build our reasonings upon in philosophical inquiries." Cajori, p. 397.

17. Cited in Manuel, *A Portrait of Isaac Newton,* pp. 154–55, and in

Richard S. Westfall, *Never At Rest: A Biography of Isaac Newton* (Cambridge: Cambridge University Press, 1980), who explores the controversy more fully, pp. 446–51. Also see Cohen's discussion of this matter in *Introduction to Newton's "Principia,"* p. 132.

18. The original statement in this Scholium read: "The case of the sixth corollary obtains in the celestial bodies; and therefore in what follows. . . ." For his acknowledgement, Newton simply added a parenthetical phrase: "The case of the sixth corollary obtains in the celestial bodies (as Wren, Halley, and Hooke of our nation have severally observed). . . ." See Cohen's *Introduction to Newton's "Principia,"* p. 135. In Cajori's edition, see p. 46.

19. Manuel, *A Portrait of Isaac Newton,* pp. 156–57. Manuel's figurative account of "midwives" delivering the *Principia* is noteworthy in itself, especially if we regard the figuration in terms of the anxieties that both Newton and the scientific community harbored about maternity. I will be discussing such matters later in this chapter.

20. Cited in Cohen, *Introduction to Newton's "Principia,"* p. 152.

21. Cohen, *Introduction to Newton's "Principia,"* pp. 153–44.

22. See A. Rupert Hall, *Philosophers at War: The Quarrel Between Newton and Leibniz* (Cambridge: Cambridge University Press, 1980).

23. Cited in Cohen, *Introduction to Newton's "Principia,"* p. 243, n. 14. Also see Brian Easlea, *Witch Hunting, Magic and the New Philosophy* (Brighton: Harvester Press, 1980), p. 183.

24. Cotes's Preface is included in Cajori's edition of the *Principia*. See pp. xxvi-xxvii.

25. Cohen, *Introduction to Newton's "Principia,"* p. 243.

26. Kuhn, *The Structure of Scientific Revolutions*. Also see Easlea's comments on the background of Newton's distrust of hypotheses, pp. 163–64.

27. Manuel, *A Portrait of Isaac Newton,* pp. 64–66. Also see Manuel's *Isaac Newton: Historian* (Cambridge, Mass.: Harvard University Press, 1963), which explores Newton's writings on history, chronology, and the interpretation of prophecy.

28. Manuel, *A Portrait of Isaac Newton,* pp. 25 and 78.

29. Westfall, *Never At Rest,* pp. 407–8.

30. Margaret Jacob, *The Radical Enlightenment: Pantheists, Freemasons and Republicans* (London: Allen & Unwin, 1981), p. 22.

31. See Easlea, *Witch Hunting*. For a discussion of why even the "radical" thinkers rejected magic and witchcraft, see Jacob, *Radical Enlightenment,* pp. 32–35.

32. Frank Manuel, *The Changing of the Gods* (Hanover: University Press of New England, 1983), p. 25.

33. Manuel, *A Portrait of Isaac Newton*, p. 18.

34. Cited in Easlea, *Witch Hunting*, p. 171.

35. Merchant, *The Death of Nature*, p. 275. Kuhn offers a similar description, in terms of his own theories about the development of science, in *The Structure of Scientific Revolutions*, pp. 105–6.

36. Hugh Kearney, *Science and Change: 1500–1700*, World University Library (New York: McGraw-Hill, 1971).

37. Easlea, *Witch Hunting*, p. ix.

38. Serres, *Hermes*, p. 83.

39. Manuel, *A Portrait of Isaac Newton*, p. 190. Also consider Manuel's comment on Newton's devotion to the father figure: "The image of this father, the yeoman Isaac Newton, soon fused with the vision of God the Father, and a special relationship was early established between the son and his father" *Portrait of Isaac Newton*, p. 28, also p. 117.

40. For Newton's letters to Bentley, see *Isaac Newton's Papers & Letters On Natural Philosophy*, ed. I. Bernard Cohen (Cambridge, Mass.: Harvard University Press, 1958), pp. 279–312. Also see Easlea's discussion of this matter, p. 182.

41. See Easlea, *Witch Hunting*, pp. 184–85.

42. See Cohen's remarks on the revisions of both treatises, *Introduction to Newton's "Principia,"* p. 258.

43. Manuel, *Portrait of Isaac Newton*, p. 162. For discussions of the tradition of alchemy and Newton's fascination with the subject, see Westfall, pp. 18–23 and Christainson, pp. 203–36.

44. See, for instance, Merchant, *The Death of Nature*, p. 214 and 275, and Keller, *Gender and Science*, p. 44.

45. See Easlea, *Witch Hunting*, pp. 169–70.

46. Cited in Easlea, *Witch Hunting*, pp. 170–71, and in Christianson, *In the Presence of the Creator*, p. 231.

47. Cited in Manuel, *A Portrait of Isaac Newton*, p. 180.

48. Easlea, *Witch Hunting*, p. 171. Also consider the remarks of John Maynard Keynes, who acquired many of Newton's papers on alchemy and who, on studying the papers, challenged the accepted notion of Newton as a "rationalist" and suggested instead that "he was the last of the magicians." Keynes's final assessment of the alchemical papers, however, only shows how firmly he himself believed in a strict if not mechanical conception of science: "Interesting, but not useful," he wrote, "wholly magical and wholly devoid of scientific value." See the discussion of Keynes's remarks in Christianson, *In the Presence of the Creator*, pp. 204–5.

49. Luce Irigaray, *This Sex Which Is Not One*, trans. Catherine Porter (Ithaca: Cornell University Press), pp. 106–7.

50. Manuel, *A Portrait of Isaac Newton*, pp. 25–28.

51. Nina Auerbach, *Woman and the Demon: The Life of a Victorian Myth* (Cambridge, Mass.: Harvard University Press, 1982), pp. 3, 228.

52. Cited in Keller, *Gender and Science*, p. 53.

53. Manuel, *A Portrait of Isaac Newton*, pp. 84–85.

54. Jacques Derrida, *Spurs*, trans. Barbara Harlow (Chicago: University of Chicago Press, 1978), p. 49.

55. Catharine Clément, "The Guilty One," *The Newly Born Woman*, trans. Betsy Wing, *Theory and History of Literature*, vol. 24 (Minneapolis: University of Minnesota Press), p. 6.

56. Irigaray, *This Sex Which Is Not One*, p. 106.

3
Newton, Pope, and the Problem of Color

Epigraphs: Hélène Cixous, "Sorties," *The Newly Born Woman*, trans. Betsy Wing, Theory and History of Literature, vol. 24 (Minneapolis: University of Minnesota Press, 1986), p. 88; Isaac Newton, *Opticks* (New York: Dover Publications, 1952), p. 160; Alexander Pope, *Epistle To a Lady*, ll. 17–20.

1. All references to Pope's poetry are to *The Twickenham Edition of the Poems of Alexander Pope*, gen. ed. John Butt (New Haven: Yale University Press; London: Methuen): vol. 1, *Pastoral Poetry and An Essay on Criticism*, ed. E. Audra and Aubrey Williams (1961); vol. 2, *The Rape of the Lock and Other Poems*, ed. Geoffrey Tillotson (1962); vol. 3, i, *An Essay on Man*, ed. Maynard Mack (1950); vol. 3, ii, *Epistles to Several Persons*, ed. F. W. Bateson (1961); vol. 4, *Imitations of Horace with an Epistle to Dr Arbuthnot and The Epilogue to the Satires*, ed. John Butt (1953); vol. 5, *The Dunciad*, ed. James Sutherland (1943). References will be noted parenthetically in the text by line number, or by canto and line number.

2. All references to Newton's *Principia* are to *Sir Isaac Newton's Mathematical Principles of Natural Philosophy and his System of the World*, trans. Florian Cajori (Berkeley: University of California Press, 1934), and will be noted parenthetically in the text by page number.

3. Michel Serres, *Hermes: Literature, Science, Philosophy*, ed. Josué V. Harari and David F. Bell (Baltimore: Johns Hopkins University Press, 1982), p. 83.

4. Newton, *Opticks, Or a Treatise of the Reflections, Refractions, Inflections*

& Colours of Light (New York: Dover Publications, 1952). All references are to this edition and will be noted parenthetically in the text by page number.

5. Marjorie Hope Nicolson, *Newton Demands the Muse: Newton's Opticks and the Eighteenth-Century Poets* (Princeton: Princeton University Press, 1968), pp. 37–38.

6. *John Milton: Complete Poems and Major Prose*, ed. Merritt Y. Hughes (New York: Odyssey, 1957), ll. 1–12.

7. Simone de Beauvoir, *The Second Sex*, p. 166.

8. See Cohen's "Preface" to the *Opticks*, p. xlix.

9. *Isaac Newton's Papers & Letters on Natural Philosophy*, ed. I. Bernard Cohen (Cambridge, Mass.: Harvard University Press, 1958), pp. 118–19.

10. Newton, *Observations Upon the Prophecies of Daniel, and the Apocalypse of St. John* (London: J. Darby and T. Browne, 1733), p. 16.

11. Ibid., p. 17.

12. See, for instance, Geoffrey Cantor's discussion of "optical discourse" as encompassing two traditions: a Lockean tradition in which precise notions were conveyed in a plain style, and an anti-Lockean tradition that attributed deeper meanings to words. Describing John Hutchinson as an anti-Lockean, he explores some of the symbolic implications of an otherwise "plain" scientific language—particularly the symbolism of the sun and its associations with God the father. "The sun," Cantor explains, "like God, cannot be diminished. Instead, it is the undiminished, unchanging fountain of light and power." "Light and Enlightenment: An Exploration of Mid-Eighteenth-Century Modes of Discourse" in *The Discourse of Light from the Middle Ages to the Enlightenment*, papers read at a Clark Library Seminar (Los Angeles: William Andrews Clark Memorial Library, 1985), pp. 70, 92. I would suggest that Newton's scientific language, despite its "plain" style, is rich in such metaphoric associations—particularly religious ones. See my discussion of this topic in Chapter Two.

13. *John Milton: Complete Poems*, Bk. 9, ll. 1135–36.

14. Northrop Frye, "The Revelation to Eve," in *Paradise Lost: A Tercentenary Tribute*, ed. Balachandra Rajan (Toronto: University of Toronto Press, 1969), p. 46.

15. Julia Kristeva, "Giotto's Joy," *Desire in Language: A Semiotic Approach to Literature and Art*, ed. Leon S. Roudiez, trans. Thomas Gora, Alice Jardine, and Leon S. Roudiez (New York: Columbia University Press, 1980), pp. 219, 222.

16. De Beauvoir, *The Second Sex*, p. 167. While the male aspires to the light of the sun, woman maintains her associations not only with darkness,

but also color. See, for instance, de Beauvoir's observation that prostitutes have traditionally been forced "to wear a special costume of many-colored cloth, ornamented with bouquets, and they had to dye their hair with saffron," p. 102.

17. Julia Kristeva, "Motherhood According to Giovanni Bellini," *Desire in Language*, pp. 247–49.

18. Julia Kristeva, "Oscillation between Power and Denial," trans. Marilyn A. August, *New French Feminisms*, ed. Elaine Marks and Isabelle de Courtivron (New York: Schocken Books, 1981), p. 167.

19. Newton, *Optica*, in *The Optical Papers of Isaac Newton*, ed. Alan E. Shapiro, vol. 1 (Cambridge: Cambridge University Press, 1984), p. 437.

20. Richard Westfall, *Never At Rest: A Biography of Isaac Newton* (Cambridge: Cambridge University Press, 1980), pp. 61, 156.

21. Frank Manuel, *A Portrait of Isaac Newton* (Cambridge, Mass.: Harvard University Press, 1968), p. 78.

22. In Marjorie Hope Nicolson and G. S. Rousseau, *"This Long Disease, My Life": Alexander Pope and the Sciences* (Princeton: Princeton University Press, 1968), pp. 267–69. Nicolson cites two other critics of "color and light" in Pope: Norman Ault, who attributed Pope's sensitivity to color to his study of painting under Charles Jervas, and Maynard Mack, whose ideas about Pope's grotto I treat in detail later. Cleanth Brooks claimed that Pope's attention to Belinda's artistry in *The Rape* puts him in line with Yeats who "could address a 'young beauty' as 'dear fellow artist.'" See "The Case of Miss Arabella Fermor" in *The Well Wrought Urn* (London: D. Dobson, 1947), p. 77. Brooks's implication is that both Pope and Yeats found a healthy source of inspiration in the beauty of women. But we should also keep in mind that Pope painted Belinda with the same "gawdy Colours" that he used to paint and criticize women in his *Epistle to a Lady*. Jean Hagstrum, for instance, calls attention to Pope's "pejorative associations" of color especially in the poems on women, which enforce Pope's satire of their "evanescent, superficial, ephemeral" nature. See *The Sister Arts: The Tradition of Literary Pictorialism and English Poetry from Dryden to Gray* (Chicago: University of Chicago Press, 1958), p. 240. Yet in exploring the implications of such studies of Pope and the "sister arts," Pollak focuses on the "sexual ideology" that has been overlooked by critics, an ideology implicit in Pope's "metaphorization of the female as a work of art." She argues that this ideology reveals not a satire of their characters, but a view of woman as "lack"—the "part and counterpart of man, whom she at the same time mirrors and completes." See *The Poetics of Sexual Myth: Gender and Ideology in the Verse of Swift and Pope* (Chicago: University of Illinois Press, 1985), p. 109.

23. Nicolson and Rousseau, *"This Long Disease, My Life,"* pp. 286, 292.

24. See Atkins's discussion of Pope's *Epistle to Arbuthnot* in *Reading Deconstruction, Deconstructive Reading* (Lexington: University Press of Kentucky, 1983), pp. 118–35. Also see Atkins's chapter on "Becoming Woman: Writing, Self, and the Quest of Difference in the *Imitations of Horace*" in *Quests of Difference: Reading Pope's Poems* (Lexington: University Press of Kentucky, 1986), pp. 99–146, where he argues that Pope, despite his desire for "manly ways," nonetheless becomes "womanly" as he himself exhibits both masculine and feminine characteristics—that is, as he loses his fixed identity as male.

25. Kristeva, *Desire in Language,* pp. 221–22. On a different occasion, Kristeva underscores the feminine associations of color by thinking of Virginia Woolf "who sank wordlessly into the river, her pockets weighted with stones. Haunted by voices, by waves, by lights, in love with colours—blue, green—seized by a sort of bizarre gaiety that brought on the fits of strangled, hooting, uncontrolled laughter remembered by Miss Brown." *About Chinese Women,* trans. Anita Barrows (New York: Marion Boyars, 1986), p. 39.

26. Ellen Pollak argues convincingly that in associating Eloisa with uncontrolled feminine desire, Pope engages in a "voyeuristic male appropriation of female eroticism in the service of a phallocentric ordering of desire in which both excess and lack are figured as feminine." See *The Poetics of Sexual Myth,* p. 186. I would only add that on an unconscious level, Pope also engaged in the very feminine desire that as a male writer he ostensibly tried to control. Also see Douglas Brooks-Davies, who identifies the feminine associations of gardens and caves with Eve and Belinda, in *Sexuality in Eighteenth-Century Britain,* ed. Paul-Gabriel Boucé (Manchester: Manchester University Press, 1982), pp. 177, 186–87. I would suggest, in addition, that the groves of *Windsor-Forest* and Eloisa's cavernous abode are also rich in the feminine associations to which Pope responded, and that he repressed.

27. See Maynard Mack, *The Garden and the City: Retirement and Politics in the Later Poetry of Pope* (Toronto: University of Toronto Press, 1969). My own understanding of Pope's landscape has much in common with Carole Fabricant's study of *Swift's Landscape* that, in its "disconcerting state of uncertainty and flux," Fabricant contrasts with Pope's landscape of artistic balance and order. See *Swift's Landscape* (Baltimore: Johns Hopkins University Press, 1982), pp. 10–16. No doubt Pope did create and inhabit a landscape of symmetry and design, yet I would also suggest that its subterranean and unconscious hallows betray the same uncertainty and flux that Swift acknowledged more explicitly. Mack, in his recent biogra-

phy of Pope, treats matters similar to those he studied in *The Garden and the City,* discussing them in the context of major events and developments in Pope's literary career. See *Alexander Pope: A Life* (New Haven: Yale University Press, 1985), especially pp. 358–66 and 384–87.

28. Cited in Mack, *The Garden and the City,* p. 26.

29. Ibid., p. 44.

30. Luce Irigaray, *This Sex Which Is Not One,* trans. Catherine Porter (Ithaca: Cornell University Press, 1985), p. 74.

31. Mack, *The Garden and the City,* p. 47.

32. Consider, for instance, Socrates's remarks about "lovers of sights and sounds" who "enjoy beautiful voices and colours and outlines," yet whose "thought is unable to take in and delight in the being of the beautiful itself." *Plato's Republic,* ed. and trans. I. A. Richards (Cambridge: Cambridge University Press, 1966), p. 100.

33. Sandra Gilbert and Susan Gubar, *The Madwoman in the Attic: The Woman Writer and the Nineteenth-Century Literary Imagination* (New Haven: Yale University Press, 1979), pp. 93–97.

34. Aubrey Williams, "The 'Fall' of China and *The Rape of the Lock,*" in *Essential Articles for the Study of Alexander Pope,* ed. Maynard Mack (Hamden, Conn.: Archon, 1964), pp. 274–90.

35. Manuel, *A Portrait of Isaac Newton,* p. 70.

36. Julia Epstein and Mark Greenberg, "Decomposing Newton's Rainbow," *Journal of the History of Ideas* 45 (January-March 1984): 117. Also see Epstein's and Greenberg's discussion of the ways in which "post-Newtonian poets" depicted "nature (often figured as a woman) yielding herself to Sir Isaac Newton, or the force of Newton's intellect figuratively ravishing nature" (p. 124).

37. Carolyn Merchant, *The Death of Nature: Woman, Ecology and the Scientific Revolution* (New York: Harper & Row, 1980), pp. 283–87.

38. See my discussion of this topic in Chapter Two.

39. Laura Brown, *Alexander Pope* (Oxford: Basil Blackwell, 1985), p. 23.

40. See Pollak's treatment of the dynamics of display in *The Rape of the Lock* in *The Poetics of Sexual Myth,* pp. 77–79.

41. Sheila Delany, "Sex and Politics in Pope's *Rape of the Lock,*" *Writing Women* (New York: Schocken Books, 1983), pp. 93–112.

42. Susan Gubar, "The Female Monster in Augustan Satire," *Signs* 3, no. 2 (Winter 1977): 380–94.

43. Robert Graves, *The White Goddess: A Historical Grammar of Poetic Myth* (1948; rpt. New York: Farrar, Straus and Giroux, 1966), p. 25.

44. Graves, *The White Goddess,* pp. 71–72. For a fascinating discussion

of whiteness and woman's magical and excessive demeanor, see Nina Auerbach's reading of Wilkie Collins's *The Woman in White,* in her *Woman and the Demon: The Life of a Victorian Myth* (Cambridge, Mass.: Harvard University Press, 1982), pp. 135–43.

<h1 style="text-align:center">4
Swift's Disruptive Woman</h1>

Epigraphs: Monique Wittig, *Les Guérillères,* trans. David Le Vey (Boston: Beacon Press, 1985), p. 93; Luce Irigaray, *Speculum of the Other Woman,* trans. Gillian C. Gill (Ithaca: Cornell University Press, 1985), p. 237; Jonathan Swift, "The Lady's Dressing Room," *The Poems of Jonathan Swift,* ed. Harold Williams, 2d ed., 3 vols. (Oxford: Clarendon Press, 1958), 2: 526–27.

1. All references to *Gulliver's Travels* are to *The Prose Works of Jonathan Swift,* ed. Herbert Davis, 14 vols. (Oxford: Basil Blackwell, 1965), 11, and all subsequent references will be noted parenthetically in the text by page number. For Gulliver's description of Laputa, see pp. 119–72. Swift's satire of empirical science in general and the Royal Society in particular has often been noted. See, for example, Kathleen Williams's comment that the magnetic quality of Laputa and Balnibarbi "suggests the limited usefulness of that understanding of the laws of the universe upon which the Newtonian era so prided itself," *Jonathan Swift and the Age of Compromise* (Lawrence: University of Kansas Press, 1958), p. 167. Also see Marjorie Hope Nicolson and Nora Mohler, "The Scientific Background of Swift's *Voyage to Laputa,*" *Annals of Science,* 2 (1937): 299–334, rpt. in Nicolson, *Science and Imagination* (Ithaca: Cornell University Press, 1956), pp. 110–54. For a more general study of the connections between the *Principia* and eighteenth-century literature, see William Powell Jones, *The Rhetoric of Science: A Study of Scientific Ideas and Imagery in Eighteenth-Century English Poetry* (London: Routledge & Kegan Paul, 1966).

2. For a good summary of this critical tendency, see Carole Fabricant, *Swift's Landscape* (Baltimore: Johns Hopkins University Press, 1982), pp. 3–4.

3. See, for instance, C. J. Rawson, *Gulliver and the Gentle Reader: Studies in Swift and Our Time* (London: Routledge & Kegan Paul, 1972), Fabricant, *Swift's Landscape;* G. Douglas Atkins, *Reading Deconstruction, Deconstructive Reading* (Lexington: University Press of Kentucky, 1983); and Ellen Pollak, *The Poetics of Sexual Myth: Gender and Ideology in the Verse of Swift and Pope* (Chicago: University of Chicago Press, 1985).

4. Edward Said, "Swift's Tory Anarchy," *Eighteenth-Century Studies* 3 (Fall 1969): 48–66.

5. See Said, "Swift's Tory Anarchy"; Rawson, *Gulliver and the Gentle Reader*; Castle, "Why the Houyhnhnms Don't Write: Swift, Satire and the Fear of the Text," *Essays in Literature* 7 (Spring 1980): 31–44; and Fabricant, *Swift's Landscape*.

6. Hélène Cixous, "Sorties," *The Newly Born Woman*, trans. Betsy Wing, Theory and History of Literature, vol. 24 (Minneapolis: University of Minnesota Press, 1986), p. 85.

7. Michel Foucault, *Madness and Civilization: A History of Insanity in the Age of Reason*, trans. Richard Howard (New York: Vintage Books, 1965), p. 9.

8. Cited in Fabricant, *Swift's Landscape*, p. 234. Also see Fabricant's discussion of Swift's descriptions of his sea travels between Ireland and England, pp. 211–13.

9. Luce Irigaray, *This Sex Which Is Not One*, trans. Catherine Porter (Ithaca: Cornell University Press, 1985), p. 111; Cixous, "Sorties," p. 90.

10. Sheila Shaw, "The Rape of Gulliver: Case Study of a Source," *PMLA* 90 (1976): 62–68.

11. For a discussion of "the theme of imprisonment pervading [Swift's] work," see Fabricant, *Swift's Landscape*, pp. 43–54.

12. Castle, "Why the Houyhnhnms Don't Write," p. 36.

13. "No-man's land" is the term used by Claudine Hermann to describe the "space" occupied by woman. See her "Women and Space and Time" in *New French Feminisms*, ed. Elaine Marks and Isabelle de Courtivron (New York: Schocken Books, 1981), p. 169.

14. Quoted in Verena Conley, *Hélène Cixous: Writing the Feminine* (Lincoln: University of Nebraska Press, 1984), p. 151.

15. References to *The Battel of the Books* and *A Tale of a Tub* are to *The Prose Works of Jonathan Swift*, ed. Herbert Davis, 14 vols. (Oxford: Basil Blackwell, 1965), 1, and will be noted parenthetically in the text by page number. For an excellent discussion of monstrous female figures in Swift, see Susan Gubar, "The Female Monster in Augustan Satire," *Signs* 3, no. 2 (Winter 1977): 380–94.

16. Fabricant, *Swift's Landscape*, pp. 6–7.

17. Irigaray, *This Sex Which Is Not One*, pp. 106, 113.

18. Hélène Cixous, "The Laugh of the Medusa" in *New French Feminisms*, p. 256.

19. My allusions here are to, respectively, "The Progress of Beauty," "On Stella's Birth-day, 1718–19," "Strephon and Chloe," and "The Fur-

niture of a Woman's Mind." All references to Swift's poetry are to *The Poems of Jonathan Swift*, ed. Harold Williams, 2d ed., 3 vols. (Oxford: Clarendon Press, 1958), and will be noted parenthetically in the text by line number.

20. See, for instance, Peter J. Schakel, *The Poetry of Jonathan Swift: Allusion and the Development of a Poetic Style* (Madison: University of Wisconsin Press, 1978); John Irwin Fischer, *On Swift's Poetry* (Gainesville: University Presses of Florida, 1978); and Felicity A. Nussbaum, *The Brink of All We Hate: English Satires on Women, 1660–1750* (Lexington: University Press of Kentucky, 1984).

21. Ellen Pollak, *The Poetics of Sexual Myth*, pp. 3, 63.

22. Johnson explains: "The differences *between* entities . . . are shown to be based on a repression of differences *within* entities, ways in which an entity differs from itself. . . . Difference is a form of *work* to the extent that it *plays* beyond the control of any subject. . . ." *The Critical Difference: Essays in the Contemporary Rhetoric of Reading* (Baltimore: Johns Hopkins University Press, 1980), pp. x–xi.

23. G. Douglas Atkins, *Reading Deconstruction, Deconstructive Reading*, p. 116.

24. Castle, "Why the Houyhnhnms Don't Write," p. 32.

25. Gayatri Chakravorty Spivak, "Love Me, Love My Ombre, Elle," *Diacritics* 14, 4 (1984): 21–22.

26. Irigaray, *This Sex Which Is Not One*, p. 113.

27. See Brown's essay on Swift, "The Excremental Vision," in *Life Against Death: The Psychoanalytical Meaning of History* (Middletown, Conn.: Wesleyan University Press, 1959), pp. 179–201.

28. It is interesting, in this context, to consider Irigaray's question: ". . . we might ask (ourselves) why sperm is never treated as an object *a?*" See her brief discussion of this question, pp. 113–14.

29. The first word of this citation was omitted from the 1710 edition. I take the full quotation and the translation from *The Writings of Jonathan Swift*, ed. Robert A. Greenberg and William B. Piper (New York: W. W. Norton, 1973), pp. 347, 418.

30. See Pollak's note on this matter in *The Poetics of Sexual Myth*, pp. 215–16, n. 38.

31. Catherine Clément, "The Guilty One," *The Newly Born Woman*, p. 7.

32. Said, "Swift's Tory Anarchy," p. 49.

33. Cixous, "Sorties," pp. 79–80.

34. Irigaray, *This Sex Which Is Not One*, p. 74.

5

Anne Finch Placed and Displaced

Epigraphs: Simone de Beauvoir, *The Second Sex,* trans. H. M. Parshely (1952; rpt. New York: Vintage Books, 1974), p. 293; Shoshana Felman, "Rereading Femininity," *Yale French Studies* 62 (1981): 42; Anne Finch, "The Consolation," *Selected Poems of Anne Finch, Countess of Winchilsea,* ed. Katharine M. Rogers (New York: Fredrick Ungar, 1979), ll. 7–8.

1. See my discussion of this archetype and its gender implications in the section of Chapter Three titled "The Journey to Light."

2. See, for instance, Peggy Kamuf, "Writing Like a Woman" in *Women and Language in Literature and Society,* ed. S. McConnell-Ginet et al (New York: Praeger, 1980), pp. 284–99; Jonathan Culler, "Reading As a Woman," *On Deconstruction: Theory and Criticism After Structuralism* (Ithaca: Cornell University Press, 1982), pp. 43–64; and *Gender and Reading: Essays on Readers, Texts, and Contexts,* ed. Elizabeth A. Flynn and Patrocinio P. Schweickart (Baltimore: Johns Hopkins University Press, 1986).

3. For a fruitful discussion of these differences between the Anglo-American and French perspectives, see *New French Feminisms,* ed. Elaine Marks and Isabelle de Courtivron (New York: Schocken Books, 1981); Toril Moi, *Sexual/Textual Politics: Feminist Literary Theory* (London: Methuen, 1985); and Alice Jardine, *Gynesis: Configurations of Woman and Modernity* (Ithaca: Cornell University Press, 1985).

4. Jardine, *Gynesis,* pp. 84–85.

5. "An Invitation to Dafnis," *Selected Poems of Anne Finch, Countess of Winchilsea,* ed. Katharine M. Rogers (New York: Fredrick Ungar, 1979), ll. 15, 17. All references to Finch's poetry are to this edition; for lengthy poems, I will note parenthetically in the text references to line numbers.

6. See the recent Clark publication with this title, David C. Lindberg and Geoffrey Cantor, *The Discourse of Light from the Middle Ages to the Enlightenment* (Los Angeles: William Andrews Clark Memorial Library, 1985).

7. See Katharine Rogers's discussion of this matter in her introductory comments to *Selected Poems of Anne Finch,* p. xvi.

8. See Reuben A. Brower, "Lady Winchilsea and the Poetic Tradition of the Seventeenth Century," *Studies in Philology* 42 (1945): 61–80, and Rogers's introductory comments to *Selected Poems of Anne Finch,* p. xvii, xxiii-xxiv.

9. Sandra Gilbert and Susan Gubar, *The Madwoman in the Attic: The*

Woman Writer and the Nineteenth-Century Literary Imagination (New Haven: Yale University Press, 1979), pp. 13, 17, 211.

10. See Rogers's introductory comments to *Selected Poetry of Anne Finch*, p. xv. Also see Rogers's essay on Finch in *Shakespeare's Sisters: Feminist Essays on Women Poets*, ed. Sandra Gilbert and Susan Gubar (Bloomington: Indiana University Press, 1979), pp. 32–46.

11. Celeste M. Schenck suggests as much when she discusses Finch in the context of women elegiac poets who "refuse or rework the central symbolisms and procedures of elegy" by deconstructing "the genre's valorization of separation" and by reconstructing "alternative elegiac scenarios that arise from a distinctly feminine psycho-sexual experience." "Feminism and Deconstruction: Re-Constructing the Elegy," *Tulsa Studies in Women's Literature* 5 (Spring 1986), pp. 13, 18. For Luce Irigaray's description of a "woman-thing," see *This Sex Which Is Not One*, trans. Catherine Porter (Ithaca: Cornell University Press, 1985), p. 111.

12. For Finch's reference to the "dazling white" robe of Solomon, see her own note to these lines, in Rogers's edition, p. 163, n. 26.

13. See Newton's *Observations Upon the Prophecies of Daniel, and the Apocalypse of St. John* (London: J. Darby and T. Browne, 1733), p. 17.

14. Catherine Clément, "The Guilty One," *The Newly Born Woman*, trans. Betsy Wing, Theory and History of Literature, vol. 24 (Minneapolis: University of Minnesota Press, 1986), p. 7.

15. "The Preface" in *Selected Poems of Anne Finch*, p. 12.

16. Ibid., p. 9.

17. This poem is not included in Rogers's *Selected Poems of Anne Finch*. See Gilbert and Gubar, *Madwoman in the Attic*, p. 478. Their source is the now out-of-print edition of Finch's verse, *The Poems of Anne Countess of Winchilsea*, ed. Myra Reynolds (Chicago: University of Chicago Press, 1903), ll. 1–13.

18. Gilbert and Gubar, *Madwoman in the Attic*, p. 525.

19. Ibid., p. 526.

20. Nancy K. Miller, "Arachnologies: The Woman, the Text, and the Critic," *The Poetics of Gender*, ed. Nancy K. Miller (New York: Columbia University Press, 1986), p. 272–74.

21. Hélène Cixous, "Sorties," *The Newly Born Woman*, p. 80.

22. See, for instance, J. Hillis Miller, "Ariadne's Thread: Repetition and the Narrative Line," *Critical Inquiry* 3 (1976): 57–78, and "Ariachne's Brooken Woof," *Georgia Review* 31 (Spring 1977): 36–48.

23. Cited in Nancy Miller, "Arachnologies," p. 275.

24. Irigaray, *This Sex Which Is Not One*, p. 111.

25. Cixous, "Sorties," p. 94.

26. See Ovid's description of this colorful weaving in Book VI of the *Metamorphoses,* vol. 1, trans. Frank Justus Miller, Loeb Classical Library (Cambridge, Mass.: Harvard University Press, 1966), p. 293.

27. Irigaray, *This Sex Which Is Not One,* p. 164.

28. Cited in Sandra Harding, *The Science Question in Feminism* (Ithaca: Cornell University Press, 1986), p. 237.

29. Carolyn Merchant, *The Death of Nature: Woman, Ecology, and the Scientific Revolution* (New York: Harper & Row, 1980), p. 174.

30. See, for instance, Sherry Ortner, "Is Female to Male as Nature Is to Culture?" in *Women, Culture and Society,* ed. M. Z. Rosaldo and L. Lamphere (Stanford: Stanford University Press, 1974).

31. Cited in Harding, *The Science Question,* p. 237.

32. Jardine, *Gynesis,* pp. 70–71.

33. See Gilbert and Gubar's discussion of this matter, *Madwoman in the Attic,* p. 99. Also see Maurice Blanchot's reading of the Orpheus and Eurydice myth as the story of the artist's desire to gaze on feminine darkness, a desire that we might understand as yet another "appropriation" of feminine space. *The Space of Literature,* trans. Ann Amock (Lincoln: University of Nebraska Press, 1982), pp. 171–72.

34. See Margaret A. Doody, "Deserts, Ruins and Troubled Waters: Female Dreams in Fiction and the Development of the Gothic Novel," *Genre* 10 (Winter 1977): 529–72.

35. See Gilbert and Gubar on this poem, *Madwoman in the Attic,* pp. 60–63.

36. See my exploration of these matters in Chapter One.

37. Irigaray, *This Sex Which Is Not One,* p. 111.

38. Gilbert and Gubar, *Madwoman in the Attic,* p. 61.

Post-Scripting

Epigraphs: Jean-François Lyotard, *The Postmodern Condition: A Report on Knowledge,* trans. Geoff Bennington and Brian Massumi, Theory and History of Literature, vol. 10 (Minneapolis: University of Minnesota Press, 1984), p. xxiv; Hélène Cixous, "Sorties," *The Newly Born Woman,* trans. Betsy Wing, Theory and History of Literature, vol. 37 (Minneapolis: University of Minnesota Press, 1986), p. 94.

1. Luce Irigaray, *This Sex Which Is Not One,* trans. Catherine Porter (Ithaca: Cornell University Press, 1985), pp. 85, 111.

2. The term *poststructural* is, like the notion of the "feminine," a descriptive term for that which seems to elude any strict definition. As definitions, for instance, strive to place words in some fixed symbolic order, a post-

structural discourse not only questions the stasis of that order, but participates in the excessive "play" of language that transgresses the fixity of structure. It is just as difficult, in surveying the diverse discourse of contemporary theory, to distinguish between "structuralist" and "poststructuralist" writers. See Terry Eagleton, for instance, who relies on the distinction even while questioning it, in *Literary Theory: An Introduction* (Minneapolis: University of Minnesota Press, 1983), pp. 134–43, and Jonathan Culler, who discusses the problems in differentiating these movements, in *On Deconstruction: Theory and Criticism After Structuralism* (Ithaca: Cornell University Press, 1982), pp. 22–30.

I use the term "poststructural" because it describes best my own sense, as well as that of many others, that in much recent theoretical discourse there is a recognition of and engagement in that which exceeds structures—metaphysical, historical, linguistic, scientific—and an attempt to come to terms with "differences" and "omissions" unaccommodated in systems of discourse.

3. See Michel Foucault, *Madness and Civilization: A History of Insanity in the Age of Reason*, trans. Richard Howard (New York: Vintage Books, 1965). Also see Foucault's *The Order of Things* (New York: Random House, 1970), and *The Archaeology of Knowledge and The Discourse on Language*, trans. A. M. Sheridan Smith (New York: Pantheon Books, 1972).

4. See Jacques Derrida's essay on "Differance" in *Margins of Philosophy*, trans. Alan Bass (Chicago: University of Chicago Press, 1982), and *Of Grammatology*, trans. Gayatri Chakravorty Spivak (Baltimore: Johns Hopkins University Press, 1974).

5. Alice Jardine, *Gynesis: Configurations of Woman and Modernity* (Ithaca: Cornell University Press, 1985), pp. 21, 24–25.

6. Irigaray, *This Sex Which Is Not One*, p. 111.

7. See Jacques Derrida's *Spurs*, trans. Barbara Harlow (Chicago: University of Chicago Press, 1978), p. 49.

8. Klaus Theweleit, *Male Fantasies, 1. Women, Floods, Bodies, History*, trans. Stephen Conway, Theory and History of Literature, vol. 22 (Minneapolis: University of Minnesota Press, 1987). Especially see Theweleit's discussion of woman's representational associations with water, floods, "all that flows," pp. 229–300.

9. See Jacques Lacan, "The Freudian Thing," *Écrits: A Selection*, trans. Alan Sheridan (New York: W. W. Norton, 1977), p. 124.

10. Lyotard, *The Postmodern Condition*, p. 60.

11. Georges Bataille, *Visions of Excess: Selected Writings, 1927–1939*, trans. Allan Stoekl, Theory and History of Literature, vol. 14 (Minneapolis: University of Minnesota Press, 1985).

12. Michel de Certeau, *Heterologies: Discourse on the Other,* trans. Brian Massumi, Theory and History of Literature, vol. 17 (Minneapolis: University of Minnesota Press, 1986).

13. Jardine describes such men as "women's *compagnons de route,* our intellectual fellow travelers into the twenty-first century." She explains that "'Woman,' as a new rhetorical space, is inseperable from the most radical moments of most contemporary disciplines . . . 'she' may be found in Lacan's pronouncements on desire; Derrida's internal explorations of writing; Deleuze's work on becoming woman; Jean-François Lyotard's calls for a feminine analytic relation; Jean Baudrillard's work on seduction; Foucault's on madness; Goux's on the new femininity; Barthes's in general; Michel Serres's desire to become Penelope or Ariadne . . . 'She' is created from the close explorations of semantic chains whose elements have changed textual as well as conceptual positions, at least in terms of valorization: from time to space, the same to other, paranoia to hysteria, city to labyrinth, mastery to nonmastery, truth to fiction," *Gynesis,* (p. 38).

14. I take the term *political reconstitution* from Thomas Laquer, who argues that during this time woman's body was regarded not only as different from the male body, but as problematic and uncontrolled because of its supposed inclinations toward excessive sexual pleasure and bleeding, and because of its reproductive capabilities. Her body in this way necessitated the reestablishment of a political hierarchy in which men, or women whose bodies were like those of men, maintained social superiority. See "Orgasm, Generation, and the Politics of Reproductive Biology," *Representations* 14 (Spring 1986): 1–41.

15. Cixous, "Sorties," p. 93.

Bibliography

Adams, Henry. *The Education of Henry Adams*. Ed. D. W. Brogan. Boston: Houghton Mifflin, 1961.

Atkins, G. Douglas. *Reading Deconstruction, Deconstructive Reading*. Lexington: University Press of Kentucky, 1983.

————. *Quests of Difference: Reading Pope's Poems*. Lexington: University Press of Kentucky, 1986.

Auerbach, Nina. *Woman and the Demon: The Life of a Victorian Myth*. Cambridge, Mass.: Harvard University Press, 1982.

Bataille, Georges. *Visions of Excess: Selected Writings, 1927–1939*. Trans. Allan Stoekl. Theory and History of Literature, vol. 14. Minneapolis: University of Minnesota Press, 1985.

Beauvoir, Simone de. *The Second Sex*. Trans. H. M. Parshley. 1953; rpt. New York: Vintage Books, 1974.

Bernheimer, Charles, and Claire Kahane, eds. *In Dora's Case: Freud-Hysteria-Feminism*. New York: Columbia University Press, 1985.

Blanchot, Maurice. *The Space of Literature*. Trans. Ann Smock. Lincoln: University of Nebraska Press, 1982.

Boucé, Paul Gabriel, ed. *Sexuality in Eighteenth-Century England*. Manchester: Manchester University Press, 1982.

Brooks, Cleanth. "The Case of Miss Arabella Fermor." *The Well Wrought Urn*. London: D. Dobson, 1947.

Brower, Reuben A. "Lady Winchilsea and the Poetic Tradition of the Seventeenth Century." *SP* 42 (1945): 61–80.

Brown, Laura. *Alexander Pope*. Oxford: Basil Blackwell, 1985.

Brown, Norman O. "The Excremental Vision." *Life Against Death: The Psychoanalytical Meaning of History*. Middletown, Conn.: Wesleyan University Press, 1959.

Cantor, Geoffrey. "Light and Enlightenment: An Exploration of Mid-Eighteenth-Century Modes of Discourse." In *The Discourse of Light from the Middle Ages to the Enlightenment*. Los Angeles: William Andrews Clark Memorial Library, 1985.

Carroll, Berenice A., ed. *Liberating Women's History: Theoretical and Critical Essays*. Urbana: University of Illinois Press, 1976.

Castle, Terry. *Masquerade and Civilization: The Carnivalesque in Eigh-*

teenth-Century English Culture and Fiction. Stanford: Stanford University Press, 1986.

———. *Clarissa's Ciphers: Meaning and Disruption in Richardson's "Clarissa."* Ithaca: Cornell University Press, 1982.

———. "Why the Houyhnhnms Don't Write: Swift, Satire and the Fear of the Text." *Essays in Literature* 7 (Spring 1980): 31–44.

Certeau, Michel de. *Heterologies: Discourse on the Other.* Trans. Brian Massumi. Theory and History of Literature, vol. 17. Minneapolis: University of Minnesota Press, 1986.

Christianson, Gale E. *In the Presence of the Creator: Isaac Newton and His Times.* New York: The Free Press, 1984.

Cixous, Hélène. "The Laugh of the Medusa." *New French Feminisms.* Ed. Elaine Marks and Isabelle de Courtivron. New York: Schocken Books, 1981, pp. 245–64.

———. "Sorties." *The Newly Born Woman.* Trans. Betsy Wing. Theory and History of Literature, vol. 37. Minneapolis: University of Minnesota Press, 1986.

Clément, Catherine. "The Guilty One." *The Newly Born Woman.* Trans. Betsy Wing. Theory and History of Literature, vol. 37. Minneapolis: University of Minnesota Press, 1986.

Coetzee, J. M. "Newton and the Ideal of a Transparent Scientific Language." *Journal of Literary Semantics* 11 (April 1982): 3–13.

Cohen, I. Bernard. *Introduction to Newton's "Principia."* Cambridge, Mass.: Harvard University Press, 1971.

———. *The Birth of the New Physics.* New York: Doubleday, 1960.

———, ed. *Isaac Newton's Papers & Letters on Natural Philosophy.* Cambridge, Mass.: Harvard University Press, 1958.

Conley, Verena. *Hélène Cixous: Writing the Feminine.* Lincoln: University of Nebraska Press, 1984.

Culler, Jonathan. *On Deconstruction: Theory and Criticism After Structuralism.* Ithaca: Cornell University Press, 1982.

Davis, Natalie Zemon. "Women on Top: Symbolic Sexual Inversion and Political Disorder in Early Modern Europe." In *The Reversible World: Symbolic Inversion in Art and Society.* Ed. Barbara A. Babcock. Ithaca: Cornell University Press, 1978.

Delany, Sheila. "Sex and Politics in Pope's *Rape of the Lock.*" *Writing Woman.* New York: Schocken Books, 1983.

Derrida, Jacques. "Differance." In *Margins of Philosophy.* Trans. Alan Bass. Chicago: University of Chicago Press, 1982.

———. *Of Grammatology.* Trans. Gayatri Chakravorty Spivak. Baltimore: Johns Hopkins University Press, 1974.

————. *Positions*. Trans. Alan Bass. Chicago: University of Chicago Press, 1982.

————. *Spurs*. Trans. Barbara Harlow. Chicago: University of Chicago Press, 1978.

Doane, Mary Ann. "The Clinical Eye: Medical Discourses in the 'Woman's Film' of the 1940s." In *The Female Body in Western Culture: Contemporary Perspectives*. Ed. Susan Rubin Suleiman. Cambridge, Mass.: Harvard University Press, 1986.

Doody, Margaret A. "Deserts, Ruins and Troubled Waters: Female Dreams in Fiction and the Development of the Gothic Novel." *Genre* 10 (Winter 1977): 529–72.

Douglas, Mary. *Natural Symbols: Explorations in Cosmology*. New York: Vintage Books, 1973.

Eagleton, Terry. *Literary Theory: An Introduction*. Minneapolis: University of Minnesota Press, 1983.

————. *The Rape of Clarissa: Writing, Sexuality, and Class Struggle in Samuel Richardson*. Minneapolis: University of Minnesota Press, 1982.

Easlea, Brian. *Witch Hunting, Magic and the New Philosophy*. Brighton: Harvester Press, 1980.

Ehrenreich, Barbara, and Deirdre English. *Witches, Midwives, and Nurses: A History of Women Healers*. Old Westbury, New York: The Feminist Press, 1973.

Epstein, Julia L. and Mark L. Greenberg. "Decomposing Newton's Rainbow." *Journal of the History of Ideas* 45 (January-March 1984): 115–40.

Fabricant, Carole. *Swift's Landscape*. Baltimore: Johns Hopkins University Press, 1982.

Felman, Shoshana. "Rereading Femininity." *Yale French Studies* 62 (1981): 19–44.

Feyerabend, Paul. *Against Method: Outline of an Anarchistic Theory of Knowledge*. Boston: Schocken Books, 1978.

Finch, Anne. *The Poems of Anne Countess of Winchilsea*. Ed. Myra Reynolds. Chicago: University of Chicago Press, 1903.

————. *Selected Poems of Anne Finch, Countess of Winchilsea*. Ed. Katharine M. Rogers. New York: Fredrick Ungar, 1979.

Fischer, John Irwin. *On Swift's Poetry*. Gainesville: University Presses of Florida, 1978.

Flynn, Elizabeth A., and Patrocinio P. Schweickart, eds. *Gender and Reading: Essays on Readers, Texts, and Contexts*. Baltimore: Johns Hopkins University Press, 1986.

Foucault, Michel. *The Archaeology of Knowledge and The Discourse on Lan-*

guage. Trans. A. M. Sheridan Smith. New York: Pantheon Books, 1972.

—————. *The Birth of the Clinic: An Archaeology of Medical Perception*. Trans. A. M. Sheridan Smith. New York: Vintage Books, 1975.

—————. *The History of Sexuality*. vol. 1. Trans. Robert Hurley. New York: Vintage Books, 1978.

—————. *Madness and Civilization: A History of Insanity in the Age of Reason*. Trans. Richard Howard. New York: Vintage Books, 1965.

—————. *The Order of Things*. New York: Random House, 1970.

Frye, Northrop. "The Revelation to Eve." In *Paradise Lost: A Tercentenary Tribute*. Ed. Balachandra Rajan. Toronto: University of Toronto Press, 1969.

Gallop, Jane. *The Daughter's Seduction: Feminism and Psychoanalysis*. Ithaca: Cornell University Press, 1982.

—————. *Reading Lacan*. Ithaca: Cornell University Press, 1986.

Gilbert, Sandra. "Forward." *The Newly Born Woman*. Trans. Betsy Wing. Theory and History of Literature, vol. 37. Minneapolis: University of Minnesota Press, 1986.

Gilbert, Sandra, and Susan Gubar. *The Madwoman in the Attic: The Woman Writer and the Nineteenth-Century Literary Imagination*. New Haven: Yale University Press, 1979.

—————, eds. *Shakespeare's Sisters: Feminist Essays on Women Poets*. Bloomington: Indiana University Press, 1979.

Graves, Robert. *The White Goddess: A Historical Grammar of Poetic Myth*. 1948; rpt. New York: Farrar, Straus and Giroux, 1966.

Greene, Gayle, and Coppelia Kahn. "Feminist Scholarship and the Social Construction of Woman." In *Making A Difference: Feminist Literary Criticism*. London: Methuen, 1985.

Gubar, Susan. "The Female Monster in Augustan Satire." *Signs* 3, no. 2 (Winter 1977): 380–94.

Hagstrum, Jean. *The Sister Arts: The Tradition of Literary Pictorialism and English Poetry from Dryden to Gray*. Chicago: University of Chicago Press, 1958.

Hall, Rupert A. *Philosophers At War: The Quarrel Between Newton and Leibniz*. Cambridge: Cambridge University Press, 1980.

Harding, Sandra. *The Science Question in Feminism*. Ithaca: Cornell University Press, 1986.

Herrmann, Claudine. "Women in Space and Time." Trans. Marilyn R. Schuster. In *New French Feminisms*. Ed. Elaine Marks and Isabelle de Courtivron. New York: Schocken Books, 1981, pp. 168–73.

Hunter, Dianne. "Hysteria, Psychoanalysis, and Feminism: The Case of

Anna O." In *The (M)Other Tongue: Essays in Feminist Psychoanalytic Interpretation*. Ed. Shirley Nelson Garner, Claire Kahane, and Madelon Sprengnether. Ithaca: Cornell University Press, 1985.

Irigaray, Luce. *Speculum of the Other Woman*. Trans. Gillian C. Gill. Ithaca: Cornell University Press, 1985.

———. *This Sex Which Is Not One*. Trans. Catherine Porter. Ithaca: Cornell University Press, 1985.

Jacob, Margaret C. *The Newtonians and the English Revolution: 1689–1720*. Ithaca: Cornell University Press, 1976.

———. *The Radical Enlightenment: Pantheists, Freemasons and Republicans*. London: Allen & Unwin, 1981.

Jardine, Alice. *Gynesis: Configurations of Woman and Modernity*. Ithaca: Cornell University Press, 1985.

Johnson, Barbara. *The Critical Difference: Essays in the Contemporary Rhetoric of Reading*. Baltimore: Johns Hopkins University Press, 1980.

Jones, William Powell. *The Rhetoric of Science: A Study of Scientific Ideas and Imagery in Eighteenth-Century English Poetry*. London: Routledge & Kegan Paul, 1966.

Kamuf, Peggy. "Writing Like a Woman." In *Women and Language in Literature and Society*. Ed. S. McConnell-Ginet et al. New York: Praeger, 1980, pp. 284–99.

Kearney, Hugh. *Science and Change: 1500–1700*. World University Library. New York: McGraw Hill, 1971.

Keller, Evelyn Fox. *Reflections on Gender and Science*. New Haven: Yale University Press, 1985.

Kelly, Joan. *Women, History, and Theory: The Essays of Joan Kelly*. Chicago: University of Chicago Press, 1984.

Kristeva, Julia. *About Chinese Women*. Trans. Anita Barrows. New York: Marion Boyars, 1986.

———. *Desire in Language: A Semiotic Approach to Literature and Art*. Ed. Leon S. Roudiez. Trans. Thomas Gora, Alice Jardine, and Leon S. Roudiez. New York: Columbia University Press, 1980.

———. "Oscillation between Power and Denial." Trans. Marilyn A. August. *New French Feminisms*. Ed. Elaine Marks and Isabelle de Courtivron. New York: Schocken Books, 1981, pp. 165–67.

———. "Woman Can Never Be Defined." Trans. Marilyn A. August. In *New French Feminisms*. Ed. Elaine Marks and Isabelle de Courtivron. New York: Schocken Books, 1981. pp. 137–41.

Kuhn, Thomas. "Comment (on the Relations of Science and Art)." *Comparative Studies in Philosophy and History* 11 (1969): 403–12.

————. *The Structure of Scientific Revolutions*. 2d ed. Chicago: University of Chicago Press, 1970.

Lacan, Jacques. *Écrits: A Selection*. Trans. Alan Sheridan. New York: W. W. Norton, 1977.

LaCapra, Dominick. *History and Criticism*. Ithaca: Cornell University Press, 1985.

Lyotard, Jean-François. *The Postmodern Condition: A Report on Knowledge*. Trans. Geoff Bennington and Brian Massumi. Theory and History of Literature, vol. 10. Minneapolis: University of Minnesota Press, 1984.

Mack, Maynard. *Alexander Pope: A Life*. New Haven: Yale University Press, 1985.

————. *The Garden and the City: Retirement and Politics in the Later Poetry of Pope*. Toronto: University of Toronto Press, 1969.

Manuel, Frank. *A Portrait of Isaac Newton*. Cambridge, Mass.: Harvard University Press, 1968.

————. *The Changing of the Gods*. Hanover: University Press of New England, 1983.

————. *Isaac Newton: Historian*. Cambridge, Mass.: Harvard University Press, 1963.

Meese, Elizabeth. *Crossing the Double-Cross: The Practice of Feminist Criticism*. Chapel Hill: University of North Carolina Press, 1986.

Merchant, Carolyn. *The Death of Nature: Woman, Ecology, and the Scientific Revolution*. New York: Harper & Row, 1980.

Miller, J. Hillis. "Ariachne's Brooken Woof." *Georgia Review* 31 (Spring 1977): 36–48.

————. "Ariadne's Thread: Repetition and the Narrative Line." *Critical Inquiry* 3 (1976): 57–78.

Miller, Nancy K. "Arachnologies: The Woman, the Text, and the Critic." In *The Poetics of Gender*. Ed. Nancy K. Miller. New York: Columbia University Press, 1986.

Milton, John. *John Milton: Complete Poems and Major Prose*. Ed. Merrit Y. Hughes. New York: Odyssey, 1957.

Moi, Toril. *Sexual/Textual Politics: Feminist Literary Theory*. London: Methuen, 1985.

Newton, Isaac. *Observations Upon the Prophecies of Daniel, and the Apocalypse of St. John*. London: J. Darby and T. Browne, 1733.

————. *Opticks, Or a Treatise of the Reflections, Refractions, Inflections & Colours of Light*. New York: Dover Publications, 1952.

————. *Sir Isaac Newton's Mathematical Principles of Natural Philosophy and his System of the World.* Trans. Florian Cajori. Berkeley: University of California Press, 1934.

Nicolson, Marjorie Hope. *Newton Demands the Muse: Newton's Opticks and the Eighteenth-Century Poets.* Princeton: Princeton University Press, 1946.

———, and G. S. Rousseau. *"This Long Disease, My Life": Alexander Pope and the Sciences.* Princeton: Princeton University Press, 1968.

———, and Nora Mohler. "The Scientific Background of Swift's *Voyage to Laputa." Annals of Science* 2 (1937): 299–334; rpt. in Nicolson. *Science and Imagination.* Ithaca: Cornell University Press, 1956.

Nussbaum, Felicity A. *The Brink of All We Hate: English Satires on Women, 1660–1750.* Lexington: University Press of Kentucky, 1984.

Ortner, Sherry. "Is Female to Male as Nature Is to Culture?" In *Women, Culture, and Society.* Ed. M. Z. Rosaldo and L. Lamphere. Stanford: Stanford University Press, 1974.

Ovid. *Metamorphoses.* vol. 1. Trans. Frank Justus Miller. Loeb Classical Library. Cambridge: Cambridge University Press, 1966.

Ozick, Cynthia. "The Moral Necessity of Metaphor: Rooting History in a Figure of Speech." *Harper's* 272 (May 1986): 62–68.

Perry, Ruth. *The Celebrated Mary Astell: An Early English Feminist.* Chicago: University of Chicago Press, 1986.

Plato. *Plato's Republic.* Ed. I. A. Richards. Cambridge: Cambridge University Press, 1966.

Pollak, Ellen. *The Poetics of Sexual Myth: Gender and Ideology in the Verse of Swift and Pope.* Chicago: University of Chicago Press, 1985.

Pope, Alexander. *The Twickenham Edition of the Poems of Alexander Pope.* Gen. ed. John Butt. 11 vols. New Haven: Yale University Press. London: Methuen, 1939–69.

Ragland-Sullivan, Ellie. *Jacques Lacan and the Philosophy of Psychoanalysis.* Urbana: University of Illinois Press, 1986.

Rawson, C. J. *Gulliver and the Gentle Reader: Studies in Swift and Our Time.* London: Routledge & Kegan Paul, 1972.

Ricoeur, Paul. *The Reality of the Historical Past.* Milwaukee: Marquette University Press, 1984.

Rogers, Katharine. *Feminism in Eighteenth-Century England.* Urbana: University of Illinois Press, 1982.

Rousseau, G. S. "Psychology." In *The Ferment of Knowledge: Studies in the Historiography of Eighteenth-Century Science.* Ed. Rousseau and Roy Porter. Cambridge: Cambridge University Press, 1980, pp. 143–210.

————. "Science and the Discovery of the Imagination in Enlightened England." *ECS* 3 (Fall 1969): 108–35.

Said, Edward. "Swift's Tory Anarchy." *ECS* 3 (Fall 1969): 48–66.

Schakel, Peter J. *The Poetry of Jonathan Swift: Allusion and the Development of a Poetic Style*. Madison: University of Wisconsin Press, 1978.

Schenck, Celeste M. "Feminism and Deconstruction: Re-Constructing the Elegy." *Tulsa Studies in Women's Literature* 5 (Spring 1986): 13–27.

Schnorrenberg, Barbara B., and Jean E. Hunter. "The Eighteenth-Century English Woman." In *The Women of England From Anglo-Saxon Times to the Present*. Ed. Barbara Kanner. Hamden, Conn.: Archon Books, 1979.

Serres, Michel. *Hermes: Literature, Science, Philosophy*. Ed. Josué V. Harari and David F. Bell. Baltimore: Johns Hopkins University Press, 1982.

Shapiro, Alan E., ed. *The Optical Papers of Isaac Newton*. vol. 1. Cambridge: Cambridge University Press, 1984.

Shaw, Sheila. "The Rape of Gulliver: Case Study of a Source." *PMLA* 90 (1976): 62–68.

Smith, Hilda L. *Reason's Disciples: Seventeenth-Century English Feminists*. Urbana: University of Illinois Press, 1982.

Smith-Rosenberg, Carroll. *Disorderly Conduct: Visions of Gender in Victorian America*. New York: Alfred A. Knopf, 1985.

Spivak, Gayatri Chakravorty. "Love Me, Love My Ombre, Elle." *Diacritics* 14, 4 (1984): 19–36.

Swift, Jonathan. *The Poems of Jonathan Swift*. Ed. Harold Williams. 2d ed. 3 vols. Oxford: Clarendon Press, 1958.

————. *The Prose Works of Jonathan Swift*. Ed. Herbert Davis, 14 vols. Oxford: Basil Blackwell, 1939–1968.

————. *The Writings of Jonathan Swift*. Ed. Robert A. Greenberg and William B. Piper. New York: W. W. Norton, 1973.

Theweleit, Klaus. *Male Fantasies, 1. Women, Floods, Bodies, History*. Theory and History of Literature, vol. 22. Minneapolis: University of Minnesota Press, 1987.

Thompson, E. P. *The Making of the English Working Class*. New York: Pantheon Books, 1964.

Turner, Victor. *The Ritual Process: Structure and Anti-Structure*. Chicago: University of Chicago Press, 1969.

Vieth, David. "Introduction" to "A Symposium on Women in Swift's Poems: Vanessa, Stella, Lady Acheson, and Celia." *Papers on Language and Literature* 14 (1978): 115–16.

Bibliography

Warner, William Beatty. *Reading* Clarissa: *The Struggles of Interpretation.* New Haven: Yale University Press, 1979.

Westfall, Richard S. *Never At Rest: A Biography of Isaac Newton.* Cambridge: Cambridge University Press, 1980.

White, Hayden. *Tropics of Discourse: Essays in Cultural Criticism.* Baltimore: Johns Hopkins University Press, 1978.

Williams, Aubrey. "The 'Fall' of China and *The Rape of the Lock.*" In *Essential Articles for the Study of Alexander Pope.* Hamden, Conn.: Archon, 1964.

Williams, Kathleen. *Jonathan Swift and the Age of Compromise.* Lawrence: University of Kansas Press, 1958.

Wittig, Monique. *Les Guérillères.* Trans. David Le Vey. Boston: Beacon Press, 1985.

Index

Index

Note on the Author

RUTH SALVAGGIO is the author of *Dryden's Dualities* (1983), and essays appearing in such journals as *Glyph Textual Studies, Philological Quarterly,* and *Women's Studies.* She is on the faculty at Virginia Polytechnic Institute where she teaches in English, Women's Studies, and Humanities.